# A Taste of the World

## CUISINE SANS FRONTIÈRES

## DISHES FROM GREAT CHEFS AROUND THE WORLD

Compiled and edited
by

### Christopher and Jean Conil

### with help from David Evans, Chairman of the

### World Master Chefs' Society

**MARTIN BOOKS**

# ACKNOWLEDGEMENTS

The authors and editors would like to thank the following sponsors and supporters of the production of this book: Sue Goddard and the American Soybean Association; Maurice Hanssen, a patron of the Cercle Epicurien Mondial and the World Master Chefs' Society; Jacques Schneider of Profile; Gordon Martin of Express Dairy; Mr Stas of G.W. White Ltd Fishmongers; wholesale butchers Ian Woodhouse, Ian Garner, K.G. Burke, G.H. Boyd; Mr Laurence Clore of Snipe and Grouse; Mr Paul Cockerton; Anthony Reisebro; Mr Karl Walter Pfestorf; the American Peanut Association; as well as the managements of the leading hotels and restaurants which have supplied the illustrations of the main dishes.

Pictured on the front cover: Compote d'Ananas Harry Chapin (page 200).
See pages 140/141 for dishes pictured on the back cover.

Published by Martin Books
Simon & Schuster International Group
Fitzwilliam House, 32 Trumpington Street, Cambridge CB2 1QY

in association with
The American Soybean Association
Centre International Rogier
Box 521, 1210 Brussels, Belgium

and the Cercle Epicurien Mondial
and the World Master Chefs' Society
282 Dollis Hill Lane, London NW2 6HH

First published 1989
Text and photographs © Cercle Epicurien Mondial 1989

ISBN 0 85941 616 X

Design: Goddard Niklas Delaney DeRoos Ltd
Photography: Nick Tomkin
Food stylists: Jean and Christopher Conil
Typesetting: Goodfellow & Egan, Cambridge
Printed and bound in Great Britain by
Butler & Tanner Ltd, Frome and London

# Contents

# $\mathscr{I}$NTRODUCTION

$\mathscr{H}$ere is a dazzling array of gourmet recipes from all the corners of the world, near and far, including contributions from leading chefs in the UK. As you explore this book and try out its delectable offerings, you can imagine yourself in Hong Kong, Venice, France, USA, Malaysia, Thailand, Japan, the Bahamas and many many other centres of gastronomic delight. The majority of the master chefs who contributed recipes for the book are all members of the prestigious Cercle Epicurien Mondial, and are eminent exponents of the culinary specialities of their own regions.

The royalties from the book are being donated to the Save the Children Fund, which works throughout the developing world, particularly in the poorest countries, to alleviate hunger, distress and disease. We are very pleased that the involvement of the Cercle Epicurien Mondial with this organisation has prompted a generous response, and such a glittering display of excellence from top chefs around the world.

We include recipes from celebrity chefs well-known in this country, such as Anton Mosimann, David Evans and Antonio Mancini, and a diverse selection from other countries' leading chefs, such as Eëro Mäkelä of Finland, Khunying Prasansook Tuntivejakul of Thailand, and Howard Bulka and John Ash of California. We are deeply indebted to all our colleagues, as each recipe does justice to the cuisine of all the countries which are represented here.

All the recipes are dedicated to taste and health; all of them can be made in the home although some of them feature the sort of exotic ingredients which one usually only savours in gourmet feasts, and which may take a little well-spent time to find. These are health-conscious recipes: soya oil and margarine are used throughout, and the chapter entitled The Gifts of Ceres is wholly devoted to the culinary delights to be made from the world's grains: the best staple diet both for health and economic reasons. Seafood also features prominently, and we are proud of the brilliant and beautiful dishes which have come from Hong Kong, Japan and other food-loving islands.

We hope you will enjoy your gourmet journey around the world with us, guided by prizewinning Master Chefs. Bonne santé et bon appetit!

Jean and Christopher Conil

# $\mathscr{N}$OTES ON $\mathscr{R}$ECIPES

$\mathscr{A}$ll recipes give ingredients in metric and imperial measures. Use any one set of measurements, but not a mixture of both, in any one recipe. All spoon measures are given in level spoons, unless otherwise stated. Eggs are standard, size 3, unless otherwise stated.

# *F*ROM *C*LOVER TO *C*REAM – Milk, Cream and Cheese

*F*rom time immemorial, man has made use of milk in his diet. Various mammals, including buffalo, camels, goats and sheep, as well as cows, produce milk for the human diet. Today's dairy animals' feed is synthesised by scientists into a balanced ration of grain, grass and legumes, elements that are equally important in our diets.

*D*airy products play a major part in the diet of growing children, expectant and nursing mothers and the elderly. Breast milk is the ideal first food for the infant. Provided that the mother's diet is satisfactory, an infant fully breast-fed will obtain from the milk, in an assimilated form, all the nutrients it needs for its first three to four months. In the poorest developing countries, where Save the Children is most active, much effort is directed towards creating health centres where hygiene, nutrition, and basic cookery are taught to mothers. In these countries, the consumption of milk under hygienic conditions can help enormously to reduce the high infant mortality rate of 175 per 1,000.

*M*ilk is particularly good in a mixed diet, as a major source of protein, calcium and riboflavin. A child under two years of age needs at least 1 litre (1¾ pints) of milk a day to provide 1,000 calories. The average adult needs only 300 ml (½ pint) of low-fat or fat-free milk a day.

## YOGURT

*Y*ogurt is made by inoculating pasteurised milk or long-life, skimmed milk with a mixture of the bacteria cultures *lactobacillus bulgaricus* and *streptococcus thermophilus*. The bacteria change the lactose they feed on to lactic acid and turn the product into an acidulated curd of varying texture according to the amount of fat or casein (the milk protein) it contains.

## CHEESE

*F*or the health-conscious consumer, low-fat cheeses are preferable to the hard cheeses. They contain on average 96 calories per 199 grams, compared with 406 in Cheddar.

*I*n modern cuisine, much use is made of low-fat cheese in mousses, soufflés, legume terrines, pizzas, flans and vegetable sauces, although the flavour is not as cheesy as that of the ripe, hard cheeses. If the flavour of the latter is wanted without the calories, we recommend using a small amount of well matured Cheddar. In eastern countries where cheese is not popular, soya bean protein is used in the preparation of the cheese-like tofu.

*T*he three major ingredients for cheese-making are milk, a culture of bacteria specific to the type of cheese, and an enzyme. Rennet, which is obtained from the stomachs of calves, has been found to be the most effective enzyme. Other enzymes, extracted from fruits such as figs (ficin), pineapple (bromelin) and pawpaw (papayin), are also used to curdle milk into a sort of junket. Lemon juice is used to make quark (a kind of German cottage cheese) and vinegar is used to curdle milk or cream in Yorkshire cheese fillings.

## BUTTER

*I*f the taste of butter is needed without all the calories, a good solution is to mix a little unsaturated oil, such as soya, with the butter. Unsalted butter is preferable for cooking purposes as it emulsifies better in rich egg sauces (such as hollandaise or béarnaise), but these sauces can equally well be made from soya margarine or a mixture of butter and margarine.

## VEGETABLE OILS

*A*n important aspect of modern cuisine is that unsaturated vegetable fats are now widely accepted as preferable to saturated fats for health and nutritional reasons. Fats that are liquid at room temperature are called oils; all oils which are labelled as being high in polyunsaturated fats and low in saturated fats are suitable for healthy eating. All oils are identical in that they have around 899 calories per 100 ml (3½ fl oz) – 45 calories per teaspoon.

*B*oth Western and Eastern peoples use soya and other oils in their diet for, indeed, meals cooked without fat are often unpalatable. Very low-fat diets are inadvisable, except when medically prescribed, because there is a danger of depleting the body of fat-soluble vitamins A and D.

*S*aturated, mono-unsaturated and polyunsaturated fatty acid content in g per 100 g of various fats and oils:

|  | Mono-unsaturated | Poly-unsaturated | Saturated |
|---|---|---|---|
| Butter | 26.10 | 2.24 | 48.97 |
| Beef dripping | 48.08 | 4.07 | 42.50 |
| Lard | 41.65 | 8.99 | 41.82 |
| Suet | 36.62 | 1.23 | 56.22 |
| Margarine, hard – made with animal and vegetable oils | 34.61 | 13.78 | 29.79 |
| Margarine, hard – made with vegetable oils only | 37.87 | 9.75 | 29.81 |
| Margarine, soft, blended – made with animal and vegetable oils | 36.47 | 15.79 | 24.47 |
| Margarine, soft, blended – made with vegetable oils only | 33.68 | 17.88 | 25.63 |
| Margarine, polyunsaturated | 15.87 | 60.15 | 19.12 |
| Low-fat spread | 15.52 | 12.06 | 10.97 |
| Coconut oil | 6.59 | 1.69 | 85.17 |
| Corn oil | 29.32 | 49.28 | 16.43 |
| Olive oil | 69.72 | 11.18 | 14.04 |
| Palm oil | 41.64 | 8.31 | 45.27 |
| Peanut (groundnut) oil | 47.85 | 28.46 | 18.83 |
| Rapeseed oil – high erucic acid | 64.28 | 24.83 | 5.35 |
| Rapeseed oil – low erucic acid | 57.20 | 31.52 | 6.60 |
| Safflower seed oil | 12.62 | 72.11 | 10.22 |
| Soya bean oil | 24.26 | 56.73 | 14.05 |
| Sunflower seed oil | 31.81 | 49.95 | 13.09 |

*Note: Margarines and low-fat spreads made from a mixture of oils and fats may vary in composition throughout the year depending on the raw materials used in their manufacture. These figures are taken from* The First Supplement of The Composition of Foods *by McCance and Widdowson.*

*S*oya oil is 100% pure vegetable oil. Good quality soya oil is bland and therefore can be used to absorb any kind of herb or spice flavour, either for macerating or frying food. This is why it is so important in sauce-making, and in stir-frying not only various vegetables, but also nuts and seeds or ground spices. The main dish itself tastes better after a quick browning in hot soya oil.

*O*ne way to achieve a healthy aspect in your cookery is to use pure soya oil in place of butter, margarine, or animal fats, which can be done in most recipes, including some cakes. It can replace fat in sauces and can be used as a base for icings. It can be used as a binding ingredient in all kinds of emulsified sauces such as mayonnaise, and it can replace all the butter in sauces such as hollandaise and its derivatives. It can be used just as widely as any other vegetable oil, such as corn, sunflower or safflower, and it is also more economical.

# *P*EAR WITH *P*ENCARREG *M*OUSSE AND *W*ATERCRESS *S*AUCE

| | |
|---|---|
| 4 ripe William or Comice pears, peeled, cored, and halved | 2 tbs soya oil |
| | 150 ml ( ¼ pint ) double cream |
| | 100 g ( 3½ oz ) Pencarreg Welsh cheese |
| FOR THE SAUCE | ( soft brie-type ), grated |
| 3 tbs soya oil | a little nutmeg |
| 2 bunches watercress | salt and pepper to taste |
| 150 ml ( ¼ pint ) double cream | 15 g ( ½ oz ) gelatine powder ( soaked in 6 tbs cold water ) |
| salt and pepper | |
| | TO GARNISH |
| FOR THE MOUSSE | 150 g ( 5 oz ) white of leek, cut in thin strips |
| 50 g ( 2 oz ) onion, chopped | 8 lettuce leaves |

*T*o make the sauce, chop the watercress leaves. Heat the soya oil and fry the watercress for 30 seconds. Stir in the cream and season. Boil for 5 minutes. To make the mousse, gently cook the onion in the soya oil until soft without browning. Add the cream and cheese. Boil for 5 minutes. Season and strain. Bring back to the boil, add the soaked gelatine and heat until dissolved. Pour this mixture into a mould. Cool until mixture sets.

Fill the cavity of each pear with cheese mousse. To serve, scald the leek strips for 10 seconds and leave to cool.

Take 4 plates and pour a pool of watercress sauce on each. Over the sauce feather a thin line of piped cream for a marbling effect. Arrange 2 pear halves on each plate, decorate with lettuce leaves and sprinkle the leek strips over the pears.    *Serves 4*                                                         **TIMOTHY DEWHIRST**

# ℛIESLING ℙAPRIKA 𝒮OUP

| | |
|---|---|
| 1 bottle Riesling wine | 2 level tsp cornflour |
| 1 slice lemon | a little sugar or honey, to taste |
| 3 or 4 cloves | 100 ml ( 3½ fl oz ) whipping cream |
| 1 small stick cinnamon | 1 tsp ground paprika |
| 3 egg yolks | 1 tbs chopped dill weed |

ℛeserving about 3 tbs of the wine to add to the finished soup, heat the wine with the lemon slice, cloves and cinnamon. When the mixture begins to boil, remove from the heat and strain.

In a bowl, beat the egg yolks with the cornflour and gradually stir in the strained wine, a little at a time, while mixing the contents like a custard. Return the pan to the heat and bring to the boil while stirring constantly until the mixture begins to thicken. For a dry wine, add sugar or honey to taste. Cool the soup, then add the reserved wine for extra flavour.

Serve in individual bowls with a dollop of whipped cream dusted over with paprika and a garnish of dill.    *Serves 4*                                                                                      MARTYN EMSEN

# ℬAKED 𝒮WEET ℙOTATO 𝒮OUFFLÉ WITH 𝒞HEESE

*𝒯he sweet potato (Ipomoea batatas) has been a staple food in the Caribbean and Latin American countries for centuries. The protein content of sweet potato is 1.6 per cent, higher than that of the common potato, which is only 0.19 per cent. This is the main reason that potato dishes should be balanced with a protein supplement such as cheese, eggs, milk, legumes (peas, beans, lentils, or nuts), fish, meat, or poultry.*

| | |
|---|---|
| 2 × 250 g ( 8 oz ) sweet potatoes, scrubbed and wiped dry | 1 tsp mixed salt and celery salt |
| 2 tsp soya oil | grated nutmeg and ginger to taste |
| 2 tbs milk | 4 egg whites |
| 50 g ( 2 oz ) soya margarine or butter | 4 tbs chopped pecan nuts |
| 50 g ( 2 oz ) cheese, grated | 25 g ( 1 oz ) hard cheese, grated |
| 2 egg yolks | |

ℋeat the oven to Gas Mark 6/200°C/400°F. Prick the sweet potatoes all over with a fork. With the point of a knife, make a small horizontal indentation around the middle of each sweet potato, to mark where it will be cut in half.

Brush each sweet potato with soya oil and wrap it in foil. Bake in the oven for 1 hour. Then cut into halves, following the marking line. Scoop out the pulp and pass it through a sieve. Blend the next 6 ingredients with the pulp.

In a clean bowl, beat the egg whites with a pinch of salt until the mixture forms stiff peaks. Fold the meringue into the creamy pulp. Fill the 4 halved skins with the mixture. Level it with a palette knife, and sprinkle over the pecan nuts and grated cheese. Place on a baking tray and bake for 25 minutes.　　*Serves 4*　　**JEAN CONIL**

# CHILLED TOMATO SOUP WITH CORIANDER AND YOGURT QUENELLES

| 10 large tomatoes, each weighing about 75 g ( 3 oz ), skinned |
| --- |
| 2 small spring onions, chopped |
| juice of 1 lemon |
| 12 coriander leaves |
| 150 g ( 5 oz ) low-fat set yogurt |
| a little sugar |
| a little cinnamon |
| salt and cayenne pepper to taste |

Cut the tomatoes into halves and squeeze out the seeds. Place the onions and the tomatoes with the lemon juice and 6 of the coriander leaves in a blender and liquidise to a thin purée.

Season to taste with the sugar, cinnamon, salt and pepper and serve in bowls, each garnished with 2 tsp yogurt and a coriander leaf.　　*Serves 4–6*　　**RALF WIEDMANN**

# Sun-dried Tomato and Four-cheese Croûtons

*Pictured on page 69.*

| |
|---|
| 50 g (2 oz) each ricotta, mozzarella, and goat's cheese |
| 50 g (2 oz) soft soya margarine |
| 1 clove garlic, chopped |
| 1 tbs chopped parsley and basil |
| 1 french bread stick, sliced slantways |
| 100 ml (3½ fl oz) soya oil |
| 50 g (2 oz) sun-dried or 250 g (8 oz) fresh tomatoes |
| 50 g (2 oz) parmesan cheese, grated |

Heat the oven to Gas Mark 6/200°C/400°F.

In a bowl, mix the first three cheeses to a paste. Add the soya margarine, garlic, and herbs. Brush the bread slices with the oil and toast one side under the grill. Spread some of the cheese mixture over each slice, and top with a piece of tomato. Sprinkle a little grated parmesan over the tomato. Place the croûtons on a baking tray and heat in the oven until the cheese is melted. *Serves 8* **HOWARD BULKA**

# Potato and Cep Gratin

*If ceps are unavailable, you can use other mushrooms for this recipe.*

| |
|---|
| 1 kg (2 lb) potatoes, peeled and sliced thickly |
| 500 g (1 lb) ceps, washed and sliced |
| 250 g (8 oz) Gruyère cheese, grated |
| salt and pepper |
| 2 cloves garlic, crushed and mixed with 50 g (2 oz) mixed butter and soya oil |
| 300 ml (½ pint) single cream |

Heat the oven to Gas Mark 6/200°C/400°F. Scald the potatoes in boiling salted water for 30 seconds. This will prevent the acid in the potatoes from curdling the cream. Drain the potato slices and arrange them in an earthenware dish with alternate layers of ceps and grated cheese until full. Heat the garlic mixture for 30 seconds. Add this to the cream with seasoning and drizzle over the potatoes and ceps. Bake in the oven for 45 minutes until soft and golden on top. *Serves 6* **PHILLIPE MILLION**

# FIELD MUSHROOMS STUFFED WITH AUBERGINE PURÉE AND CHEESE

*The field or cultivated variety of mushroom in Britain is* Agaricus campestris. *The cep, or boletus, is a wild variety also used for this dish. Select large, fresh mushrooms with cap diameters of about 5 cm (2 inches).*

| | |
|---|---|
| 8 large mushrooms | 1 tbs tomato pulp, chopped |
| 1 aubergine, sliced | 1 tsp chopped basil |
| 4 tbs soya oil | juice of ½ lemon |
| 1 medium onion, chopped | 50 g ( 2 oz) Cheddar cheese, grated |
| 2 cloves garlic, chopped | salt to taste |
| 1 green chilli, de-seeded and chopped | 8 spinach or chard leaves, to garnish |

Remove the stems from the mushrooms and peel the caps. Chop the stems. Sprinkle salt over the sliced aubergine and leave to drain for 30 minutes. Then rinse in running water and drain well.

Heat 2 tbs of the oil in a pan and sauté the onion, garlic, chopped mushroom stems and chopped chilli for 4 minutes. Remove from the pan. Heat the remaining oil and fry the aubergine slices, covered, for 2 minutes until soft. Stir in the tomato pulp and cook for 1 minute. Leave to cool. Combine all the cooked ingredients, and mince or purée. Season to taste. Add basil and lemon juice.

Grease a baking tin, and place the 8 mushroom caps in it, inside upwards. Spoon some of the mixture onto each cap. Sprinkle over the grated cheese. Brown under the grill for 3 minutes.

Take 4 plates, and arrange 2 spinach leaves, overlapping, on each plate, with 2 filled mushrooms in the centre.　　*Serves 4*　　　　　　　　　　　　　　　　　　　　　　　　　　　　　　　**GEORGE SAINT**

# CHEESE MOUSSE WITH ORANGE BRIOCHE

*Pictured on page 34.*

| FOR THE MOUSSE | 3 tbs mixed soya margarine and butter |
|---|---|
| 15 g ( ½ oz ) powdered gelatine | 1 egg, beaten with 1 tbs milk and a pinch sugar |
| 15 g ( ½ oz ) caster sugar | 3 tbs orange juice |
| 250 g ( 8 oz ) cooking or dessert apples, peeled, cored, | 25 g ( 1 oz ) caster sugar |
| and cut into wedges | |
| 150 ml ( ¼ pint ) sweet, sparkling wine or champagne | FOR THE SAUCE |
| 50 g ( 2 oz ) mascarpone or cream cheese | 500 g ( 1 lb ) fresh raspberries |
| 5 tbs double cream, whipped lightly | 50 g ( 2 oz ) icing sugar |
| | juice of ½ lemon |
| FOR THE ORANGE BRIOCHE | |
| 200 g ( 7 oz ) plus 1 tbs bread flour | TO DECORATE |
| ½ tsp salt | peel and segments of 1 orange |
| 15 g ( ½ oz ) sugar | 2 kiwifruits, peeled and sliced |
| 15 g ( ½ oz ) fresh yeast | 50 g ( 2 oz ) sugar |
| 3 tbs milk, warmed | 8 mint leaves |
| 1 egg, beaten | |

Heat the oven to Gas Mark 7/220°C/425°F.

To prepare the mousse, blend together the ground gelatine and the sugar. Poach the apples in the champagne until the fruit is soft. Dissolve the gelatine and sugar in this mixture. Set aside the apples and all but 3 tbs of the syrup. Combine the 3 tbs of syrup with the cheese. Leave until cold, then fold in the whipped cream. Oil four 100 ml oval moulds. Fill these with the cheese mixture and place in the refrigerator. Meanwhile prepare the brioches. Put the flour in a bowl, making a well in the centre and add the salt and sugar. In a cup, mix the yeast with the lukewarm milk. Stir this into the well and sprinkle on 1 tbs of flour. Allow to ferment for 10 minutes, then mix the ingredients. Add the egg, and beat the dough for 8 minutes until stiff.

Dot the mixture with butter and margarine and leave to rest, covered with a cloth, until the dough has risen to twice its volume. Knock back the dough by kneading and mixing the soft butter into it. Divide into 8 well-formed balls. Grease 8 individual tin moulds with margarine and dust the insides with flour. Shake off the surplus flour. Place a ball of dough in each tin. Brush with the egg, milk, and sugar mixture. Allow to prove until the mixture rises over the brim of each mould. Brush the top with egg wash again and bake in the oven for 30 minutes. Meanwhile, boil the orange juice and caster sugar together until it has reduced by ⅔ of its volume and is sticky. Unmould the brioches and glaze with the orange syrup while still hot.

Make a sauce by mixing together the raspberries, icing sugar, and lemon juice. Purée and strain.

Prepare the decoration by boiling the orange peel with sugar and a little water until the water evaporates and the peel is dried. Then boil 50 g (2 oz) sugar with 1 tbs water until the sugar is almost caramelised. Add the orange segments and leave the syrup to cool.

Take 4 plates and place half a brioche and one cheese mould on each plate. Cover with the other halves of the brioches. Pour on a pool of raspberry sauce and decorate with slices of kiwifruit. Sprinkle crystallised orange peel over each brioche, and place a wedge of crystallised orange, or an apple wedge, and 2 mint leaves, over the cheese mould. *Serves 4*                     GEORGE McNEILL

# *Jerusalem Jamboree and Cheese Mousse*

*Jerusalem artichokes tend to be rather misshapen and knobbly. They are best in October and delicious hot with a lemon dressing. They can be eaten raw too. This recipe uses both cooked and raw artichokes. Pictured on page 33.*

| | |
|---|---|
| 4 tbs soya oil | 1 clove of garlic, crushed |
| 250 g (8 oz) Jerusalem artichokes, peeled and sliced | salt and pepper |
| 250 g (8 oz) field mushrooms, sliced | |
| 150 g (5 oz) onion, sliced thinly in strips | TO GARNISH |
| juice of 1 lemon and grated rind of ½ lemon | lettuce and chicory leaves |
| 150 g (5 oz) plain curd or cream cheese | 4 Jerusalem artichokes, peeled and sliced thinly |
| 2 egg whites, beaten | 2 radishes, sliced |
| 1 tsp mint leaves, chopped | ½ cucumber, split and sliced thinly |

*H*eat the oven to Gas Mark 6/200°C/400°F.

Heat the oil in a pan and toss the artichokes, mushrooms and onions for 6 minutes. Season and flavour with half the lemon juice. Pass the mixture through a sieve to obtain a purée.

In a bowl, combine the cheese, artichoke purée, egg whites, lemon, and mint leaves. Add garlic and seasoning.

Grease 4 small basins with soft margarine and fill them with the mousse mixture. Place in a baking tray half-filled with hot water and bake in the oven for 20 minutes.

Divide the lettuce and chicory leaves between 4 plates and arrange the artichoke slices over them. Place a cheese mousse in the centre. Decorate with slices of radish and cucumber around each mousse. Sprinkle with the remaining lemon juice at the last minute.     *Serves 4*                     GORDON McGUINESS

# Aubergine Papeton

*Aubergines are ripe when their colour becomes an overall black-purple or ivory-white, depending on the variety. The skin is the main source of flavour. A member of the same family as the potato and tomato, the aubergine has an affinity with both vegetables, as well as with peppers. Pictured on page 33.*

| | |
|---|---|
| 2 medium aubergines | 2 eggs, beaten |
| 75 g (3 oz) soya margarine | 5 tbs double cream or low-fat yogurt |
| 3 tbs soya oil | 2 sprigs basil, chopped |
| 1 small onion, chopped | juice of ½ lemon |
| 1 clove garlic, chopped | 2 tbs grated Cheddar or parmesan cheese |
| 2 medium tomatoes, skinned, de-seeded and chopped | salt and pepper to taste |
| 1 small chilli, chopped | |

Heat the oven to Gas Mark 6/200°C/400°F. Using a potato-peeler, peel one of the aubergines to obtain regular skin ribbons. Scald these ribbons for 30 seconds. Spread the margarine thickly inside 4 individual metal bowls. Arrange the ribbons in them in a crisscross pattern, leaving the ends to overlap to wrap the filling.

Slice the unpeeled aubergine, and cut the peeled aubergine into cubes. Wash in plenty of water to remove the bitter juice. Rinse and wipe dry. Heat the oil in a pan and fry the aubergine, onion and garlic pieces for 5 minutes until soft, without browning. Add the chopped tomato and chopped chilli. Cook for 3 more minutes. Season to taste and cool the mixture completely.

Blend the eggs with the cream or yogurt. Add basil and lemon juice. Season to taste. Combine the aubergine and egg mixtures. Fill the 4 basins and cover with the overlapping aubergine ribbons. Place the basins in a tray half-filled with hot water. Bake in the oven for 35 to 40 minutes, until set like baked custard.

Turn out each papeton onto a plate and sprinkle over the grated cheese. Serve with a tomato sauce, such as Creole Sauce (see page 170). *Serves 4*　　　　　　　　　　　　　　　　　　　　　　　**AIMÉ MÉTTÉTAL**

# Pancake Soufflé with Winter Salad

| | |
|---|---|
| 1 egg, beaten | TO GARNISH |
| 150 ml (¼ pint) milk | mixed winter salad leaves |
| 75 g (3 oz) wholemeal flour | 3 tbs soya oil |
| 1 tsp mixed celery salt and black pepper | 1 tbs cider vinegar |
| | 2 olives, stoned and chopped |
| FOR THE FILLING | 1 tsp made Dijon mustard |
| 150 g (5 oz) ripe brie, minus rind | 1 tbs chopped parsley |
| 1 egg, beaten | salt and pepper to taste |
| 4 egg whites | |
| 1 tsp salt | |

Heat the oven to Gas Mark 6/200°C/400°F. Prepare a smooth batter by combining the egg, milk, and flour. Add the seasoning. Rest the batter for 15 minutes. Lightly oil an 18 cm (7 inch) frying pan, and make four pancakes with the batter.

To prepare the filling, blend the brie with the egg, and add the salt. In a separate, clean bowl, beat the egg whites, with a pinch of salt added to improve texture. When the whites form peaks, blend in the cheese mixture lightly but thoroughly. Spoon the mixture onto each pancake. Fold over and place on a greased tray. Bake in the oven for 8 minutes to set the mixture.

On 4 plates, arrange some salad leaves. Blend the remaining ingredients in a liquidiser and sprinkle over the leaves. Place a pancake on each plate and serve immediately. *Serves 4* **ANTONIO MANCINI**

# Normandy Fondue

*This fondue mixture is also good spread on toasted brioches and served hot at a party with dry white wine.*

| |
|---|
| 50 g ( 2 oz ) soya margarine |
| 4 cloves garlic, chopped |
| 300 ml ( ½ pint ) dry wine |
| 750 g ( 1 ½ lb ) Gruyère cheese, grated |
| 3 tbs kirsch or calvados |
| 12 slices french bread, toasted |

*Blend* the margarine and garlic together. Melt the mixture in a saucepan until it froths. Then stir in the wine and grated cheese. Simmer, stirring with a wooden spoon, for 8 minutes until you have a smooth paste. Just before serving, add the kirsch. Serve in a heated fondue pot with the toasted bread on a separate plate, and leave the guests to help themselves by dipping the bread into the fondue.

*Serves 4–6*

**PATRICK POMMIER**

# Cream of Pumpkin Soup

*Pictured on page 34.*

| | |
|---|---|
| 4 tbs soya oil | ½ tsp mixed ground ginger and cinnamon |
| 2 cloves garlic, chopped | salt to taste |
| 1 large onion, chopped | |
| 250 g ( 8 oz ) potatoes, peeled and diced | |
| 500 g ( 1 lb ) ripe red pumpkin pulp, diced | TO GARNISH |
| 1 litre ( 1¾ pints ) water | 150 g ( 5 oz ) bread croûtons, fried in soya oil |
| 600 ml ( 1 pint ) milk | 100 g ( 3½ oz ) cheese, grated |

*Heat* the oil in a sauté pan and stir-fry the garlic and onion for 1 minute without browning. Add the potatoes and pumpkin. Cover with water and boil until the vegetables are soft. Strain or liquidise the ingredients to a soft purée. Reheat, add the milk, and season to taste with the ginger, cinnamon, and salt.

The soup can be served in the dried skin of a pumpkin, or in individual bowls with fried bread croûtons and grated cheese sprinkled over.     *Serves 8–12*

**BILL GALLAGHER**

# CHRISTOPHENE MARROW STUFFED WITH GOAT'S CHEESE

*The Christophene marrow* (Sechium edule), *which is available in Britain during the winter from supermarkets or Indian shops, is also known as chow-chow or chayote. The skin should be smooth and ridged.*

| | |
|---|---|
| 2 × 375 g (12 oz) Christophene marrows | 1 green chilli, de-seeded and chopped |
| 150 g (5 oz) goat's cheese, rinded and chopped | 1 tsp curry powder |
| 1 egg, beaten | 1 tbs Cheddar cheese, grated |
| 1 medium onion, chopped | 1 tsp desiccated coconut |
| 1 clove garlic, chopped | salt to taste |
| 3 tbs soya oil | |

Boil the marrows in salted water for 20 minutes. Cut in half and discard the stones. Scoop out the pulp, retaining the skins as shells for the filling.

Heat the oven to Gas Mark 6/200°C/400°F, or turn the grill to high. In a bowl, combine the pulp, goat's cheese and egg. In a pan, stir-fry the onion and garlic for 2 minutes in the oil. Add the chilli and cook for 30 seconds. Mix in the curry powder and stir for 5 seconds. Add to the pulp mixture and blend well. Fill each skin to the top with the pulp mixture. Sprinkle over the grated cheese and coconut, and place the filled marrows on a baking tray. Bake in the oven for 15 minutes or glaze under the grill for 5 minutes.     *Serves 4*

**KEN ANDERSON**

# Avocado Mousse

| |
|---|
| 3 large unblemished avocados, peeled and stoned |
| 7 g ( ¼ oz) or 2 sheets gelatine |
| juice of ¼ lemon |
| 1 leaf fresh tarragon or a few mint leaves, chopped |
| 2 tbs thick mayonnaise |
| 300 ml ( ½ pint) whipping cream |
| salt and pepper to taste |

Sieve the avocados into a bowl. Soften the gelatine in water for 1 minute, then dissolve over heat for 2 minutes. Add to the avocado purée and season to taste. Add the lemon juice and chopped tarragon or mint to the mayonnaise, and stir into the purée. Leave to cool completely. Whip the cream and fold it in.

Fill four lightly oiled moulds and chill for 1 hour. Either unmould on plates or decorate with peeled, sliced cherry tomatoes around each mould, with a few stoned black olives for contrast. Or scoop out four medium tomatoes and fill the cavities with the avocado mousse. Or serve the mousse piped inside Chinese cabbage leaves. Avocado mousse is also an excellent dip to serve with *crudités*.     *Serves 4*     JEAN-PAUL BATTAGLIA

# Tomato and Cheese Roulade

| | |
|---|---|
| 4 tbs soya oil | 4 tbs mango chutney |
| 1 small onion, chopped | ½ tsp made strong yellow mustard |
| 8 tomatoes, skinned, de-seeded and chopped finely | 1 small bunch watercress |
| 2 tbs wholemeal flour | |
| 6 eggs, separated | TO GARNISH |
| seasoning to taste | 4 tomatoes, sliced thinly |
| 50 g ( 2 oz) Cheddar cheese, grated | 2 avocados, sliced thinly |

Heat the oven to Gas Mark 6/200°C/400°F. Line a 30 cm × 20 cm (12 × 8-inch) swiss-roll tin with greaseproof paper, and brush 2 tbs of the oil over the paper. Heat the remaining oil in a pan and stir-fry the onion and tomatoes for 4 minutes. Add the flour and cook for 1 minute. Season to taste. Leave the mixture to cool in a bowl. Blend in the egg yolks, and check the seasoning. In a clean bowl, beat the egg whites with a pinch of salt. When stiff, very gently fold into the tomato mixture. Spread it evenly onto the tin and bake in the oven for 20 minutes. Turn onto a sheet of greaseproof paper and cool.

To make the filling, blend together the cheese, mango chutney and mustard in a bowl. Add the watercress leaves, and spread this mixture over the sponge. Roll the mixture, using the greaseproof paper under the sponge as a lever. Cut in slices and serve on plates garnished with the tomatoes and avocados.

*Serves 4*                                                                                                       **CHRISTOPHER CONIL**

# Spinach and Tyn Crug Roulade

| | |
|---|---|
| 4 eggs, separated | 100 g (3½ oz) Tyn Crug mature Welsh Cheddar |
| ½ tsp salt | cheese, or other hard cheese, grated |
| 150 g (5 oz) spinach, chopped | salt and pepper |

| FOR THE FILLING | TO GARNISH |
|---|---|
| 25 g (1 oz) soya oil | a few different-coloured salad leaves |
| 25 g (1 oz) flour | a few chicory leaves |
| 150 ml (¼ pint) milk | 4 tsp salad dressing |
| 50 g (2 oz) onion, chopped | 8 small slices of Tyn Crug Welsh Cheddar |

Heat the oven to Gas Mark 5/190°C/375°F. In a clean bowl, beat the egg whites and salt until stiff. Blend in the egg yolks and add the chopped spinach. Place the mixture in a swiss-roll tin lined with foil or heat-resistant film. Bake in the oven for 16 minutes. Unmould onto a sheet of greaseproof paper.

To make the filling, heat the oil and add the flour to make a roux. Stir in the milk and the raw onion. Boil for 5 minutes. Season to taste and allow to cool. Mix the cheese into the paste. When cold, spread this thick cheese paste over the spinach roulade and roll up. Wrap in foil to form a cylindrical shape. When wanted unwrap and cut into 8 thick slices.

To serve, arrange nests of mixed lettuce and chicory leaves on four plates. Sprinkle over a little salad dressing. Place 2 slices of the cheese roulade in the centre of each nest and top with 2 slices of Cheddar. Serve hot or cold.    *Serves 4*                                                                                     **LEWIS KEAL**

# Siberian Pelmeni

*Traditional pelmeni is pasta, stuffed with cheese, fish, or meat, which is frozen before being cooked. This gives the pasta a special texture and opaque appearance, almost like rice pasta. In this adaptation, which I served to a Soviet Air Minister many years ago, I was able to reproduce the original, to the Minister's satisfaction.*

| FOR THE PASTA | 1 tbs soured cream |
|---|---|
| 375 g (12 oz) bread flour | 2 tbs mixed fresh herbs (parsley, thyme, and basil) |
| 25 g (1 oz) ground semolina | 1 clove garlic, chopped |
| 1 egg, beaten | 1 egg, hard-boiled, shelled, chopped, and sieved |
| 1 tbs soya oil | 50 g (2 oz) walnuts, chopped very finely |
| 125 ml (4 fl oz) water | salt and black pepper |
| 1½ tsp celery salt | |
| 50 g (2 oz) mixed butter and oil | TO GARNISH |
| | 4 tomatoes, sliced |
| FOR THE FILLING | 2 tbs mixed fresh herbs (dill, basil, and parsley) |
| 100 g (3½ oz) cream cheese | 50 g (2 oz) Cheddar cheese, grated |

Sift the flour and celery salt over a pastry board. Make a well in the centre and pour in the beaten egg, soya oil and water. Gradually mix to a dough, then roll to a ball. Rest the dough for 30 minutes. Dust ground semolina and flour over the pastry ball and roll out to 5 mm (¼ inch) thick. Using a plain 5 cm (2-inch) pastry cutter, cut into rounds.

In a bowl, combine all the filling ingredients to form a smooth but stiff paste. If too soft, add more walnuts or chopped, hard-boiled egg. Brush the pastry rounds with water, and spoon some of the mixture onto the centre of each, about 15 g (½ oz) per pelmeni. Fold over, and curve the turnovers with the pointed ends connected together to look like a hat. Oil a tray and place all the prepared pelmeni on it. Freeze for 4 hours. When frozen, wrap with greaseproof paper or polythene sheet. Store in a box in the freezer until required.

Boil some salted water and poach the frozen pelmeni in it for 25 minutes. Drain well. Heat the butter and oil, and gently reheat the pelmeni for 6 minutes. To serve, take 4 plates, and place 4 tomato slices and 2 cooked pelmeni on each. Sprinkle the tomatoes with herbs, and the pelmeni with cheese.     *Serves 4*     **JEAN CONIL**

# *T*HE *G*IFTS OF *C*ERES – Grains, Pasta and Pulses

*C*ereal grains derive their common name from the goddess Ceres, thought by the Romans to rule over all vegetation. Cereal grains include rice, oats, rye, barley, corn (maize), millet, and sorghum, as well as wheat. In both Semitic and Christian countries, bread has always been the staff of life; and to make bread you need wheat flour. Wheat and rice, as the most important of the cereal grains, today provide more nourishment for the peoples of the world than any other food.

Arable land planted with wheat will provide food for more people than the same land used for producing non-cereal food, such as meat, milk and poultry. It is estimated that about 3.5 kg (8 lb) of grain is required to produce 500 g (1 lb) of meat. This weight of wheat offers far greater quantities of many essential nutrients than does the 500 g (1 lb) of meat. Because of the world's exploding population, it would be practical to return from our present 'meat economy' to greater dependence on wheat-flour foods. Wheaten foods provide generous quantities of carbohydrates, protein, certain vitamins and minerals. A diet with large amounts of cereal protein and only small amounts of protein from animal sources is sufficient. Heart disease and the associated afflictions that plague so many people in the West are much less common in other parts of the world where people eat larger amounts of wheat, rice, or other grains. There is growing evidence that diets which include foods high in hard, saturated animal fat and cholesterol produce a greater incidence of coronary diseases. This is the main reason that we have emphasized throughout our recipes the use of soya oil as a product suitable for healthy diets.

Canned, chilled, frozen, dried or ready-to-eat packaged foods often contain some wheat or are flour-based, and they include many different kinds of crackers, biscuits, soups, sauces and puddings. No other type of food finds its way to the table in so many forms.

Cereals go well with other rich sources of protein; like the partnership of rice and peas, corn and beans, pies, poultry in rich sauces, French crêpes, cheese pizzas, and Cornish pasties. Would you eat a burger without a bun? Then we have the enormous selection of pasta foods, a huge variety of which are found in China, although our recipe for Fresh Pasta Carousel (see page 24) comes from Italy. It would seem that there are as many ways of making and serving pasta as there are people to enjoy them. Found in a variety of shapes and textures, they include rice noodles, which are simply soaked in water and then deep-fried so crisp as to crumble at the least touch; and wheat noodles, which are thought to have been introduced to Italy by Marco Polo, inaugurating the pasta industry there without grateful acknowledgement to the Chinese inventors.

Above all, in the West, we eat most of our meals with bread. Several hundred varieties of loaves have been developed over the centuries from the flat, unleavened pitta to the Indian chapati. We have enriched our bread with milk, eggs, fats and mineral supplements to make it as nutritious as possible, and we have varied the myriad ways of cooking it to make it as delicious as possible.

# Afghanistan Rice Kedgeree with Mung Beans

| FOR THE MEATBALLS | 1 pinch mixed spices, e.g. cinnamon, ground cloves, |
|---|---|
| 500 g (1 lb) minced lamb | pepper, paprika, ground ginger |
| 1 small onion, chopped | 1 litre (1¾ pints) water |
| ½ tsp each of ground cumin and coriander | 1 tsp curry powder |
| 1 tbs mint leaves, chopped | 150 g (5 oz) mung beans, half-cooked |
| 1 egg | salt to taste |
| 1 tbs flour | |
| 3 tbs soya oil | FOR THE SAUCE |
| | 2 tbs soya oil |
| FOR THE PILAFF | 1 small onion, chopped |
| 3 tbs soya oil | 1 clove garlic, chopped |
| 1 large onion, chopped | 500 g (1 lb) tomatoes, skinned, de-seeded, and chopped |
| 2 cloves garlic, chopped | 1 tbs tomato purée |
| 150 g (5 oz) short-grain rice | salt, pepper, and sugar to taste |

Prepare the meatballs by combining all the ingredients except the oil. Shape the mixture into small balls. Heat the oil and fry the meatballs until cooked all over.

To make the pilaff, heat the oil and sweat the onion and garlic for 2 minutes. Add the rice and stir so that it absorbs the oil. Sprinkle on the spices and curry powder and cover with the water. Add the well-washed mung beans. Bring to the boil, cover with a lid, and simmer for 30 minutes. Add salt to taste.

To prepare the tomato sauce, heat the oil and stir-fry the onion for 4 minutes. Add the rest of the ingredients and cook for 4 minutes only. Coat the meatballs with the tomato sauce, and serve on the rice. The Afghans eat this dish with yogurt.     *Serves 4*

**JEAN CONIL**

# *M*ushroom *P*ancakes

*Apparently the Ancient Romans thrived on mushroom dishes, but this particular recipe was developed during the Napoleonic wars by numerous chefs. The cognac added to the delicate filling is a touch of genius. Wild mushrooms, such as ceps and morels can also be used. Pictured on page 67.*

| FOR THE PANCAKE BATTER | 1 small shallot, chopped |
|---|---|
| 2 eggs, beaten | 250 g (8 oz) mushrooms, washed and quartered |
| 300 ml (½ pint) full-cream milk | 100 ml (3½ fl oz) double cream |
| 1 tsp salt | pinch saffron powder |
| 100 g (3½ oz) wholemeal flour | salt and pepper |
| | 1 tbs cognac (optional) |
| FOR THE FILLING | 4 sprigs watercress, to garnish |
| 3 tbs soya oil | |

*In* a bowl, first mix the eggs and milk with the salt, and then blend in the flour to a smooth consistency. Leave to rest for 30 minutes, then make the pancakes in a well-greased 12 cm (5-inch) pan.

To make the filling, heat the oil and stir-fry the shallot until soft, then add the mushrooms and cook for 3 minutes only. Discard surplus fat. Add the cream, saffron, and seasoning. Gently simmer for 5 minutes. Flavour with the cognac if you wish.

Fill each pancake with mushroom filling and fold over. Serve hot with a sprig of watercress.

*Serves 4*                                                                                      **PIERRE CONIL**

# Fresh Pasta Carousel
## IN Three Different Sauces

| FOR THE | FOR THE SCALLOP SAUCE |
|---|---|
| **BLACK FETTUCCINI (THIN NOODLES)** | 1 tbs olive or soya oil |
| 100 g (3½ oz) strong flour | 3 tbs tomato pulp, chopped |
| 1 small egg, beaten | 1 small shallot, chopped |
| 1 tsp octopus ink | 50 g (2 oz) cleaned scallops, diced |
| ⅓ tsp salt | 3 tarragon leaves, chopped |
| | salt and pepper to taste |
| FOR THE | |
| **GREEN FETTUCCINI** | FOR THE SCAMPI SAUCE |
| 100 g (3½ oz) strong flour | 1 tbs olive or soya oil |
| 1 small egg, beaten | 1 clove garlic, chopped |
| 25 g (1 oz) spinach or rocket | 2 tbs chopped spinach or rocket |
| 1 tbs water | 3 tbs chopped tomato pulp |
| ⅓ tsp salt | 2 scampi, diced |
| | salt and pepper to taste |
| FOR THE | |
| **WHITE PASTA** | FOR THE TOMATO SAUCE |
| 100 g (3½ oz) strong flour | 1 tbs olive or soya oil |
| 1 small egg, beaten | 1 tbs tomato purée |
| 2 tbs mixed oil and water | 3 tbs tomato pulp, diced |
| ⅓ tsp salt | salt and pepper to taste |

Prepare each pasta in a separate bowl by combining the ingredients. Roll out and cut into thin layers 15 cm (6 inches) long, and with a knife or pasta-machine cut into thin noodles, or fettuccini. Boil each type of pasta separately for 2 minutes and drain.

Make the sauces separately. Heat the oil, stir-fry all the ingredients for 3 minutes, and season to taste. On each plate, arrange a small portion of each pasta. Ladle on a little of each sauce to produce different textures and flavours. *Serves 4* SERGIO MEI

# Vegetable Millefeuille in Pastry Leaves

| | FOR THE SAUCE |
|---|---|
| 250 g (8 oz) ready-made puff pastry | |
| 1 egg yolk | 25 g (1 oz) shallots, chopped |
| 125 g (4 oz) spinach leaves | 3 tbs dry white wine |
| 125 g (4 oz) mangetouts, topped and tailed | 3 tbs light stock |
| 8 baby carrots | 100 ml (3½ fl oz) double cream |
| 8 baby turnips | 15 g (½ oz) unsalted butter |
| 8 small sprigs broccoli | 2 tbs lemon grass (or tarragon, chervil, or mint) |
| 8 small sprigs cauliflower | juice of ½ lemon |
| 50 g (2 oz) unsalted butter | salt and pepper to taste |
| salt and black pepper to taste | |

Heat the oven to Gas Mark 4/180°C/350°F. Roll out the puff pastry to 3 mm (⅛-inch) thickness. Brush with the beaten yolk and let it dry for 15 minutes. Place the pastry on a greased tin and prick it with a fork. Bake to a pale yellow for 12 minutes. Cool and cut into strips 5 cm (2 inches) wide. Boil the vegetables for 3 minutes. Drain well, then season and add the butter.

To prepare the sauce, boil the chopped shallots in the wine and stock for 4 minutes, until soft. Add the cream and butter and reduce by half. Season to taste. Lastly, flavour the sauce with the fresh, chopped lemon grass herb and the lemon juice.

To serve, arrange a layer of pastry on each plate. Top with sliced vegetables and coat with the sauce. Cover with another layer of pastry. A pool of sauce can be poured beside each pastry.  *Serves 4*  **JENS P. KOLBECK**

# Vegetable Dolmas Jordanian-Style

| | |
|---|---|
| 4 carrots, peeled and split | 2 red peppers, split and de-seeded |
| 4 turnips, peeled and split | 2 green peppers, split and de-seeded |
| 4 mooli, peeled | 4 large, ribbed tomatoes, de-seeded |
| 4 courgettes, scooped out | |
| 4 onions, peeled and split | FOR THE SECOND STUFFING |
| 8 vine leaves, blanched | 100 g (3½ oz) pilaff rice |
| | 1 tbs soya or olive oil |
| FOR THE FIRST STUFFING | 1 small onion, chopped |
| 200 g (7 oz) easy-cook long-grain rice | 1 clove garlic, chopped |
| 25 g (1 oz) onion, chopped | 50 g (2 oz) pine nuts |
| 1 clove garlic, chopped | 1 tsp mixed cumin, pepper, salt, |
| 50 g (2 oz) tomato pulp, chopped | and cinnamon |
| 1 tsp mixed chopped fresh mint and parsley | |
| juice of 1 lemon | 4 small aubergines, halved |
| grated peel of ½ lemon | soya oil for deep-frying |
| 1 tsp mixed cumin and cinnamon | |
| | FOR THE THIRD STUFFING |
| 2 potatoes, peeled and sliced | 2 tbs soya oil |
| 2 large onions, sliced | 150 g (5 oz) mixed red and green peppers, chopped |
| 1 bouquet garni | 1 small onion, chopped |
| 1½ tbs soya or olive oil | 1 clove garlic, chopped |
| 2 large tomatoes, sliced | 1 tbs chopped parsley or coriander |
| salt and pepper to taste | salt and pepper to taste |

To prepare the first stuffing, wash the easy-cook rice and leave to soak for 30 minutes. Drain. Stir in the chopped onion and garlic, tomato pulp, chopped herbs, lemon juice and peel, seasoning, and spices. Pack each root vegetable, the courgettes and the vine leaves three-quarters full, leaving room for the rice to expand. In the bottom of a casserole, place a layer of potatoes and onions and the bouquet garni. Arrange the stuffed vegetables on top, packed tightly together so that they do not split open during cooking. Sprinkle a little oil on top. Cover vegetables with sliced tomatoes. Season, and add enough water just to cover. Wedge a lid on top to keep the vegetables compressed. Cook gently, covered, for 1 hour on a low heat.

Heat the oven to Gas Mark 6/200°C/400°F. To prepare the second stuffing (for the peppers and tomatoes), boil the pilaff rice for 20 minutes and drain. Heat the oil and stir-fry the onion and garlic for 2 minutes. Add the pine nuts, fry for 1 minute and then mix with the cooked rice. Season to taste and blend in the mixed spices.

Allow to cool, then use to stuff the scooped-out tomatoes and peppers. Put them in a pan, add some water (about half-way up the sides of the vegetables) and a little oil, cover with foil and make some holes to allow steam to escape. Cook for 30 minutes.

Cut the aubergines into halves, making cavities for the stuffing. Score the skin lengthways and across. Deep-fry them in soya oil for 4 minutes. To fill the aubergines, heat the oil and stir-fry the ingredients for the third stuffing for 3 minutes, then pile into each aubergine half.

To serve, place the stuffed vegetables on an attractive large platter, alternating the items for colour and variety.     *Serves 4*                                                              AL WALBRECKER

# *M*USHROOM *S*TROGANOFF

*This is a vegetarian dish which was popular with the imperial family of Russia. Cultivated or wild varieties of mushroom or a mixture of both can be used in this dish.*

| | |
|---|---|
| 6 tbs soya oil | 1 tbs chopped mixed fresh herbs (dill, tarragon, and |
| 1 onion, cut into thin strips | parsley), plus extra to decorate |
| 1 small turnip, peeled and cut into thin strips | |
| 1 mooli, peeled and cut into thin strips | FOR THE ACCOMPANIMENT |
| 500 g (1 lb) different varieties of mushroom, sliced | 500 g (1 lb) noodles, cooked |
| 150 ml (¼ pint) soured cream | 50 g (2 oz) butter |
| 1 tbs vegetable extract or soya sauce | 2 tbs soya oil |
| salt and black pepper | 50 g (2 oz) Cheddar cheese, grated |
| 1 tbs tomato pulp, chopped | salt and pepper to taste |

*In* a large wok, heat the oil and toss the onion, turnip and mooli for 3 minutes without letting them colour. Add the mushrooms and stir-fry for 3 more minutes. Stir in the cream, and boil for 2 minutes. Season to taste. Finally add the vegetable extract, tomato pulp and mixed herbs. Toss the hot noodles in a pan with the butter, oil, and grated cheese. Season to taste.

On 4 plates, place some cooked noodles and surround them with the mushroom Stroganoff. Sprinkle chopped herbs over the noodles.     *Serves 4*                                              JEAN·CONIL

# Pumpkin and Rice Pie

| |
|---|
| 100 g (3½ oz) patna rice |
| 1 kg (2 lb) pumpkin, peeled, de-seeded, and cubed |
| 2 small pieces ginger, chopped |
| 3 tbs soya oil |
| 1 small onion, chopped |
| 100 g (3½ oz) hard cheese, grated |
| salt and pepper |

Boil the rice in twice its volume of water for 15 minutes and drain. Heat the oven to Gas Mark 7/225°C/425°F. Boil the pumpkin and one piece of ginger with water to cover for 10 minutes. Drain and mash to a purée. In an earthenware dish, place a layer of rice and a layer of pumpkin purée. Heat 2 tbs of the oil and stir-fry the onion and second piece of ginger for 2 minutes. Add this to the pie and sprinkle with plenty of cheese. Season to taste and bake in the oven for 12 minutes until golden.      *Serves 4*      MICHEL LOUSTEAU

# American Muffins

*This nutritious American muffin has been popular since the 17th century. Served hot with butter and cherry jam, it is a snack that children will enjoy.*

| | |
|---|---|
| 175 g (6 oz) wholemeal flour | 100 g (3½ oz) quick porridge oats |
| 100 g (3½ oz) dark rye flour | 300 ml (½ pint) buttermilk or yogurt |
| 175 g (6 oz) fine corn meal (polenta) | 1 large egg, beaten |
| 25 g (1 oz) baking powder | 3 tbs clear honey, warmed |
| ½ tsp salt | 3 tbs soya oil |

Heat the oven to Gas Mark 6/200°C/400°F. Sift together the flours, corn meal, baking powder, and salt. Mix in the oats. In another bowl, combine the buttermilk or yogurt, egg, oil, and honey. Blend the two mixtures together to make a soft, elastic dough batter. Grease some bun tins, spoon in the batter, and bake for 20 minutes. Serve warm with jam.      *Serves 8*      CHRISTOPHER CONIL

# Havengore Bounty

*Christopher Conil's memories of the bread he ate in his grandmother's farmhouse in a Picardy village prompted him to develop this tasty snack. The filling can be varied by the use of different cheeses, corned beef, chicken or ham. Pictured on page 67.*

| FOR THE BREAD | 1 egg, beaten |
|---|---|
| 500 g (1 lb) strong white flour | pinch sugar |
| ½ tsp salt | |
| pinch saffron powder | FOR THE FILLING |
| 2 tsp powdered milk | 250 g (8 oz) baked beans |
| 3 tbs soya oil | 100 g (3½ oz) onion, chopped |
| 25 g (1 oz) yeast | 250 g (8 oz) cooked potatoes, diced |
| 1 egg, beaten | 125 g (4 oz) Lymeswold soft cheese |
| 250 ml (8 fl oz) lukewarm water | pinch celery powder |
| | pinch curry powder |
| FOR THE GLAZE | 1 tbs chopped parsley |
| 1 tbs milk | salt and pepper to taste |

Heat the oven to Gas Mark 6/200°C/400°F. Mix together the flour, salt, saffron powder and powdered milk, then add the oil. Blend thoroughly. Pour the water into a bowl, then add the yeast and egg, stirring well. Blend this with the flour and knead well to a smooth and elastic dough. Place in an oiled, polythene bag and prove until double in size. Divide the dough into 8 buns, and rest for 5 minutes. Lightly dust with flour and roll out in flat circles 5mm (¼ inch) thick. Mix together the glaze ingredients, and brush some over each round.

Combine in a bowl all the filling ingredients. Spoon a portion onto each round of dough. Wet the edges and fold over. Crimp the sides to seal the pasty, and decorate with a strip of plaited dough, if wished. Brush with the glaze again. Arrange the pasties on 2 greased trays 30 cm (12 inches) × 13 cm (5 inches). Allow to rest for 30 minutes at room temperature before baking. Bake for 25 minutes, then serve with a tossed salad of chicory and lemon dressing.     *Serves 8*                    **CHRISTOPHER CONIL**

# Mexican Enchiladas

*Corn tortillas, made from masa harina, are still the Mexicans' staple food. Masa harina is preferable to ordinary corn meal (polenta), as it has been treated with lime water and is not so gritty. Supermarkets sell the made tortillas too.*

| | |
|---|---|
| **FOR THE TORTILLAS** | 500 g ( 1 lb ) cooked and well-dried spinach leaves |
| 500 g ( 1 lb ) masa harina | salt and pepper to taste |
| 50 g ( 2 oz ) bread flour | 1 red chilli, de-seeded and chopped |
| 125 ml ( 4 fl oz ) water | 250 g ( 8 oz ) curd cheese |
| 1 tsp salt | |
| 1 tbs soya oil | **FOR THE SAUCE** |
| | 15 g ( ½ oz ) soft margarine |
| **FOR THE ENCHILADAS** | 15 g ( ½ oz ) flour |
| 50 g ( 2 oz ) soya margarine | 600 ml ( 1 pint ) mixed cream and milk |
| 3 tbs soya oil | 1 green chilli, de-seeded and chopped |
| 1 onion, chopped | salt to taste |
| 2 cloves garlic, chopped | 100 g ( 3½ oz ) hard cheese, grated |

Heat the oven to Gas Mark 6/200°C/400°F. To make the tortillas, in a bowl mix together all the ingredients into a fine, elastic dough that is firm but moist. Divide into 12 balls. Place each ball on dusted wax or a polythene sheet and roll into a pancake 13 cm (5 inches) in diameter. Cook on a griddle pan for 2 minutes, turning the tortillas once. Keep the tortillas stacked and wrapped in a napkin. If you wish to curve them for filling, leave to cool on an oiled rolling pin.

To make the enchilada stuffing, heat the oil and margarine and toss the onion in it until soft, then add the garlic and spinach, and simmer for 5 minutes. Remove from the heat and season. Add the chilli and cheese, and leave to cool. Fill each tortilla with mixture and roll them. Place these enchiladas in 8 individual buttered dishes.

To make the sauce, heat the margarine in a pan and blend in the flour. Cook until the roux looks like wet sand. Stir in the cream and milk, and bring to the boil gently. Cook, stirring with a spoon, until the sauce is smooth. Add the chopped chilli, and salt to taste. Coat each tortilla with this sauce. Sprinkle over grated cheese and bake for about 20 minutes until golden. Serve with a tomato salad.     *Serves 8*     **JEAN CONIL**

# Country Pasties

*There was a time when the best turnovers were made with rich puff pastry as a casing. Today we recognise the importance of cutting down on butter in our pastries, and here a plain water and flour dough is adequate for a new version of meat pasty. Pictured on page 67.*

| FOR THE PASTRY | FOR THE STUFFING |
| --- | --- |
| 500 g ( 1 lb ) plain flour | 250 g ( 8 oz ) lean lamb, minced |
| 125 ml ( 4 fl oz ) warm water | 150 g ( 5 oz ) mixed carrots, onions, leeks, and celery, cubed |
| 1 egg, beaten | 1 egg, beaten |
| 1 tbs soya oil | salt and black pepper to taste |
| 1 tsp salt | 1 egg yolk, beaten |

Heat the oven to Gas Mark 6/200°C/400°F. In a bowl, combine the pastry ingredients and knead the paste to a dough. Gather into a ball and rest for 30 minutes. Divide into 6 balls. Dust with flour and roll them into circles 13 cm (5 inches) in diameter.

In a bowl, combine all the stuffing ingredients, except the beaten egg yolk. Season to taste. Divide into 6 small meatballs. Wet the edges of each pastry circle, and place a meatball in the centre. Fold the pastry over, and crimp the edges to seal the pasties. Brush with the egg yolk and place on a greased baking tray. Bake on the middle shelf of the oven for 30 minutes. Serve hot. *Serves 6* **CHRISTOPHER CONIL**

# LATIN AMERICA PUMPKIN BREAD

*Pumpkin is available in many supermarkets. It can be used for soups or tarts but also for a host of dishes, such as this bread, which are unfamiliar to Western gourmets.*

| |
|---|
| 500 g ( 1 lb ) wholemeal flour |
| 50 g ( 2 oz ) baking powder |
| 1 tsp salt |
| 1 tsp mixed cinnamon and allspice |
| 100 g ( 3½ oz ) fine corn meal ( polenta ) |
| 250 g ( 8 oz ) soya margarine, plus extra for greasing |
| 100 g ( 3½ oz ) treacle |
| 15 g ( ½ oz ) honey |
| 3 eggs, beaten |
| juice and grated peel of 1 lime |
| 250 g ( 8 oz ) pumpkin purée |

Heat the oven to Gas Mark 4/180°C/350°F. Sift together the flour, baking powder, salt, and spices, then rub in the corn meal, mixing well. Whip the soft margarine with the treacle and honey, and stir in the eggs. When the mixture is fluffy, blend in the lime juice and peel and the pumpkin purée. Gradually beat in the flour mixture to make a batter of dropping consistency.

Spread soft margarine evenly inside 2 loaf tins. Line them with greaseproof paper and grease the paper. Fill the tins two-thirds full. Bake for 45–50 minutes. The bread is ready when a needle inserted in the centre emerges dry. Cool in the tins, and turn out. Peel off the paper and slice.     *Serves 8*     **CHRISTOPHER CONIL**

*Jerusalem Jamboree and Cheese Mousse (page 13), Aubergine Papeton (page 14)*

Top: *Cheese Mousse with Orange Brioche (page 12)*, below left: *Cheese Puddings with Cloudberry Sauce (page 185)*, below right: *Cream of Pumpkin Soup (page 16)*

# Pitta Bread Stuffed with Broad-bean Fritters

*Pittas are usually stuffed with a savoury, vegetarian filling such as cheese, tomato, avocado, or even these delicious broad-bean fritters. Pictured on page 67.*

| | |
|---|---|
| 500 g ( 1 lb) bread flour | 1 small onion, chopped |
| 1 tsp salt | 500 g ( 1 lb) broad beans, boiled, skinned, and mashed |
| 250 ml ( 8 fl oz) lukewarm water | 2 tbs seasoned flour |
| 1 sachet active yeast | salt and pepper |
| 2 tsp sugar | juice of ½ lemon |
| | lettuce leaves or pickled cucumber slices, to garnish |
| **FOR THE FILLING** | |
| 3 tbs soya oil | |

Sift the flour and salt in a bowl and warm for 5 minutes. Remove 1 cup of the flour. In a cup, blend the warm water and yeast. Let it ferment for 10 minutes with a pinch of flour until it foams. Make a well in the centre of the sifted flour and fill with the liquid fermented yeast. Add the remaining flour and knead to a dough for 5 minutes. Gather into a ball and cover with a cloth or wrap in a polythene bag. Allow to prove for 30 minutes until double in size.

Heat the oven to Gas Mark 7/220°C/425°F. Knock the dough back with your knuckles to remove air pockets. Knead again and divide into 12 balls. Cover and let it swell again for 15 minutes. Roll out each ball into a round. Dust with flour to make the rolling easier. Leave for 15 minutes and then roll again into oval shapes. Arrange these pitta buns on a greased tray and bake for 5 minutes, turning half-way through.

Heat the oil and stir-fry the onion for 2 minutes. Strain the oil and add the onion to the bean paste. Shape the paste into 12 balls. Dip in seasoned flour and shallow-fry in the same oil until golden. Season and sprinkle with lemon juice. Slit each pitta bun to make a pocket and fill it with a broad-bean fritter and a leaf of lettuce or a slice of pickled cucumber. Eat while hot.     *Serves 6–8*     **CHRISTOPHER CONIL**

# CHAPATIS

*This Indian bread is the griddle pancake which has been modified through the centuries as Indians have travelled all over the world. The dough is fried as an accompaniment to curried dishes.*

| |
|---|
| 500 g ( 1 lb ) bread flour |
| 1 tsp curry powder |
| 1 pinch chilli powder |
| 3 tbs soya oil |
| 1 tsp salt |
| 100 ml ( 3½ fl oz ) warm water |
| 50 g ( 2 oz ) liquid clarified butter |

In a bowl or on a pastry board, heap together the flour and spices and make a well. Stir in the oil, add the salt, and rub the mixture between your fingers to get a crumble. Stir in the water to make the mixture into a dough. Knead for 5 minutes. Rest the dough for 30 minutes, then divide it into 16 balls. Flatten the balls, either with the palms of your hands or with a rolling pin, into round cakes 15 cm (6 inches) in diameter. Grease a griddle and cook them one by one like pancakes. (Do not grease the pan but instead brush them with butter as they are cooked.) If the chapatis inflate like balloons, flatten them with a spatula to remove the air. They will keep hot wrapped in foil and placed on a hot plate.

Alternatively, if you simply deep-fry the pancakes in oil until crisp – about 2 minutes, then drain them on a colander lined with absorbent paper, you have puris.     *Serves 16*     **M. SATISH**

# CHINESE MEDLEY OF VEGETABLES AND MUSHROOMS

| FOR THE TARO BASKET | FOR THE SAUCE |
|---|---|
| 500 g (1 lb) taro, peeled | 8 tbs water or vegetable stock |
| 25 g (1 oz) salt | 1 tbs cornflour |
| 25 g (1 oz) cornflour | 1 tsp sugar |
| soya oil for deep-frying | 1 tsp salt |
|  | 2 tbs soya sauce |
| FOR THE FILLING |  |
| 50 g (2 oz) each of: | TO GARNISH |
| field mushrooms, or black Chinese mushrooms, | 4 large mushrooms |
| lotus root, | 6 baby corn cobs |
| water chestnuts, | 2 carrots |
| mangetouts, | 2 sticks green celery |
| celery, | 1 bamboo root |
| fennel, | 5 tbs soya oil |
| carrots, | salt and pepper to taste |

To make the basket you require two colanders, one slightly smaller than the other. Using a mandoline cutter, slice the taro in a crisscross pattern to obtain waffle-shaped slices 3mm (⅛ inch) thick. Cut the remaining taro into 2 cm (¾-inch) strips for the base of the basket. Soak the sliced taro in salted water for 1 hour. Drain well and pat dry. Rub the slices in cornflour. Form the woven basket by overlapping the slices around the sides of the larger well-oiled colander. Place the strips to form the base of the basket across the bottom. Fit the smaller colander over the taro to hold the basket together. Deep-fry in soya oil for 5 minutes until crisp then remove. Take out the smaller colander and lift out the basket. Drain well.

To make the filling, peel and slice the vegetables and mushrooms. Top and tail the mangetouts. Blanch the vegetables for 2 minutes and drain well. Heat the oil in a wok and sauté the vegetables for 3 minutes. Add the stock and diluted cornflour to the mixture to bind the vegetables. Cook for 1 more minute. Add the sugar, salt, and soya sauce. Drain with a slotted spoon. Cut the garnish vegetables to the width and length of the mangetouts. Cut the baby corn cobs in half. Blanch quickly all the sliced vegetables and corn cobs. Toss the mushrooms in oil for 1 minute and drain. Season. Place the taro basket on a serving dish and pile in the filling. Around the basket arrange rows of the garnish vegetables, overlapping each other neatly.

*Serves 12*                                                                    **LAM SING-LUN**

# Beanie Pizza Pie

| FOR THE DOUGH | 1 small onion, chopped |
|---|---|
| 250 g (8 oz) flour | 1 clove garlic, chopped |
| 1 tsp salt | 50 g (2 oz) tomato purée |
| 1 tsp clear honey | 250 g (8 oz) fresh tomato pulp, chopped |
| 100 ml (3½ fl oz) warm water | salt and pepper |
| 1 tsp dried yeast | 100 g (3½ oz) baked beans in tomato sauce |
| 1 tsp soya oil, plus extra for brushing | 1 tsp chopped oregano or fresh mint leaves |
| | 2 large tomatoes, sliced |
| FOR THE FILLING | 100 g (3½ oz) mozzarella cheese, crumbled or |
| 3 tbs soya oil | cut into slices |

To make the dough, sift the flour and salt into a mixing bowl. Stir together the honey and warm water, and sprinkle on the yeast and a pinch of flour. Allow to ferment for about 12 minutes until it froths. Make a well in the flour and pour in the yeast mixture. Gently mix the flour and yeast to make a plastic dough. Knead for 10 minutes. Add the oil as you knead.

Roll out the dough thinly and cut out 16 circles with a 5 cm (2-inch) cutter. Place on greased baking trays and brush each small pizza with soya oil. Rest them for 15 minutes.

Heat the oven to Gas Mark 6/200°C/400°F. Heat the oil in a pan and stir-fry the onion for 4 minutes. Add the garlic and cook for 30 seconds. Next add the tomato purée and pulp, and cook for 10 minutes. Season to taste. Blend in the baked beans and herbs. Check the seasoning. Spoon the filling over each pizza base. Place a tomato slice and some cheese on top of each one. Bake for 20 minutes until golden and crisp.

*Serves 4*

**CHRISTOPHER CONIL**

# Michigan Bean and Beef Pie

| FOR THE DOUGH | FOR THE FILLING |
| --- | --- |
| 500 g ( 1 lb ) bread flour | 50 g ( 2 oz ) soya oil |
| 1 tsp salt | 1 medium onion, chopped |
| 1 tsp sugar | 1 clove garlic, chopped |
| 25 g ( 1 oz ) baking powder | 250 g ( 8 oz ) minced beef |
| ¼ tsp grated nutmeg | 500 g ( 1 lb ) baked beans, drained |
| 75 g ( 3 oz ) soya margarine | 1 tbs tomato purée |
| 300 ml ( ½ pint ) milk | 1 tsp oregano |
| 1 egg, beaten | salt and black pepper to taste |

Heat the oven to Gas Mark 6/200°C/400°F. To make the dough, sift the flour, salt, sugar, baking powder and nutmeg into a bowl. Rub in the margarine. Stir in the milk and blend to a soft, elastic dough. Divide the mixture into 16 balls. Dust with flour and flatten to rounds 1 cm ( ½ inch ) thick.

To make the filling, heat the oil and stir-fry the onion and garlic for 1 minute. Blend in the meat and brown for 3 minutes only. Add the beans, then stir in the tomato purée. Season to taste and sprinkle on the oregano. Place the bean and meat mixture in an earthenware dish and cover evenly with the scone rounds. Brush the tops with the beaten egg and bake on the middle shelf of the oven for 25–30 minutes.

*Serves 8*                                                                        CHRISTOPHER CONIL

# 𝒮EAFOOD

𝒯t is difficult to believe how simple it is to catch an octopus. Just show it a white flag and it will be there in a flash to grab it, although we do not advise holiday-makers to try it! If you want to cook an octopus, you must first of all make sure that it has been beaten and rubbed with oil for at least half an hour. You can then boil it and serve it cold with lemon dressing, or fry it and serve it with rice, tomato, and garlic sauce. You can even use the ink to flavour sauce or colour pasta.

More prosaically, most consumers prefer their seafood a little less exotic. From the nutritional aspect, fish fall into two categories: white fish and oily fish. This classification depends on the amount of oil in the fresh fish, irrespective of whether it is a freshwater or a sea fish. Sardine, mackerel, trout, salmon, tuna, and herring are oily fish. All flat fish, such as plaice, sole, turbot, and halibut, and round types, such as cod, hake, and haddock, are white fish. Whatever the fish, it must be very fresh, with firm flesh, fresh scent, bright eyes, red gills, and plenty of scales.

Fish bones are of two types, namely cartilage or soft bones, found in ray, skate, and dog fish, and hard bones ossified with calcium salts which are inedible. Some fish, such as whitebait and small sardines, have softer bones, which can be eaten for their calcium content. Bones and fish heads impart flavour to stocks. For good, clear stocks, use bones from gelatinous white fish such as sole, turbot, and cod.

Fish eggs, called roe, are rich in protein whether they are from the herring or the sturgeon, which produces caviar. Soft roe is called milt and is good grilled on toast.

Shellfish include crustaceans and molluscs, which are biologically distinct from each other and from fish. Crustaceans, whose shells yield the unique calcium flavour found in bisques and lobster Newburg sauces, include shrimps, huge crawfish (clawless lobsters), true lobsters, soft- and hard-shell crabs, the river prawns known as écrevisses or crayfish, and the numerous varieties of ocean prawn. Molluscs include snails, clams, cockles, abalones, mussels, octopuses, and oysters.

Vitamin A is found in all crustaceans and oysters, cockles contain iron, and all shellfish provide calcium and phosphorus. All seafood provides a high percentage of protein equal to that of meat and poultry. Fish proteins are highly digestible, particularly those of white fish, which are best poached for lighter diets.

## COOKING FISH

Although there is a fashion for raw, marinated fish, Japanese or Scandinavian style, most people prefer their fish lightly cooked in oil or butter. The French love fish chowders with saffron and fennel stock. In Britain, fish and chips remains popular, eaten in northern towns with mushy peas.

The modern tendency to steam fish wrapped in vegetable leaves, to obtain a natural flavour, has caught on with gourmets, but the shallow-fry and stir-fry methods still provide the best flavour. It is important also to realise that the deep-frying method does not necessarily load the fish with too much fat if the frying is done at the correct temperature.

Oily fish are best grilled, but white fish gain in flavour when deep-fried in a good, polyunsaturated oil, such as soya. The flavour is intensified when the fish is fried after being coated with nuts and spices.

# Fish Stock

| |
|---|
| 2 tbs soya oil |
| 1 large onion, sliced vertically |
| 1 carrot, sliced |
| 500 g ( 1 lb ) white-fish bones ( sole or cod ) |
| 150 ml ( ¼ pint ) white wine |
| 750 ml ( 1¼ pints ) water |
| 1 bouquet garni |
| 3 peppercorns, crushed |

Heat the oil and gently shallow-fry the vegetables and fish bones for 6 minutes, without browning. Pour in the wine and water. Add the bouquet garni and peppercorns. Boil for 25–35 minutes. Strain through a nylon sieve. Use for sauces, chowder, or to baste large fish such as bass.                    JEAN CONIL

# Seafood Kebab Princess Anne

*Pictured on back cover and page 140.*

| |
|---|
| 500 g ( 1 lb ) salmon, filleted |
| 250 g ( ½ lb ) monkfish or cod, filleted |
| 1 red pepper |
| 1 yellow pepper |
| 1 green pepper |
| 8 cubes of pineapple |
| soya oil, for brushing |
| salt and pepper to taste |

Cut the fish into 2.5 cm (1-inch) cubes. Cut the peppers into 4 cm (2-inch) squares. Alternate all the ingredients on 4 kebab sticks. Brush with soya oil and sprinkle with salt and pepper. Grill for 5 minutes, turning after 2 minutes. Serve the kebabs with any of the following sauces: Chinese Watermelon Salad Dressing (page 168), Green Mexican (page 173), Almond and Lime (page 174), Israel Hazeret (page 169), Jamaican Pawpaw (page 171), Creole (page 170). Accompany them with side salads.    *Serves 4*    JEAN CONIL

# Sole Fillets in Saffron Sauce

*Pictured on page 104.*

| | |
|---|---|
| 4 × 450 g (15 oz) Dover sole fillets | salt and pepper |
| (bones and heads to be used for stock-making) | juice of ½ lemon |
| 2 tbs soya oil | |
| 300 ml (½ pint) Fish Stock (see page 41) | TO GARNISH |
| 75 ml (3 fl oz) dry white wine | 24 mint leaves (half for |
| 4 strands saffron | cooking and half for decoration) |
| 25 g (1 oz) soya margarine and | 1 truffle, sliced (optional) |
| 25 g (1 oz) flour creamed together | 4 stuffed olives, sliced |

Place the cleaned fillets, slightly beaten to break up the fibres, in an earthenware dish, which has been well-greased with soya oil. Cover with a third of the fish stock and add wine, saffron, seasoning and half of the mint leaves. Cover with well-oiled paper and bake for 10 minutes at Gas Mark 4/180°C/350°F.

Drain the fish liquor and reboil in a saucepan to make the sauce. Add the remaining fish stock. Boil for 8 minutes to reduce it by half. Thicken the sauce with the margarine and flour paste. Boil for 4 minutes and strain. Season to taste, and add the lemon juice.

On 4 plates, pour pools of sauce and then arrange on them the 4 fish fillets. Decorate with mint leaves, slices of truffle and sliced olives.     *Serves 4*                                          **MICHEL SIMIOLI**

# Malaysian Spicy Seafood Soup

*Traditionally the fish ingredients in this recipe are not filleted or skinned before being added to the soup. But it is easier to eat if this is done beforehand and the shells and bones used in the stock.*

| |
|---|
| 900 ml (1½ pints) Fish Stock (see page 41) |
| 3 stalks lemon grass (use white part only, in 2 cm (1-inch) lengths), or lemon mint |
| 1 knob galangal or ginger, skinned and sliced |
| 4 kaffir lime or mint leaves, shredded |
| 2 sprigs coriander leaves, including roots |
| 2 small chillies, pounded to a paste |
| 4 king prawns |
| 2 small crabs (dissected into 4 parts) |
| 12 mussels, cleaned and well scrubbed |
| 2 small squid, cleaned and sliced |
| 150 g (5 oz) sea bream or snapper, filleted and skinned (use the bones for stock) |
| 3 tbs fish essence |
| salt and pepper to taste |
| 2 limes |
| 1 tsp honey or palm sugar |
| 4 basil leaves, to garnish |

*H*eat the fish stock then add the lemon grass or lemon mint, kaffir or mint leaves, galangal or ginger, chillies and coriander roots. Bring to the boil, then add all the fish. Cook for 10 minutes and then add the fish essence and seasoning. Simmer for 2 more minutes, then season to taste and add the honey or palm sugar. Lastly flavour the soup with lime juice and thin rind cut into small strips. Garnish each portion with fresh basil and coriander leaves. *Serves 4*                    **SOO PENG WAH**

# Monkfish Blanquette with Prime Vegetables

*Pictured on page 68.*

| | |
|---|---|
| 12 each: | 25 g (1 oz) butter |
| baby carrots, turnips, and courgettes | 2 tbs double cream |
| 4 small leeks, whites only | seasoning to taste |
| 250 g (8 oz) thin french beans, topped and tailed | juice of 1 lemon |
| 1 red pepper, cut into strips and blanched | |
| 4 × 150 g (5 oz) monkfish, filleted | TO GARNISH |
| 150 ml (¼ pint) Fish Stock, made with sole bones (see page 41) | 4 basil leaves |
| 3 tbs vermouth | 4 slices cooked beetroot |
| 3 shallots, chopped | 4 carrots, carved into roses |

Blanch all the vegetables separately for 4–5 minutes. Refresh in iced water until cold. Drain well. Poach the fish fillets in the stock for 3 minutes. Do not boil, but gently simmer. Drain, retaining the stock, and keep warm. Boil the vermouth and shallots for 5 minutes, until the shallots are soft. Add the stock, reduce by half, and whisk in the butter to emulsify the sauce. Boil the cream and gradually add it to the sauce. Season to taste. Add the lemon juice.

Reheat the fish in the sauce. Pour the sauce onto 4 plates. Lay out the fish fillets and arrange the reheated vegetables all around. Decorate with the basil, beetroot, and carrots. *Serves 4* **STEPHANE LEDAY**

# Shrimp Dumplings

| | |
|---|---|
| 25 g (1 oz) fresh salmon, filleted and minced | 1 tbs Fish Stock (see page 41) |
| 50 g (2 oz) fresh scallops, coral included, cleaned and minced | ½ tsp chopped ginger |
| 25 g (1 oz) soya margarine | 1 tsp rice vinegar |
| 1 egg, beaten | salt and pepper |
| ½ shallot, chopped | 250 g (8 oz) puff pastry or |
| 50 g (2 oz) peeled, cooked shrimps or prawns, minced or chopped | Chinese won ton or ravioli paste |

*In* a bowl, combine the minced salmon and scallops. Blend in the soya margarine and beaten egg. Add the rest of the ingredients, except the pastry. Chill the mixture for 30 minutes.

Heat the oven to Gas Mark 6/200°C/400°F. Meanwhile roll out the pastry 5 mm (¼ inch) thick and cut regular squares with sides of 6.5 cm (2½ inches). Place a spoonful of the mixture on each square. Brush the edges with water and wrap the dumplings like a purse by folding the corners. Rest for 25 minutes.

Bake the dumplings for 15 minutes, or fry them in oil, or boil them for 5 minutes in salted water.
*Serves 4*                                                                                    HOWARD BULKA

# Shallow-Fried Fish and Shark Fins Otani

| | |
|---|---|
| 4 × 50 g (2 oz) shark fins (dried) | 4 × 150 g (5 oz) fish fillets (snapper, bream, large mackerel, |
| 250 ml (8 fl oz) Fish Stock (see page 41) | tilefish or fresh shark-steak minus bone) |
| 100 ml (3½ fl oz) concentrated veal stock | salt and pepper to taste |
| 7 g (¼ oz) ground ginger | |
| 50 g (2 oz) green onions, chopped | TO GARNISH |
| 3 tbs saké (rice wine) or sherry | 4 artichoke bottoms (fresh or canned) |
| 2 tbs butter | 4 tomatoes, skinned, de-seeded, and chopped |
| juice of 1 lemon | 1 sprig coriander |
| 3 tbs soya oil | 1 truffle, sliced, or 4 black mushrooms |

*Soak* the shark fins in water for 1 hour, then boil for 5 minutes. Clean by hand. Separately bring another pot of water to the boil. Add the ginger and green onions. Blanch the fins in this boiling water and then rinse in fresh water several times. Drain.

Combine the two stocks. Flavour with ginger, onion, saké or sherry, and seasoning. Braise the blanched fins in this stock mixture, simmering for 6 hours with the pot tightly covered. Remove when cooked and keep warm. Boil the stock for 30 minutes to reduce it by a third, to a syrupy sauce. Whisk in the butter, and add two-thirds of the lemon juice.

Heat the soya oil and shallow-fry the fish fillets for 6–8 minutes. Season to taste. Sprinkle on the remaining lemon juice. Boil the fresh artichoke bottoms until tender.

To serve, place 1 cooked fish fillet and 1 piece of shark fin on each plate. Coat with the sauce. Decorate with 1 artichoke bottom, filled with chopped tomato and topped with a coriander leaf. Decorate with a truffle slice or a black mushroom.     *Serves 4*                                                          HARUO FURUYA

# White Scallop Ravioli in Soya Butter Sauce

| |
|---|
| 1 tbs red wine vinegar |
| 150 ml ( ¼ pint) Fish Stock (see page 41) |
| 1 tbs soya sauce |
| 125 g (4 oz) dried chinese mushrooms, soaked |
| 500 g (1 lb) scallops |
| 2 tbs soya oil, for frying |
| 40 won ton wrappers |
| 2 eggs, beaten |
| 125 g (4 oz) soya margarine, chilled and diced |
| 125 g (4 oz) butter, chilled and diced |
| 2 bunches chives, chopped |
| salt and pepper to taste |

Put the wine vinegar, fish stock and soya sauce together in a pan, bring to the boil, then simmer until reduced by half. Cook the soaked mushrooms according to the packet instructions, cool, then chop them finely. Cut the white parts of each scallop into 4 pieces, heat the oil and sauté them for 1–2 minutes. Lay out 20 of the won ton wrappers, put the scallop pieces on them, and add some chopped mushrooms to each. Using a brush, wet the edges of the wrappers with the beaten eggs. Cover and seal with the remaining wrappers. Warm up the wine vinegar mixture, and whip in the cold margarine and butter and chives. Poach the ravioli in salted water for 10–15 minutes, then serve with the sauce.     *Serves 4*     **SERGE DANSEREAU**

# River Trout with Fresh Herbs

| | |
|---|---|
| 4 river trout, each weighing about 200 g (7 oz), | 2 tbs parsley, chopped finely |
| cleaned, filleted and carefully boned | 2 tbs dry white wine |
| (or 8 fillets, each weighing about 80 g/3 oz) | 2 tbs Madeira (medium dry) |
| 2 tbs mixed herbs, finely chopped (see note) | salt and freshly ground pepper |
| 50 g (2 oz) butter | |

Pat dry the trout, season with salt and pepper and coat generously with half the mixed herbs. Soften the butter in a sautéing pan with a close-fitting lid and add the trout with the rest of the mixed herbs and the parsley. Sprinkle over the wine and Madeira. Cover at once and allow the trout to poach gently for 2–3 minutes (poach fillets for 1½ minutes only). Remove the trout and place on a hot serving dish. Stir the cooking juices, adjust the seasoning, and pour over and around the fish. Serve at once.

Note: The fresh herbs could include chives, thyme, marjoram, tarragon, dill, coriander leaves, celery leaves and basil, and perhaps a little rosemary. You can poach the fish whole instead of filleted, if you wish, and remove the fillets when the fish is tender. It is becoming more acceptable to serve fish with skin, but this, too, is a matter of preference.    *Serves 4*                                    **ANTON MOSIMANN**

# Tuna-Filled New Zealand Kiwifruit

*Make sure that you choose the largest fruit you can find – there are eight sizes of New Zealand kiwifruit – to take the filling of creamy tuna mayonnaise. Eat with a knife and fork. Pictured on page 142.*

| | |
|---|---|
| 99 g (3½ oz) can tuna in brine | salt and pepper |
| 2 level tbs mayonnaise | |
| 2 level tbs strained Greek natural yogurt | T O  G A R N I S H |
| 1 spring onion, trimmed | paprika pepper |
| 4 New Zealand kiwifruit | sprigs of watercress |

Drain the tuna and transfer it to a small bowl. Using a fork, mash it with the mayonnaise and yogurt. Add the finely sliced onion and adjust the seasoning. Peel the kiwifruit, and stand each one upright on a small serving plate. Make four vertical cuts through the centre point *almost* to the base. Carefully pull the segments apart to form a 'flower'. Spoon a quarter of the tuna mixture into the centre of each. Serve garnished with a dusting of paprika and sprigs of watercress.    *Serves 4*                                    **PAT SHARREN**

# $\mathcal{S}$ALMON $\mathcal{R}$OLL STUFFED WITH $\mathcal{P}$OMFRET AND $\mathcal{C}$HIVE $\mathcal{M}$OUSSE

$\mathcal{P}$*ictured on page 104.*

| | |
|---|---|
| 150 g ( 5 oz) pomfret fish fillet, skinned | 40 g ( 1½ oz) lemon grass leaves, chopped |
| 1 level tsp salt | 15 g ( ½ oz) butter or soya margarine ( optional ) |
| 1 egg, beaten | salt and pepper to taste |
| 100 ml ( 3½ fl oz) double cream | |
| 25 g ( 1 oz) chives | TO GARNISH |
| 500 g ( 1 lb) salmon fillet, skinned | 40 g ( 1½ oz) each carrot and pumpkin |
| | 125 g ( 4 oz) bok-choy or spinach |
| FOR THE SAUCE | 4 cherry tomatoes, skinned |
| 200 ml ( 7 fl oz) Fish Stock (see page 41 ) | 1 bunch chervil |
| 200 ml ( 7 fl oz) single cream | |

$\mathcal{M}$ince the pomfret fish, add the salt and egg, and gradually add the cream. Pass the mixture through a sieve. Add the chopped chives and refrigerate for 30 minutes.

Cut the salmon into 4 large or 8 small slices and flatten them gently with a mallet. Spread the pomfret and chive mousse on each slice, then roll the slices. Wrap the rolls in foil and poach in the fish stock for 8 minutes. Remove and keep warm.

To make the sauce, boil the fish stock to reduce it by half. Then add the cream and boil again for 2 minutes. Add the chopped lemon leaves. Whisk in the butter if desired. Season to taste.

Shape 8 small balls from the carrot and pumpkin. Boil for 3 to 4 minutes in salted water and drain. Boil the bok-choy until cooked and drain. Arrange the rolls on 4 plates with a pool of sauce beside each roll. Overlap a few bok-choy or spinach leaves and decorate with the carrot and pumpkin balls, a tomato and some chervil.     *Serves 4*                                                                 **GORDON CLAPPERTON**

# Steamed Fish Curry in Young Coconut Milk

| | |
|---|---|
| 4 large cabbage leaves, minus ribs | 2 slices galangal root |
| 4 young coconuts | 6 leaves lemon grass |
| 500 g ( 1 lb ) white fish fillets or mackerel | 50 g ( 2 oz ) sliced kaffir lime rind |
| 600 ml ( 1 pint ) coconut milk | 50 g ( 2 oz ) pounded shrimp meat |
| 150 ml ( ¼ pint ) Fish Stock ( see page 41 ) | 1 tsp salt |
| 4 fresh coconut shells | 2 tbs soya oil or water |
| 5 tbs cream of coconut milk | |
| | TO GARNISH |
| FOR THE CURRY PASTE | 1 large red chilli, cut into long strips |
| 4 red chillies, de-seeded and chopped | 2 kaffir lime leaves, cut into strips |
| 2 shallots, chopped | 4 coriander leaves |
| 1 clove garlic, chopped | |

Blanch the cabbage leaves in boiling water for 2 minutes. Refresh in iced water, drain, and pat dry. Remove half of the outer covering of the young coconuts and cut the flesh into small pieces. Skin the fish fillets and cut into pieces 5 cm (2 inches) square. Pound or liquidise the curry paste ingredients with a little water or soya oil.

In a bowl, combine the curry paste, the fish and half the coconut milk. Then add the fish stock and the remaining coconut milk. Blend thoroughly. Line 4 fresh coconut shells with the blanched cabbage leaves. Fill them with fish mixture. Coat with cream of coconut milk. Wrap in foil and steam for 20 to 30 minutes.

Serve warm in the same shells, each decorated with strips of chilli and lime leaves and a coriander leaf.    *Serves 4*    **KHUNYING PRASANSOOK TUNTIVEJAKUL**

# ℐILVER 𝒲HITING ℬUTTERFLY

| | |
|---|---|
| 500 g ( 1 lb ) silver whiting fillets | 5 tbs dry white wine |
| 1 tsp soya sauce | 25 g ( 1 oz ) shallot, chopped |
| juice of 1 lemon | 1 sprig parsley |
| 2 tbs seasoned flour | 10 peppercorns, crushed coarsely |
| 2 eggs, beaten | 150 g ( 5 oz ) fresh, unsalted soft butter or soya margarine and butter |
| 100 ml ( 3½ fl oz ) soya oil | |
| 150 g ( 5 oz ) potatoes, peeled and sliced thinly | T O   D E C O R A T E |
| seasoning to taste | 10 baby red peppers, sliced |
| | 8 lime leaves |
| F O R   T H E   S A U C E | 1 small bunch chives |
| 1 bay leaf | 4 small carrots, carved like flowers |

ℳarinate the fish fillets in a mixture of the soya sauce with seasoning and lemon juice for several hours. Rub the fish in seasoned flour and dip in the beaten eggs. Heat the oil and shallow-fry the fish on both sides until golden (5 minutes). Remove and drain on a napkin to absorb excess oil. Deep-fry the potato slices like crisps. Drain well and season.

To make the sauce, boil all the ingredients except the butter or margarine, reducing the mixture by half. Strain through a nylon sieve. Reheat and gradually emulsify the sauce with the butter or margarine. Adjust the seasoning.

Arrange circles of sliced red peppers, the fish, and the crisps, so as to make the dish look like a butterfly. Decorate with lime leaves, chives and carrot flowers. Pour on the peppercorn and wine sauce.

*Serves 4*

**WALTER RAEBER**

# Crown Scallop with Noodles and Chervil Sauce

| | |
|---|---|
| 12 large scallops | pinch cayenne pepper |
| 3 tbs soya oil and butter | juice of ½ lemon or lime |
| | 2 basil leaves |
| FOR THE SAUCE | 1 sprig chervil, chopped |
| 3 tbs mixed soya oil and butter | |
| 2 shallots, peeled and chopped | TO GARNISH |
| 1 red pepper, de-seeded and diced finely | 250 g (8 oz) noodles, of three different colours |
| 150 ml (¼ pint) Fish Stock (see page 41) | 1 truffle, sliced (or use white mushrooms) |
| 5 tbs single cream | 2 tbs Madeira wine |
| 2 tbs butter | 1 sprig dill |
| salt and pepper | 1 tbs sesame seeds, toasted |

Bring a pan of salted water to the boil and cover with a colander. Place the scallops in it and steam until they open. Remove the scallop meat, discarding the back bags. Separate the red coral from the white flesh and wash under running water. Cut the scallops into thin slices laterally. Leave the coral uncut. Heat the butter and soya oil in a sauté pan and gently cook the scallops for 2 minutes. Remove and drain.

To make the sauce, heat the butter and oil, and stir-fry the shallots and pepper strips for 1 minute. Add the fish stock and boil until reduced by half. Whisk the cream in and boil for 4 minutes. Season to taste. Lastly add the lemon or lime juice and a pinch cayenne pepper. Boil the noodles separately by colour. Drain well.

Reheat the scallops slightly in sauce and add the basil leaves and chervil. Serve on 4 plates, with a border of different-coloured noodles, plaited together if you wish. Decorate with truffle or mushroom slices soaked for 5 minutes, or cooked for 4 minutes, in the wine. Also decorate each plate with a little sprig of dill. Sprinkle the toasted sesame seeds over the fish.     *Serves 4*                    **ANTONIO MANCINI**

# *P*LAICE *F*ILLETS WITH *L*ENTILS

*P*ictured on page 70.

| | |
|---|---|
| 2 × 150 g (5 oz) plaice fillets | 2 tbs soya oil |
| 8 tbs lentils, soaked for 2 hours | 1 tsp clear honey |
| 1 tbs chopped onion | salt and pepper to taste |
| 1 tbs chopped carrot | |
| 1 tsp cider or red wine vinegar | TO GARNISH |
| 1 tbs medium-dry sherry | 1 sprig coriander leaves |
| 1 tbs butter or soya margarine | 1 wedge lemon |
| 2 tbs seasoned flour | |

*C*ook the lentils in water with the onion, carrot, vinegar, sherry, and some salt for 30 minutes until tender. Drain and check seasoning. Blend in a small amount of butter or soya margarine. Rub the plaice fillets in seasoned flour and shake off the surplus. Brush with soya oil and grill for 8 minutes. From time to time, brush on a little butter for flavour. Heat the honey and brush on. Season to taste.

Place the fish on a plate with the lentils beside it and garnish with a sprig of coriander leaves and a wedge of lemon.  *Serves 1*                                            EËRO MÄKELÄ

# *W*HITE *T*UNA *M*EDALLIONS IN *C*ORIANDER *S*AUCE

| | |
|---|---|
| 1 small Christophene marrow (chow-chow), peeled | 1 onion, chopped |
| 2 carrots, peeled | 1 small red chilli, de-seeded and cut into thin strips |
| 1 small beetroot, peeled | 1 clove garlic, chopped |
| 2 sprigs broccoli | 500 g (1 lb) tomatoes, skinned, de-seeded, and chopped |
| 10 pieces tuna fish, 25 g (1 oz) each | 28 coriander leaves, chopped |
| 3 tbs seasoned flour | 1 sprig thyme |
| 3 tbs soya oil | 1 sprig parsley, chopped |
| | salt and pepper to taste |
| FOR THE SAUCE | |
| 3 tbs soya oil | |

$\mathcal{T}$rim the Christophene marrow, carrots, and beetroot into olive shapes. Trim the broccoli. Cook all the vegetables in a little water for 6 minutes. Drain and keep warm. Dip the tuna medallions in the seasoned flour. Heat the oil and fry the tuna for 5 minutes.

To make the sauce, heat the oil and stir-fry the onion, chilli, and garlic for 3 minutes. Add the tomatoes and simmer for 10 minutes until thick. Pass the sauce through a strainer. Reheat and season. Add fresh coriander leaves, thyme, and parsley.

Pour a pool of the sauce on 2 plates. Arrange 5 tuna pieces on each plate and garnish with the cooked vegetables.    *Serves 2*                                                          **BARRY ANDREWS**

$\mathcal{B}$AKED $\mathcal{B}$ASS WITH
$\mathcal{R}$OSEMARY AND $\mathcal{P}$OTATOES

| |
|---|
| 1 × 2 kg (4½ lb) sea bass, gutted, scaled, washed, and wiped dry |
| salt, pepper, and celery salt |
| 1 sprig rosemary |
| 1 sprig sage |
| 1 kg (2 lb) potatoes, 1 left whole and remainder sliced |
| 200 ml (7 fl oz) olive or soya oil, or mixture of both |
| 200 ml (7 fl oz) dry white wine |
| 300 ml (½ pint) Fish Stock (see page 41) or water |
| 1 large onion, cut into wedges |

$\mathcal{H}$eat the oven to Gas Mark 6/200°C/400°F. Season the bass with half of the salt, pepper, celery salt, rosemary leaves, and sage. Insert the whole potato in the open belly. Lay fish on its stomach in a deep tray. Arrange the sliced potatoes around the fish. Cover generously with olive and soya oil mixture, white wine, and fish stock. Season again, adding the rest of the sage and rosemary and the onion wedges. Bake for 30–35 minutes, basting the fish and potatoes regularly.

Bring to the table in the same dish, cutting the fish in front of the guests.    *Serves 4*    **AUGUSTO BORGHESE**

# Seafood Jambalaya

| |
|---|
| 3 tbs soya oil |
| 1 onion, chopped |
| 1 green and 1 red pepper, de-seeded and cut in strips |
| 125 g (4 oz) long-grain rice |
| 300 ml (½ pint) Fish Stock (see page 41) |
| 500 g (1 lb) assorted small shellfish (mussels, clams, cockles), cleaned |
| 1 sprig of thyme |
| 1 sprig of coriander |
| a little salt and pepper |

Heat the oil in a large shallow pan. Stir-fry the onion and peppers for 3 minutes, then add the rice and fish stock. Cover the pan and cook for 15 minutes. At this stage add the shellfish and cover again. Cook for 5–8 minutes. Season to taste and add a few thyme and coriander leaves. Serve in the shallow pan in which the jambalaya was cooked.     *Serves 4*                                    **ORDONO DAMASO**

# Seafood Kebabs Mountain Shadow

| | |
|---|---|
| 500 g (1 lb) swordfish, skinned, filleted, and cubed | 8 coriander seeds |
| 8 prawns, peeled | 2 cloves garlic, chopped |
| 8 scampi, peeled | salt, pepper, and ground cumin |
| 16 small scallops | |
| 2 onions, quartered and layers separated | FOR THE PECAN RICE |
| red pepper, cut into 8 square pieces | 4 tbs soya oil |
| 8 mushroom caps | 1 onion, chopped |
| 8 bay leaves | 75 g (3 oz) pecan nuts, chopped |
| | 175 g (6 oz) easy-cook mixed wild rice |
| FOR THE MARINADE | 600 ml (1 pint) Fish Stock (see page 41) |
| 150 ml (¼ pint) orange juice | salt and pepper |
| juice of 1 lime | pinch marjoram and thyme |
| 1 tsp tequilla | 1 tbs butter |
| 3 tbs soya oil | |

*W*ash and drain all cut fish and shellfish. Mix together the marinade ingredients and soak the fish in the mixture for 30 minutes. Remove the fish, drain, and pat dry. Impale the fish, onion, pepper, mushrooms and bay leaves on 8 skewers, alternating ingredients for variety and colour. Mix the ingredients of the marinade together like a dressing.

Boil the marinade mixture for 2 minutes.

To prepare the rice, heat the soya oil and stir-fry the onion for 3 minutes. Then add the nuts and rice and simmer for 3 minutes, while stirring. Add the fish stock, herbs and seasoning and boil for 20–25 minutes. Stir in the butter.

On each of 4 plates, spoon some rice and place 2 kebabs on top. Hand the marinade dressing separately.     *Serves 4*                                                                    **W. RAEBER**

*L*OBSTER IN *F*ISH *J*ELLY

*P*ictured on page 104.

| 2 × 750 g (1½ lb) live lobsters |
| --- |
| 1.75 litre (3 pints) Fish Stock (see page 41) |
| 1 tbs tomato purée |
| salt, pepper and a pinch of cayenne pepper, to taste |
| |
| **TO GARNISH** |
| lemon slices |
| coriander leaves |

*W*ash the live lobsters in clean running water for 10 minutes, and bring the fish stock to the boil. Kill the lobsters by inserting a needle between the eyes. Immerse the lobsters in boiling stock and cook for 12 minutes. Remove from the heat and cool in the stock until cold. Remove the lobsters from the cold stock. Shell the lobsters and cut the flesh in slices. Crack the claws and remove the flesh. Reheat the fish stock, add the tomato purée and strain after 4 minutes. Cool.

To serve, pour a pool of the semi-liquid fish jelly on 4 plates, and arrange lobster slices on top. Decorate with the lemon slices and coriander leaves.     *Serves 4*                                          **YANNIS KOULOUROS**

# Fillets of Salmon Trout in Red Wine Sauce

| | |
|---|---|
| 4 × 175 g (6 oz) salmon fillets | salt and black pepper to taste |
| 4 tbs soya oil | 50 g (2 oz) unsalted farm butter |
| 2 shallots, chopped | 4 sprigs broccoli, cooked |
| 250 ml (8 fl oz) red wine | 4 white mushrooms, cooked in butter |
| 4 tsp chopped tarragon | |

Skin and trim the salmon fillets into neat shapes. Heat the oil and gently fry the fish, skinned side up. Add the chopped shallots and cook for 2 minutes. Turn the fish over and cook for 2 more minutes. Remove the fish and keep warm.

To make the sauce, discard a little of the oil and add the wine. Boil until reduced by half. Whisk the butter into the sauce. Add the seasoning and tarragon.

Pour a pool of the sauce and arrange 1 fillet of fish on each plate. Garnish with a sprig of broccoli and a white mushroom. *Serves 4*

**MARTYN EMSEN**

# Grilled Scotch Salmon with Lemon Mint Sauce

| | |
|---|---|
| 4 × 250 g (8 oz) salmon steaks | 1 shallot, chopped |
| 2 tbs soya oil | 2 tbs fish essence or Fish Stock (see page 41) |
| 4 sprigs fresh mint, to garnish | 2 tbs soft butter |
| | 2 tbs soya margarine |
| FOR THE SAUCE | 1 tsp chopped mint leaves |
| 3 tbs lemon juice | peel of ½ lemon, grated |
| 3 tbs medium white wine | salt and pepper to taste |

*F*irst make the sauce. Boil the lemon juice, wine, shallot, and fish essence until reduced by half. At this stage, whisk in the butter and margarine to obtain a fine emulsion. Season, then blend in the chopped mint and a little grated lemon peel. Brush the salmon steaks with oil and grill for 2–3 minutes on each side. Remove the central bone and skin.

Serve on 4 plates with a pool of the sauce and a decoration of fresh mint leaves. New potatoes, also cooked with mint leaves, go well with this dish.     *Serves 4*                                    **PASCAL DIRRINGER**

## *F*ISH *F*INGER *S*ATAY

| |
|---|
| 10 shallots, chopped |
| 5 cloves garlic, chopped |
| 5 red or green chillies, de-seeded |
| 1 tsp salt |
| good pinch palm sugar |
| 3 tbs soya oil |
| 1 kg ( 2 lb ) white fish ( cod, haddock, whiting ), minced |
| 150 g ( 5 oz ) peeled, cooked, minced prawns or shrimps, or paste |
| 200 ml ( 7 fl oz ) coconut milk |
| soya oil |

*P*owder the first 5 ingredients. Heat 2 tbs of the soya oil and stir-fry for 3 minutes to develop flavour. Blend with the minced fish and prawns. Stir in the coconut milk to obtain a smooth mixture. Divide this fish paste into small balls, about 25 g (1 oz) each, and spear them on 25 wooden satay sticks. Brush with the remaining soya oil, and charcoal-grill or deep-fry for 3 minutes. Serve with assorted salad leaves and various dips.     *Serves 5*                                    **PETER DAVIS**

# Baked Seafood Parfait Kenmare with Avocado Sauce

*Pictured on page 103.*

| | |
|---|---|
| 4 × 150 g (5 oz) Dover sole fillets | 6 tarragon leaves |
| lemon juice, mixed with soya oil and water | small bunch dill weed |
| 100 g (3½ oz) salmon fillets, skinless | 1 tsp curry powder |
| 50 g (2 oz) monkfish fillet | 1 tsp paprika |
| 8 large prawns, de-veined | 1 garlic clove, chopped |
| 4 × 50 g (2 oz) scallops, with roe | 8 sprigs of dill, to garnish |
| 8 spinach leaves | |
| 150 g (5 oz) cod or hake fillet | FOR THE SAUCE |
| 300 ml (½ pint) single cream | 100 ml (3½ fl oz) Chablis or |
| 2 eggs, beaten | dry white wine |
| 1 egg white | 300 ml (½ pint) single cream |
| 2 tbs soya oil | 1 ripe avocado, peeled, stoned, and mashed |
| 25 g (1 oz) fennel, chopped | juice of 1 lemon |
| 100 g (3½ oz) spring onions, chopped | salt and pepper to taste |

Flatten the sole fillets with a small mallet to break up the fibres. Soak them in lemon juice mixed with a little soya oil and water. Dice the salmon, monkfish and prawns into 1 cm (½ inch) cubes. Wrap the scallops in the spinach leaves. Mince the cod or hake in a blender and gradually add 8 tbs of the cream, eggs and egg white. Refrigerate this fish paste for 20 minutes. Heat the soya oil and gently simmer the fennel, onions, tarragon, dill, spices and garlic for 3 minutes. Add this flavouring mixture to the minced fish paste, over a bowl of ice cubes. Place the diced fish in the minced fish paste, stirring gently with a wooden spoon. Heat the oven to Gas Mark 4/180°C/350°F. Grease a 13 cm × 7.5 cm (5 inches × 3 inches) earthenware terrine dish with plenty of soya oil. Drain the sole fillets and pat dry. Arrange them in a row across the dish with ends coming over the edges of the dish. Place half the fish mixture over the fillets and arrange a row of the wrapped scallops. Top with the remaining mixture until full. Fold the ends of the sole fillets over the top of the mixture. Cover with a lid and bake for 40 minutes. Remove from oven. Drain excess liquid from the baked fish terrine, retaining it for the sauce.

To make the sauce, boil this liquid down to one-third of its volume. Add the wine and remaining cream and boil down by half. Season to taste. Add the avocado and the lemon juice. Pour a pool of the sauce onto each plate and arrange 2 slices of this fish parfait. Decorate with dill sprigs. Serve with asparagus, broccoli, or spinach and mint-flavoured boiled new potatoes. *Serves 8* **JOHN MORRIN**

# Stuffed Lobster Tails Hong Kong-Style

*Pictured on page 70.*

| | |
|---|---|
| 8 × 500 g (1 lb) lobsters, cleaned and washed | 1 egg, beaten |
| 500 ml (18 fl oz) soya oil | |
| | FOR THE COATING |
| FOR THE STUFFING | 100 g (3½ oz) seasoned flour |
| 5 tbs soya oil | 2 eggs, beaten |
| 1 tsp curry powder | 4 tbs water |
| 1 tsp flour | 250 g (8 oz) fresh breadcrumbs |
| 75 g (3 oz) boned, skinned chicken, chopped | |
| 50 g (2 oz) onion, chopped | TO GARNISH |
| 75 g (3 oz) mushrooms, chopped | 4 tbs soya oil |
| 25 g (1 oz) celery, chopped | 1 stick celery, thinly sliced |
| 2 shallots, chopped | 3 shallots, chopped |
| 250 g (8 oz) ham, chopped | 1 red pepper, de-seeded and shredded |
| salt and pepper to taste | 4 chinese leaves, shredded |
| 250 ml (8 fl oz) mixed water and coconut milk | |

Bring to the boil 4.5 litres (1 gallon) salted water. Immerse the lobsters and cook for 8 minutes. Remove from the heat and leave to cool. Remove from the pan, reserving the stock. Cut off the lobster tails. With a fork, extract the tail meat in one pull. Cut the meat into slices. Next extract also the meat from the claws. Reserve the clean tail shells. The head shells can be used for lobster stock or soups.

Prepare the stuffing for the empty shells. Heat the soya oil in a wok and stir-fry all the dry stuffing ingredients. After 4 minutes add the coconut milk and the reserved stock and cook for 4 more minutes. Cool and season to taste. Drain off the liquid. Blend a beaten egg into the stuffing ingredients to bind the mixture. Mix together the coating ingredients and use to coat the mixture before filling each tail. Cut inside the shell with scissors, leaving only the red part of the shell and the filling exposed.

Heat 500 ml (18 fl oz) soya oil in a wok and deep-fry all the filled tails for 3 minutes until golden. Drain well.

To prepare the garnish, heat the soya oil and sauté the lobster meat, celery, shallots and pepper. Cook for 3 minutes. Place a heap of shredded chinese leaves on a large platter and sprinkle over a few strips of red pepper, celery and lobster meat. Top with the fried lobster tails in a circle. Serve with a sauce of your choice (see page 165). *Serves 8* **IP WAH**

# *Sole Sunset Strips* WITH *Grapefruit Dressing*

| | |
|---|---|
| 4 × 100 g (3½ oz) Dover sole fillets | 1 tbs balsamico vinegar |
| | 6 coriander seeds |
| **FOR THE MARINADE** | 1 sprig dill |
| 150 ml (¼ pint) pink grapefruit juice | |
| 4 tbs soya oil | **TO GARNISH** |
| 1 green chilli, de-seeded and chopped | 8 each radicchio and curly lettuce leaves |
| 1 tsp grated lime peel | 16 pink grapefruit segments |
| 1 sprig parsley | 1 red pepper, cut into thick strips |
| 1 mint leaf | 1 stick each celery and fennel, cut into thin strips |
| salt and pepper | 50 g (2 oz) fresh cranberries |
| 1 tsp Dijon mustard | 2 avocados, peeled, stoned, and sliced |

Cut the sole fillets into strips 4 cm (1½ inches) long and 5mm (¼ inch) thick. Liquidise all of the marinade ingredients except the coriander seeds and the dill. Place in a shallow dish and marinate the sole in this mixture for 8 hours in the fridge. Sprinkle the coriander seeds over the fish, and add the dill sprig.

To serve, arrange the lettuce and radicchio leaves on 4 plates. Top with the drained fish. Decorate with the rest of the ingredients. Drizzle over some of the marinade.     *Serves 4*     **STEPHEN WHITNEY**

# *Sole Soufflé* with *Crayfish and Caviar*

| | |
|---|---|
| 75 g (3 oz) sole fillet | 150 g (5 oz) crayfish or scampi shells, chopped |
| 1 tsp soft soya margarine or butter | 1 shallot, chopped |
| | 5 tbs dry white wine |
| **FOR THE SOUFFLÉ** | salt and pepper |
| 150 g (5 oz) sole fillet, minced | 125 ml (4 fl oz) double cream |
| 75 g (3 oz) scallop with coral, minced | 2 tbs butter |
| 2 egg whites | |
| salt and pepper | **TO GARNISH** |
| 75 g (3 oz) raw scampi or crayfish | 1 tbs snipped chives |
| 300 ml (½ pint) Fish Stock (see page 41) | 1 tbs caviar |
| | 6 asparagus tips, cooked |
| **FOR THE SAUCE** | 2 crayfish with shells, boiled |
| 2 tbs soya oil | 6 strands chives |

Heat the oven to Gas Mark 6/200°C/400°F. Flatten the sole fillet with a wooden mallet and cut into strips. Spread a little margarine or butter on two individual pastry moulds 4 cm (1½ inches) deep and 7.5 cm (3 inches) diameter. Line with two rounds of greaseproof paper, and place the strips of sole inside the moulds.

To make the soufflé, blend the minced ingredients together in a bowl over a basin of ice cubes. Beat the egg whites with a pinch of salt to form soft peaks and fold into the minced fish mixture. Season to taste.

Poach the scampi in the fish stock for 4 minutes. Remove and retain the stock. Leave the scampi to cool, then dice and add to the soufflé mixture. Fill the two moulds to the top with this mixture. Bake in the oven for 20 minutes.

To make the sauce, heat a little oil and shallow-fry the shells and the shallot for 5 minutes to develop flavour. Add the wine and 3 tbs of the poaching stock and boil for 12 minutes. Strain. Boil for 4 minutes then season. Blend in the cream and boil for 4 more minutes. Check seasoning. Whisk a little butter into the sauce.

To serve, turn out each soufflé onto a plate. Pour sauce around, and sprinkle chives and caviar over the sauce. Decorate each plate with 3 asparagus tips, a boiled crayfish and 3 strands of chives.    *Serves 2*

**DAVID THOMAS RYAN AND NIGEL FROST**

# Prawns with Peanut and Coconut Dressing

| | |
|---|---|
| 4 cabbage leaves | 600 ml ( 1 pint) coconut milk |
| 75 g ( 3 oz) bean sprouts | 65 g ( 2½ oz) palm sugar |
| 75 g ( 3 oz) cabbage, shredded | 16 lemon leaves |
| 75 g ( 3 oz) french beans, topped and tailed | salt and pepper to taste |
| 250 g ( 8 oz) prawns, boiled and shelled | |
| | TO GARNISH |
| FOR THE DRESSING | 25 g ( 1 oz) peanuts |
| 5 tbs soya oil | 75 g ( 3 oz) long red chillies, |
| 75 g ( 3 oz) shallots, chopped | de-seeded and sliced into rings |
| 2 cloves garlic, chopped | bean sprouts |
| 15 g ( ½ oz) ginger root, chopped | long beans |
| 75 g ( 3 oz) peanuts | |

Blanch the cabbage leaves in salted water. Refresh in iced water. Drain, pat dry, and remove the ribs. Blanch the bean sprouts, shredded cabbage, and beans separately. Fill each cabbage leaf with a mixture of these vegetables. Shape the stuffed leaves like rolls, then cut them into 8 small rounds.

To make the dressing, heat the soya oil and stir-fry the shallots, garlic, ginger, and peanuts for 3 minutes until brown. Drain, and dry on absorbent paper or towels to remove surplus oil. Blend with the coconut milk, add the sugar and lemon leaves, and simmer for 8 minutes, until you have a syrupy dressing. Season to taste.

To serve, arrange some prawns in the centre of each plate with a cabbage roll on either side. Coat the prawns with dressing. Garnish with peanuts, chilli rings, bean sprouts and long beans, tied up in knots if you wish. *Serves 4*                                                                    ANTON WUERSCH

# Minced Bahamian Crawfish with Peas and Rice

| | |
|---|---|
| 2 tbs soya margarine | 50 g (2 oz) celery, chopped |
| 4 × 150 g (5 oz) crawfish tails, boiled, shelled, and | 50 g (2 oz) green pepper, diced |
| chopped | 500 g (1 lb) easy-cook long-grain rice, washed, |
| 1 onion, chopped | soaked for 5 minutes, and drained |
| 1 green pepper, de-seeded and chopped | 100 g (3½ oz) tomato purée |
| 3 small celery sticks, chopped | 1 tsp black pepper |
| 1½ tbs tomato purée | pinch ground thyme |
| juice of 2 small limes | 1 litre (1¾ pints) hot water |
| 1 red chilli, de-seeded and chopped | 300 g (10 oz) black, black eye, borlotti or |
| 1 tsp ground thyme | kidney beans, cooked |
| salt to taste | salt to taste |
| | |
| FOR THE RICE | TO GARNISH |
| 3 tbs soya oil | 1 lemon, divided into segments |
| 50 g (2 oz) onion, chopped | 2 ripe pawpaws, peeled and sliced |

Heat the margarine and stir-fry the chopped crawfish and onion for 5 minutes. Add the pepper and celery and simmer gently. Blend in the tomato purée, then season with the lime juice, red chilli, and thyme. Cook for 5 minutes. Check salt.

To cook the peas and rice Bahamian style, heat the oil in a heavy-bottomed pan, and stir-fry the onion, celery, and pepper. Cook for 3 minutes until tender. Add the rice and leave for 2 minutes to absorb the oil. Stir in the tomato purée. Season with salt, pepper, and thyme. Cover with the hot water and add the beans. Bring to the boil, cook for 20 minutes, then simmer for 15 minutes at a lower temperature.

To serve, fill the empty tail shells of the crawfish with the fish mixture. Grease 4 small dariole moulds with soya margarine and fill them with the hot rice mixture. Press with a spoon to pack the rice tightly. Unmould on the plate beside the crawfish tail. Decorate with segments and pawpaw slices.   *Serves 4*   **EDWIN JOHNSON**

# Saucy Creole Plaice

| | |
|---|---|
| 3 tbs soya oil | a little salt and pepper |
| 1 medium onion, chopped | |
| 50 g (2 oz) celery, chopped | TO GARNISH |
| 25 g (1 oz) red pepper, diced | 250 g (8 oz) mixture of long-grain rice and wild rice |
| 1 tbs plain flour | a few mint leaves |
| 5 tbs single cream | |
| 15 g (½ oz) fine breadcrumbs | FOR THE CREOLE SAUCE |
| 250 g (8 oz) cooked crabmeat | 450 g (15 oz) tomatoes, skinned, de-seeded, and chopped |
| 50 g (2 oz) cooked, diced prawns | 1 tbs soya oil |
| 1 tbs chopped mixed fresh herbs | 1 garlic clove, chopped |
| 6 fillets of plaice, skinned | 1 red chilli, de-seeded and chopped |
| 3 tbs soya oil and butter, mixed, for | a little salt |
| brushing fillets and greasing | |

Heat the oven to Gas Mark 4/180°C/350°F. Heat the soya oil in a pan and stir-fry the onion, celery, and red pepper for 6 minutes. Sprinkle in the flour to absorb the oil and thicken the mixture. Stir in the cream and heat the mixture for 4 minutes. Mix in the breadcrumbs, crabmeat, prawns, and herbs. Season to taste. Cool.

Spread the fish fillets on a board, skin side upward. Fill each fillet with the stuffing and roll up. Secure the rolls with cocktail sticks. Place the fillets sideways on a shallow dish. Brush each with a mixture of soya oil and butter. Season. Cover with greased foil. Bake for 15 minutes.

To make the creole sauce, place all the ingredients except the seasoning in a food blender and liquidise to a purée. Boil the sauce for 5 minutes. Season.

Cook the rice according to the instructions on the packet.

On 4 plates arrange a bed of cooked rice. Top each with 1 or 2 fish fillets. Decorate with mint leaves. Pour a little sauce on half of the fish.     *Serves 4*                    **JEREMIE GARLICK**

# Stuffed Sole with Two Sauces

*Pictured on page 70.*

| FOR THE STUFFING | FOR THE LOBSTER SAUCE |
|---|---|
| 2 tbs soya oil | 2 tbs soya oil |
| 1 small onion, chopped | 250 g (8 oz) lobster shells with crushed legs and coral |
| 4 white mushrooms, chopped | 1 small shallot, chopped |
| 2 tbs parsley, chopped | 1 small carrot, chopped |
| 50 g (2 oz) ham, chopped | 2 tarragon leaves |
| 1 tbs breadcrumbs | 150 ml (¼ pint) Fish Stock, made with dry sparkling |
| 1 egg white | wine or champagne (see page 41) |
| salt and pepper | 1 tbs tomato purée |
| 4 × 75 g (3 oz) sole fillets | 2 strands saffron |
| | 1 tbs brandy |
| FOR THE VELOUTÉ CREAM SAUCE | 2 tbs cream |
| 150 ml (¼ pint) Fish Stock, made with dry sparkling | salt, pepper, and pinch of cayenne or chilli powder |
| wine or champagne (see page 41) plus | |
| 3 tbs champagne | TO GARNISH |
| 15 g (½ oz) soya margarine | 4 tsp each red and black caviar or lumpfish roe |
| 15 g (½ oz) flour | 4 baked puff pastries cut into moon-shaped fleurons |
| 2 tbs thick cream | 4 large prawns or 8 shrimps, shelled and cooked |
| juice of ½ lemon | sprig of dill |
| salt, pepper and a pinch of cayenne | |

Prepare the stuffing for the fish. Heat the oil in a pan and stir-fry all the ingredients, except the egg white and seasoning, for 4 minutes. Season and blend in the egg white to bind the mixture. Cool and, when cold, spread thickly on each sole fillet. Roll up and tie with string, or pin with toothpicks. To make the velouté cream sauce, first place the stuffed fillets in a saucepan side by side. Cover with the stock and poach for 10 minutes. Remove the fish and keep warm. Divide each stuffed fillet in two laterally. Reboil the liquor and add the champagne. Season to taste after 3 minutes' fast boiling. Thicken the sauce with a paste made by creaming the flour with the soya margarine. Boil the sauce for 3 minutes, until thick. Strain. Add 2 tbs of thick cream then check the seasoning. Add the lemon juice and a pinch of cayenne pepper. To make the lobster sauce, heat the soya oil in a pan and stir-fry the next 4 ingredients for 5 minutes. Add the stock and boil for 15 minutes with the tomato purée and saffron. Strain the sauce into another pan. Add the brandy and cream, and simmer for 2 minutes. Season so that the sauce is hot and peppery. To serve, pour one pool of white sauce and one of lobster sauce on either side of each plate. Arrange the pieces of sliced, stuffed sole on each sauce, making sure to keep the centre clear. Place a spot of black caviar on the fish on the pink sauce, and a spot of red caviar on the fish on the white sauce. Arrange the rest of the garnishes. *Serves 4* **MARTIN BAUMANN**

# *Straits of Melaka Prawns in Pineapple Curry Sauce*

| | |
|---|---|
| 750 g (1½ lb) king prawns | 15 g (½ oz) galangal, chopped |
| 1 onion, peeled and cut in 2 | 20 g (¾ oz) lemon grass, chopped |
| 1 bouquet garni | 175 ml (6 fl oz) fish and prawn stock |
| salt and pepper to taste | 250 g (8 oz) fresh pineapple, diced |
| FOR THE SAUCE | 100 ml (3½ fl oz) double cream |
| 150 ml (¼ pint) soya oil | |
| 65 g (2½ oz) shallots, chopped | TO GARNISH |
| 40 g (1½ oz) candlenut, chopped | 150 g (5 oz) asparagus tips, |
| 40 g (1½ oz) red chillies, de-seeded and chopped | cooked lightly |
| 40 g (1½ oz) turmeric root, chopped | 12 pickled pink peppercorns |

*B*oil the prawns in water with the onion, bouquet garni, and seasoning for 6 minutes. Shell the tails but leave the heads and antennae.

Heat the oil and stir-fry the shallots until pale golden. Add all the chopped ingredients, and sauté to enhance the flavour. Stir in the fish stock and boil for 15 minutes. Add the diced pineapple and simmer for 5 minutes. Lastly blend in the cream, and check the seasoning.

Pour the pineapple sauce on 4 plates. Arrange the prawns and asparagus tips and sprinkle over the peppercorns. Serve with steamed white rice and boiled wild rice. *Serves 4* **WALTER RAEBER**

*Pitta Bread stuffed with Broad-bean Fritters (page 35), Mushroom Pancakes (page 23), Country Pasties (page 31) and Havengore Bounty (page 29)*

Top: *Canadian Salmon Millefeuille Napoleon (page 75)*, below: *Monkfish Blanquette with Prime Vegetables (page 44)*

*Swordfish with Tempura of Vegetables (page 80), Steamed Halibut with Clam Sauce and Shrimp Dumplings (page 74),*
*Sun-dried Tomato and Four-cheese Croûtons (page 10)*

Top left: *Stuffed Lobster Tails Hong Kong-style* (*page 59*), top right: *Plaice Fillets with Lentils* (*page 52*), below left: *Stuffed Sole with Two Sauces* (*page 65*), below right: *Crayfish Tartlets in Tarragon Cream Sauce* (*page 71*)

# CRAYFISH TARTLETS IN TARRAGON CREAM SAUCE

*Pictured left.*

| | |
|---|---|
| 150 g (5 oz) prepared puff or flaky pastry | 150 g (5 oz) mixed carrots, celery, and shallots, chopped |
| 24 crayfish or large prawns, unshelled | 1 tbs tomato purée |
| 2 tbs mixed soya oil | 150 ml (¼ pint) dry white wine |
| unsalted butter | 3 leaves tarragon |
| 2 tbs brandy | 2 sprigs parsley |
| | salt, pepper, and pinch cayenne pepper |
| FOR THE SAUCE | 1 tsp sugar (optional) |
| 2 tbs soya oil | 100 ml (3½ fl oz) double cream |

Heat the oven to Gas Mark 6/200°C/400°F. Roll out the pastry to a thickness of 5 mm (¼ inch), and cut 4 rounds about 5 cm (2 inches) in diameter (larger than the tartlet tins). Grease the tartlet tins with soya oil and line them with pastry rounds. Prick the pastry and rest for 15 minutes. Fill with dry baked beans or peas. Bake in the oven for 20 minutes. Remove the beans and cool.

To obtain a good Nantua type of sauce, use the uncooked crayfish or prawn shells. Shell the crayfish and prawns. Break the shells into small pieces. Heat the oil in a pan and sauté the mixed vegetables and shells for 12 minutes. Add the tomato purée, wine and 5 tbs water and boil for 15 minutes. Strain this stock. Reheat, blend in the cream, add the herbs and boil for 8 minutes. Season to taste, adding a little sugar if you like. Liquidise the sauce.

Heat the soya oil and butter, and cook the shelled prawns or crayfish for 5 minutes. Drain off the fat. Pour on the brandy and set alight. Extinguish it by adding the sauce. Simmer the mixture for 3 minutes. Check the seasoning. To serve, place the warm pastry tartlets on 4 plates. Spoon some of the mixture onto each.

*Serves 4*

EËRO MÄKELÄ

# Bavarois and Dublin Bay Prawn Kebabs with Sole Mousse

| FOR THE KEBABS | 4 egg yolks, beaten |
|---|---|
| 12 large Dublin Bay prawns (langoustines), peeled | salt, nutmeg, and cayenne pepper to taste |
| 250 g (8 oz) sole fillets, minced | |
| 200 ml (7 fl oz) double cream | FOR THE TOMATO PRAWN STOCK |
| 2 egg whites | 2 tbs soya oil |
| 25 g (1 oz) softened butter | 100 g prawn shells and fish bones |
| 4 strands saffron | 2 shallots, chopped and sliced |
| 2 tbs seasoned flour | 4 sprigs fennel, chopped |
| 4 egg yolks, beaten | 1 bouquet garni |
| 250 g (8 oz) breadcrumbs | 1 tomato, skinned, de-seeded, and chopped |
| 100 ml (3½ fl oz) soya oil | 100 ml (3½ fl oz) water |
| salt and pepper to taste | 100 ml (3½ fl oz) Alsace white wine |
| | salt and pepper |
| FOR THE BAVAROIS | |
| 3 tbs soya oil | FOR THE SAUCE |
| 200 g (7 oz) mixed carrots, celery, and | 150 ml (¼ pint) double cream |
| onions, diced | 75 g (3 oz) prawns, cooked and diced |
| 150 g (5 oz) prawn shells | |
| 100 ml (4 fl oz) cream | TO GARNISH |
| 100 ml (4 fl oz) milk | 100 g (3½ oz) mixed carrot, celery, and |
| 1 tsp tomato purée | leek, cut into thin strips and blanched |
| 2 eggs, beaten | 4 sprigs dill |

To prepare the kebabs with sole mousse, gradually blend the minced sole fillets with the double cream and egg whites. Add the softened butter and saffron. Chill on ice to make the mixture cool and well homogenised. Impale 3 peeled prawns on each of 4 wooden satay sticks. Season the sole mousse, and pipe it over the tops of the prawns, using a plain nozzle. Dip this side lightly in seasoned flour, then in egg yolks, and finally in breadcrumbs, evenly. Repeat this operation until all the prawns and sole mousse are used. Store in the refrigerator until ready to fry. Heat the oven to Gas Mark 6/200°C/400°F.

Make the bavarois by heating the soya oil and stir-frying the diced vegetables until light golden. Add the prawn shells and tomato purée for colour. Stir in the cream and milk, bring to the boil, and simmer for 20 minutes. Strain this prawn sauce into a bowl and cool it. Add the beaten eggs and yolks as for custard. Strain again. Season with salt, nutmeg and a tiny pinch of cayenne pepper. Grease 4 150 ml (¼ pint) ramekin dishes and fill them with the prawn custard. Place in a tray half-filled with hot water. Bake on the medium shelf in the oven for 45 minutes.

To prepare the tomato prawn stock, heat the soya oil and gently shallow-fry the shells and bones with the shallots, fennel, bouquet garni and tomato. Add the water and wine, and boil for 25 minutes. Strain. Boil again to reduce by two-thirds. Add the cream and reduce by one-third. Season, then add the diced, cooked prawns. Heat the soya oil and shallow-fry the kebabs for 2 minutes, until golden. Drain on absorbent paper-towels. On each of 4 plates, unmould a prawn custard. Add a kebab and pour on 2 tbs of sauce. Decorate with the blanched vegetable strips and a sprig of dill.    *Serves 4*                                          **DAVID EVANS**

# *S*PAGHETTI WITH *C*LAM *S*AUCE

| |
|---|
| 125 g (4 oz) thin spaghetti |
| 3 tbs soya oil |
| 2 cloves garlic, chopped |
| 125 g (4 oz) clams, shelled |
| 3 tbs Parmesan cheese |
| 1 tbs chopped parsley |
| salt and pepper to taste |

*S*imply boil the spaghetti for 12 minutes in salted water and drain it. Heat the oil in a pan, sauté the garlic for 1 minute, then add the clams and the spaghetti. Sauté for 4 minutes. Season to taste and sprinkle over the Parmesan cheese and the parsley.    *Serves 2*                                          **ANGELO TORESSIN**

# Steamed Halibut with Clam Sauce and Shrimp Dumplings

*Pictured on page 69.*

| | |
|---|---|
| 4 × 50 g (2 oz) halibut fillets | **FOR THE SAUCE** |
| 8 Shrimp Dumplings (see page 44) | 8 littleneck (American) clams |
| | juice of 1 lemon |
| **FOR THE MARINADE** | juice of 2 oranges |
| 2 tbs red miso (soya paste) | 150 ml (¼ pint) water |
| 2 tbs saké (rice wine) | 1 bouquet garni |
| 2 tbs mirin (sweet rice wine) | 150 ml (¼ pint) soya yogurt or soft tofu |
| 1 tbs soya sauce | salt and pepper to taste |
| 1 tbs soya oil | |
| | **TO GARNISH** |
| | 1 tbs black sesame seeds |
| | a little dill |

In a bowl, blend the marinade ingredients. Place the fish fillets in a shallow dish with the marinade. Cover with clingfilm and leave for 3 hours in the refrigerator. When ready to steam, remove the fish, drain and wipe dry with a cloth.

Steam the fish in a wooden sieve over a pan of boiling water, allowing 1 minute per 2.5 cm (1-inch) thickness of fish as a guide.

To make the sauce, boil the clams for 3 minutes with the lemon juice, orange juice, water and bouquet garni. Strain the liquid through a cloth. Discard the shells and use the clam meat only. Boil the liquor and reduce its volume by half.

To the reduced liquor add 150 g (5 oz) soft tofu, whisking it in a little at a time for a smooth emulsion. Season to taste. Reheat the clams in the sauce without boiling it.

On each of 4 plates, arrange a steamed halibut fillet with a little sauce over, 2 shrimp dumplings, and a few clams. Sprinkle sesame seeds over the fish, and decorate with dill.     *Serves 4*     **HOWARD BULKA**

# Canadian Salmon Millefeuille Napoleon

*Pictured on page 68.*

| | FOR THE SAUCE |
|---|---|
| 250 g (8 oz) puff pastry or filo pastry | |
| 5 tbs soya oil | 2 tbs soya oil |
| 1 shallot, chopped | 1 shallot, chopped |
| 150 ml (¼ pint) Fish Stock (see page 41) | 100 ml (3½ fl oz) dry white wine |
| 500 g (1 lb) salmon fillet, skinned and cut into 4 pieces | 1 bunch watercress, stems and leaves separated |
| 25 g (1 oz) each carrot, celery, leek, turnip, and | 300 ml (½ pint) double cream |
| fennel, cut into thin strips | juice of ½ lemon |
| salt and pepper | salt and pepper |

Heat the oven to Gas Mark 6/200°C/400°F. Oil a baking tin. Roll out the pastry 5 mm (¼ inch) thick and cut into an oblong or a strip 7.5 cm (3 inches) wide and the length of the tin. Prick the surface evenly with a fork all over. Rest for 20 minutes then bake for 15 minutes until golden (not brown). Cool and cut into 8 small oblong pieces 7.5 cm (3 inches) long.

Heat 1 tbs of the soya oil and sauté the shallot for 30 seconds. Add the fish stock, seasoning, and fish fillets, and poach the fish for 5 minutes. Heat 4 tbs of the soya oil in a sauté pan. Shallow-fry the mixed vegetable strips for 1 minute. Keep them *al dente*. Remove and drain.

To prepare the sauce, heat a little oil in a pan and stir-fry the shallot for 30 seconds. Add the wine and the watercress stems. Boil until reduced in volume by two-thirds. Strain the liquor. Boil again with the cream and reduce by half. Strain, and add the chopped watercress leaves and lemon juice. Season to taste.

On each of 4 plates, pour a pool of sauce on one side. Arrange a slice of pastry. Cover with a fish fillet, and top with vegetable strips. Place another layer of pastry on top.

Serve with roasted potatoes, and flavoured with saffron powder.     *Serves 4*     **GEORGE McNEILL**

# CRUNCHY FISH STIR-FRY

| | |
|---|---|
| 500 g (1 lb) rock salmon or monkfish, boned | 1 tbs soya sauce |
| 1 tbs cornflour | 4 tbs fish or vegetable stock, or water |
| 2 tbs soya oil | 2 tsp chilli sauce |
| 50 g (2 oz) American peanuts | pinch brown sugar |
| 1 red pepper, de-seeded and sliced | 75 g (3 oz) bean sprouts |
| 1 leek, sliced | salt to taste |
| 175 g (6 oz) broccoli, cut into florets | |

Cut the fish into thin strips, then place in a bowl and sprinkle with salt. Leave for 20 minutes and then pat dry with kitchen paper and toss in the cornflour. Heat the oil in a large frying pan or wok, add the peanuts and fry until browned. Remove with a slotted spoon. Add the fish to the pan and stir-fry until firm. Remove from the pan. Add to the pan the pepper, leek, and broccoli, and stir-fry for 1 minute. Mix together the soya sauce, stock, chilli sauce, and sugar and add to the pan, stirring well. Add the peanuts and fish, lower the heat, cover, and cook for 2–3 minutes. Add the bean sprouts and heat through. Serve with rice.      *Serves 4*      **JOHN ASH**

# POTATO LATKES WITH SMOKED SALMON AND CHIVES

| |
|---|
| 1 kg (2 lb) potatoes, peeled |
| 1 onion |
| 3 eggs, well beaten |
| 2 tbs strong flour |
| 2 tbs snipped chives |
| 275 g (9 oz) smoked salmon, cut into small strips |
| 150 ml (¼ pint) soya oil |
| salt and pepper to taste |

Shred or grate the potatoes with the onion to keep them from browning. Squeeze the excess liquid through a sieve. In a bowl, mix the potato and onion with the beaten eggs, flour, and chives. Season to taste. Blend in the smoked salmon. Rest for 5 minutes.

Heat the oil in a shallow pan. Press some of the potato mixture into a large serving spoon, and then carefully slide it off the spoon into the hot oil. Fry the latkes until quite golden on both sides and crisp around the edges. Drain well on absorbent paper or towels. Repeat the process until all the latkes (about 30) are fried. Serve as soon as possible with a small mixed salad flavoured with lemon juice and yogurt. Serve separately yogurt or soured cream with chives in it.     *Serves 4*          OLARC CASYNS

# BRILL FILLETS IN A SWEET AND SOUR SAUCE

| | |
|---|---|
| 4 × 150 g ( 5 oz ) brill fillets ( or any other flat fish ), skinned | 1 tbs tomato purée |
| 3 tbs soya oil or butter | 1 tbs soya sauce |
| salt and pepper | 2 slices fresh ginger |
| | salt and pepper to taste |
| FOR THE SAUCE | |
| juice of 1 orange | TO GARNISH |
| 1 tbs sherry vinegar | 1 orange, segmented |
| 2 tbs honey | 4 mint leaves |
| 1 small green chilli, sliced and de-seeded | 1 tbs thinly grated orange peel |

Grill the brill fillets for 8 minutes, brushing them with oil or butter. Keep warm. Liquidise the sauce ingredients. Boil for 3 minutes and check seasoning.

Take 4 plates, and pour a pool of the sauce on each. Arrange the fish fillets with orange segments in a pretty pattern. Place a mint leaf and some strips of orange peel on each.     *Serves 4*          PATRICK LABOULY

# Sole and Prawns with Sauternes Wine in Fricassée

| | |
|---|---|
| 8 sole fillets | salt and pepper to taste |
| 1 kg ( 2 lb) Dublin Bay prawns or scampi | |
| 300 ml ( ½ pint) Fish stock (see page 41), made with | TO DECORATE |
| Sauternes, and the sole bones and prawn shells | 100 g ( 3½ oz) each carrot, turnip, cucumber, cooked |
| 6 tbs double cream | 1 tbs mixed fresh herbs (parsley, |
| 250 g ( 8 oz) butter | tarragon, chives) |

Cut the sole fillets into small square pieces. Shell the prawns and remove the intestinal vein from the tails. Boil the stock to reduce its volume by half. Then whisk in the cream and 150 g (5 oz) butter until it has all been used up. Season to taste. Heat the remaining butter and stir-fry the scampi and sole for 3 minutes only. Season to taste.

Pour a pool of sauce on each plate and arrange the fish on top. Decorate with the carrot, turnip, and cucumber. Finally, sprinkle the fresh herbs over the fish and serve hot.     *Serves 4*     **ANDRÉ GAUZÈRE**

# Fish Chowder

| | |
|---|---|
| 500 g (1 lb) strong flour | ½ tsp cornflour |
| 25 g (1 oz) ground semolina | 150 ml (¼ pint) double cream |
| 4 eggs, beaten | salt and pepper to taste |
| 4 tbs soya oil | 1 tbs lemon juice |
| 1 heaped tsp salt | |
| 500 g (1 lb) fish bones and heads, from assorted fish fillets | TO GARNISH |
| 1 onion, studded with 3 cloves | 50 g (2 oz) soya margarine |
| 150 ml (¼ pint) each dry white Alsace wine and water | 150 g (5 oz) each onions, mushrooms, and |
| 1 bouquet garni | leeks cut into strips |
| 500 g (1 lb) assorted fish fillets (trout, bass, | 1 tsp vinegar |
| eel, pike), cut into 75 g (3 oz) pieces | 4 sprigs coriander |

To prepare the ravioli dough, mix together the flour and semolina. Blend in the eggs, oil, and salt. Knead a little. Gather to a ball and rest, covered with a cloth. Roll the ravioli paste out to 5 mm (¼ inch) thick. Cut into 8 squares, 10 cm (4 inches) in size. Boil in salted water for 10 minutes, like pasta. Remove and place in warm water until ready to serve.

Place the fish bones and onion in a saucepan, and cover with water and wine. Add the bouquet garni and boil for 20 minutes. Strain the broth into a flat, deep metal dish. Poach the fish fillets in this broth for 4 minutes and remove with a slotted spoon. Transfer the stock to a small saucepan and boil. Mix the cornflour and cream in a cup and gradually stir it into the boiling stock. Cook for 4 minutes, until thick. Season to taste and add the lemon juice.

Heat the margarine and stir-fry the onions, mushrooms, and leeks for 2 minutes. Add the vinegar and let the liquid evaporate. Leave the mixture to cool.

To serve the fish, pour a pool of sauce on 4 plates. Arrange 1 square of ravioli pasta on each, and over it a mixture of fish. Coat the fish with a little sauce. Top with another square of ravioli, and finally decorate with a little of the mixed vegetable strips. Place a sprig of coriander or other greenery on top as the final touch.   *Serves 4*                                                                        JEAN CONIL

# Scrambled Eggs with Red Peppers and Clams

| | |
|---|---|
| 8 large clams | 1 large tomato, skinned, de-seeded, and chopped |
| 3 tbs olive oil | 4 basil leaves |
| 1 small onion, chopped | 4 eggs, beaten |
| 2 cloves garlic, chopped | 2 tbs double cream or fromage blanc |
| 1 red pepper, split, de-seeded, and chopped | salt and pepper |

Heat the clams to open the shells. Remove the flesh and dice it. Clean the shells. Heat the oil, and sauté the onion and garlic for 30 seconds. Add the red pepper and clams, and simmer for 4 minutes. Then blend in the tomato pulp and juice and the basil and cook for 1 more minute. In a separate bowl, mix the eggs, cream, and seasoning. When ready to serve, scramble the eggs in the pan with the other cooked ingredients, stirring all the time.

To serve, daintily fill each half clam shell with the mixture and serve as a starter. Any surplus can be used to stuff large grilled mushrooms or baked tartlets. *Serves 4* ANDRÉ GAUZÈRE

# Swordfish with Tempura of Vegetables

*Pictured on page 69.*

| | |
|---|---|
| 6 × 250 g (8 oz) swordfish pieces, gutted, washed, | 2 red peppers, de-seeded and cut into 12 triangles |
| and seasoned | 18 green beans, topped and tailed |
| 2 tbs soya oil | 18 asparagus spears, cut 7.5 cm (3 inches) long |
| | 6 button mushrooms |
| FOR THE BATTER | 6 slices of yam, peeled |
| 450 ml (¾ pint) water, made into ice cubes | 6 baby aubergines, sliced |
| 450 ml (¾ pint) water | 3 tbs seasoned flour |
| 300 g (10 oz) bread flour | 1.5 litres (2½ pints) soya oil |
| 25 g (1 oz) salt | |
| | TO SERVE |
| FOR THE TEMPURA | 250 ml (8 fl oz) Chilli Vinaigrette (see page 165) |
| 6 king prawns | 250 ml (8 fl oz) Wasabi Condiment (see page 165) |

$\mathcal{B}$rush oil over fish and grill for 8 minutes. Keep warm. In a bowl, blend all the batter ingredients into a smooth paste. Rub all the tempura ingredients in the seasoned flour, shake off the surplus, and pass in batter.

Heat the soya oil in a fish kettle to 180°C (350°F) and fry each group of ingredients until the whole mixture is cooked. Drain well on absorbent paper.

On each of 6 large platters, place 2 small bowls in the centre, one holding chilli vinaigrette and the other wasabi condiment. Beside the bowls place a piece of grilled fish, and arrange the tempura neatly around.    *Serves 6*                                                                                     HOWARD BULKA

## FISHERMAN'S CASSEROLE

| | FOR THE MARINADE |
|---|---|
| 4 × 200 g (7 oz) mackerel, or shad, bonito steaks, or whiting | |
| 100 g (3½ oz) flour | 25 g (1 oz) paprika |
| 500 g (1 lb) potatoes, peeled and sliced | 2 small chillies, crushed |
| 8 small shallots | 5 tbs soya oil |
| 1 onion, sliced | 2 cloves garlic, chopped |
| 4 baby carrots, peeled | 1 tsp ground cumin |
| 1 lemon, peeled and sliced | 2 tbs chopped coriander |
| 500 g (1 lb) tomatoes, blanched and sliced | salt and pepper to taste |
| 1 litre (1¾ pints) water or Fish Stock (see page 41) | |

$\mathcal{H}$eat the oven to Gas Mark 5/190°C/375°F. Remove the fins and heads of the fish. Wash and cut each into two, and coat in the flour. Mix together the marinade ingredients and marinate the fish for 15 minutes.

Oil an earthenware casserole, and arrange the carrots on the bottom, followed by half of the potatoes, then the shallots. Arrange the marinated fish over these, then the rest of the potatoes, the sliced onion, lemon, and tomatoes. Mix the remaining marinade with the stock, pour over, and bake without a lid in the oven for 45 minutes.    *Serves 4*                                                                                     MOHAMED DAHO

# *Steamed Food Osaka*

*Pictured on page 104.*

| | |
|---|---|
| 1 × 250 g (8 oz) abalone, fresh or canned | 3 tbs single cream |
| 1 mooli (daikon), peeled and grated | 3 tbs soured cream |
| 1 small lobster, weighing about 300 g (10 oz) | salt and pepper to taste |
| 8 fresh mussels, cleaned | 1 white mushroom, diced |
| 1 oyster | 1 courgette, diced |
| | 1 small truffle, diced |
| FOR THE SAUCE | 3 tbs single cream |
| 4 tbs soya oil | |
| lobster shell, chopped | TO GARNISH |
| 150 g (5 oz) mixed carrot, celery, and onion, chopped | 2 baby carrots |
| 1 bouquet garni | 2 olive-shaped turnips |
| 150 ml (¼ pint) Fish Stock (see page 41) | 2 sprigs broccoli |
| 1 tbs tomato purée | 4 small sticks celery |
| 1 tomato, skinned, de-seeded, and chopped | fresh basil and nasturtium flower for |
| 1 egg yolk | presentation of sashimi |

Slice the abalone and mix with the grated mooli. Steam for 2 hours. Cut the lobster in two lengthways. Remove the coral and reserve, and remove the flesh from the tail. Discard the gravel from the head. Chop the shell. Steam the lobster meat for 12 minutes. Steam the mussels and the oyster for 4 minutes.

To make the lobster sauce, heat the soya oil in a sauté pan and stir-fry the lobster shell until red. Add the chopped vegetables and the bouquet garni to the fish stock and tomato purée. Boil for 20 minutes, then strain. Reheat. Add the chopped tomato pulp and reboil.

Mix together the egg yolk and cream in a bowl, and gradually whisk it into the sauce. Season. Simmer until it thickens slightly.

Simmer the mushroom, the courgette, and the truffle in the cream for 3 minutes. Arrange the seafood on a dish. Coat with the mushroom, courgette, and truffle sauce. Pour over the lobster sauce. Steam the vegetable garnish for 6 minutes. Arrange it artistically around the seafood.     *Serves 2*     **MAKOTO SHIMADA**

# BIRDS OF MANY FEATHERS – Poultry and Game

$\mathscr{A}$ selection of birds bred for food has been grouped together in this chapter. It includes quails, guinea fowl, turkey, and wild duck, but mostly chicken.

From the nutritional point of view, all birds are edible, whether tame or not. They all have the same bone structure, but the taste of their flesh varies enormously according to the food they eat. All species on farms can be fed with controlled, balanced diets to produce high-quality meat. Apart from moral considerations, free-range birds are much better than battery hens, for the simple reason that freedom of movement is more healthy.

A feed mixture of grains, gravel, and milk powder may sound odd to the layman, but birds need gravel to grind the grain they swallow. Barley contributes to better flavour and higher fat content, and a combination of milk and corn has produced good results. Modern bird husbandry has provided very sophisticated feeds, which also include lentils, peas, beans, and cooked soya beans. A powder containing sulphate of iron, sodium, and carbonate of calcium (from oyster shells), gives good-coloured yolks and hard, thick egg shells.

It is important to take precautions to ensure that poultry does not contaminate other foods after it has been purchased. It must therefore be stored separately. It is wise to wash the poultry after it has been drawn and to soak it in water containing distilled spirit vinegar, which can be rinsed off in running water afterwards.

In cooking, there are many varieties of plant that have antiseptic properties, including mustard, cloves, garlic, onions, spearmint, thyme, and even dill. Eastern cuisine is full of recipes that include hygienic preparations, such as marinating in various sauces.

On average, after preparing and cooking poultry, we are left with 55 per cent cooked meat (52 per cent if we eliminate the edible skin). The flavour of the bird is in the skin, where the fat is able to concentrate it on roasting at high temperature. All bones, skin, and giblets should be used to produce concentrated stocks for soups or sauces. The best way to extract high flavour is to part-roast these ingredients prior to boiling them in water.

The cooking time depends on the thickness of the flesh and its conformity in relation to the bone structure. The larger the bird, the lower the cooking temperature should be after the initial high searing period. The succulence of the bird after cooking depends a great deal on this searing process to seal in the juice. Slow and low temperatures will dehydrate the bird.

The modern Eastern style of boning birds for many dishes saves time and fuel, the stir-fry method being very popular. The long casserole dishes have lost favour and are unnecessary as the poultry sold retail no longer includes old birds, which are sold to soup manufacturers. So we are dealing with roasting birds most of the time. Large turkeys can now be bought boned in rolled joints and even in the form of escalopes to be cooked like veal or pork with the same recipes.

The best way to flavour a bird for roasting is to introduce various herbs inside the body cavity. It may be sage for ducks, thyme for guinea fowl, and onion, mint and lemon for poultry: the range is unlimited. Garlic or slices of raw truffle can be placed between the skin and the flesh.

## THE NUTRITIONAL VALUE OF POULTRY AND WILD BIRDS

All poultry has a protein content of 18 per cent, which is higher than that of beef and pork. White poultry is lower in fat than butcher meats, except for certain species of tame duck and geese. This is why modern cooks use wild ducks for their leanness. Poultry also contains vitamin B and minerals, and is often recommended for those on invalid diets.

Cooked chicken, wrapped to prevent drying and kept in a refrigerator, should be consumed within three days or, if stuffed, within a day. It is more hygienic to reheat the cooked chicken on high heat for 14 minutes to kill germs.

The cooking of poultry requires quality fat. Bearing in mind that butter is best for flavour, there is no harm in combining unsaturated oil and butter to lower the percentage of cholesterol. Much spicier flavours are preferred in modern cooking, and with the use of fruit sauces, butter can be left out in most recipes. In this book we have advocated the use of soya oil as a substitute.

*Mexican Chicken with Corn and Red Chillies*

| | |
|---|---|
| 4 tbs soya oil | a little salt and pepper |
| 4 trimmed chicken breasts | 75 g (3 oz) sweetcorn kernels, cooked |
| 2 red chillies, split, de-seeded, and chopped | |
| 1 red pepper, split, de-seeded, and cut in strips | TO GARNISH |
| 1 medium onion, cut into thin rings | 1 large tomato, sliced |
| 150 ml (¼ pint) chicken stock | 2 sprigs of fresh mint |

Heat the oil in a shallow pan and cook the chicken breasts for 12 minutes until brown. Remove the chicken and place in a casserole dish. In the same pan, using the same oil, stir-fry the chillies, pepper, and onion for 3 minutes.

Cover the chicken with this mixture and pour the chicken stock over. Season to taste. Cook for 35 minutes, covered with a lid, adding the sweetcorn for the last 8 minutes' cooking.

Serve the chicken on individual plates with a slice of fresh raw tomato and fresh mint leaves on each. *Serves 4*                ORDONO DAMASO

# Chicken Ciara Maria Supreme

*Pictured on page 103.*

| | |
|---|---|
| 4 × 175 g (6 oz) chicken breasts, with under-fillets | FOR THE SAUCE |
| 50 g (2 oz) seasoned flour | 25 g (1 oz) mixed soya oil and butter |
| 1 egg, beaten | 50 g (2 oz) shallots, chopped |
| 50 g (2 oz) breadcrumbs | 1 tbs tarragon vinegar |
| 25 g (1 oz) sesame seeds | 150 ml (¼ pint) single cream |
| 500 ml (18 fl oz) soya oil, plus a little extra for brushing | 1 tsp Pernod or pinch star anise powder |
| | 25 g (1 oz) butter |
| FOR THE STUFFING | a good pinch of paprika |
| 1 egg, beaten | |
| 150 ml (¼ pint) cream | TO GARNISH |
| 50 g (2 oz) chives, snipped | a few strands of saffron |
| 1 tsp chopped dill | 2 tomatoes, peeled and halved |
| 50 g (2 oz) white crab meat, cooked | 4 crab claws, cooked |

Remove the skin of each chicken breast, leaving the breastbone in place. Peel away the under-fillet from each breast. Brush each breast with oil and place it between 2 sheets of polythene. With a wooden mallet gently flatten the breast as thin as possible without tearing the flesh. Repeat this operation for all 4 breasts.

To prepare the stuffing, mince the under-fillets to a paste. Place in a bowl. Blend with the egg, and beat for 30 seconds, adding the cream while mixing. At this stage, add the chives, dill, and the crab meat. Season and refrigerate for 20 minutes. Spread the mixture equally over each breast of chicken. Roll tightly in cigar shapes. Coat in seasoned flour, then dip in the beaten egg and a mixture of breadcrumbs and sesame seeds. Wrap in foil and freeze for 20 minutes, so that the chicken rolls will retain their shape. Heat the soya oil in a pan and shallow-fry the chicken breasts for 8 minutes. Pat dry with a cloth.

To make the sauce, heat the oil and butter in a pan and shallow-fry the shallots for 30 seconds, until translucent. Add the vinegar and reduce by half. Blend in the cream. Boil for 8 minutes to reduce it to a syrupy consistency. Season. Add the Pernod or star anise, butter and paprika.

Pour a pool of the sauce on each of 4 plates and sprinkle with a few strands of saffron. Place a chicken breast on each plate. Leaving the bone side intact, cut each breast into 3 slices per portion. Place half a tomato and a crab claw beside each breast. Serve with moulded pilaff rice.     *Serves 4*     JOHN MORRIN

# *Chicken Pie* WITH *Scorzonera* (SALSIFY)

*Scorzonera is the black-skinned variety of the salsify root. It was for centuries regarded as a medicinal plant, but was then adopted as a culinary vegetable by the cooks of Louis XIV. It is now established as one of the most tasty root vegetables.*

| | |
|---|---|
| 8 tbs soya oil | salt and pepper to taste |
| 1 oven-ready 2 kg (4½ lb) roasting chicken, cut into 8 pieces | |
| 4 shallots, chopped | FOR THE |
| 2 cloves garlic, chopped | MEATBALLS |
| 100 ml (3½ fl oz) chicken stock | 250 g (8 oz) minced pork or beef |
| 150 ml (¼ pint) dry white wine or cider | 1 egg |
| 2 ceps or field mushrooms, sliced | 1 tbs chopped parsley |
| 100 ml (3½ fl oz) single cream | juice of 1 lemon |
| 1 bouquet garni | 1 tbs flour |
| 500 g (1 lb) scorzonera (salsify) roots | 1 tbs soya margarine |

*H*eat the oven to Gas Mark 6/200°C/400°F. Heat 4 tbs of the soya oil in a sauté pan and shallow-fry the chicken pieces for 8 minutes, until golden. Remove the chicken to a pie dish.

In the same oil, fry the shallots and garlic for 1 minute. Drain off the oil. Add the chicken stock, wine, and mushrooms. Boil for 2 minutes. Blend in the cream. Cover the chicken in the pie dish with the wine mixture. Add the bouquet garni and season to taste. Bake in the oven for 20 minutes. Strain the chicken liquor into a pan and reduce it by half. Pour it back over the chicken pieces. Cover with a lid and simmer in the oven at the same temperature for another 15 minutes. Blend the meatball ingredients, adding seasoning, and divide the mixture into 25 g (1 oz) meatballs. Fry in the remaining oil for 6 minutes. Drain well. Keep warm.

Wash the scorzonera, brushing carefully, in plenty of water. Peel and cut into small chunks 5 cm (2 inches) long. Boil in salted water to which you have added the lemon juice and a paste made up of the flour and margarine; this will form a crust to prevent browning caused by exposure to the air.

Place 2 pieces of chicken and 2 meatballs on each plate. Blend the scorzonera with the sauce, and pour over the chicken.    *Serves 4*                                                             **ALBERT PARVEAUX**

# Chicken Toukrah Mauritius-style

| | FOR THE DRESSING |
|---|---|
| 1 × 1 kg (2 lb) chicken, cut into 8 pieces | |
| 2 cloves garlic | 2 tbs soya oil |
| 1 piece ginger | juice of 1 lemon |
| 2 cloves | salt and pepper, to taste |
| 5 mint leaves | few sprigs fresh mint, chopped |
| 5 coriander leaves | |
| 2 cardamom seeds | TO GARNISH |
| 3 peppercorns | 4 small potatoes, par-boiled |
| 1/3 tsp anise seeds | 4 eggs, hard-boiled |
| 1/2 cinnamon stick | 1/2 tsp yellow food-colouring |
| 1/2 tsp ground turmeric | soya oil for deep-frying |
| 1 red chilli, de-seeded and chopped | 8 lettuce leaves |
| 125 ml (1/4 pint) yogurt | 1/2 cucumber, cut into strips |
| 1 tomato, skinned, de-seeded, and chopped | salt to taste |
| 1 onion, chopped | |
| 3 tbs soya oil | |

Grind all the spices and herbs in a mortar to a paste. Dilute this paste with the yogurt, and add the chopped tomato and onion. Blend with the soya oil. Marinate the chicken pieces in this mixture overnight. Heat the oven to Gas Mark 6/200°C/400°F. Place all the ingredients in a casserole dish, cover with a lid, and bake in the oven for 45 minutes. Put all the dressing ingredients in a glass jar with a lid, and shake until well mixed. Roll the eggs and the potatoes in the colouring. Deep-fry in soya oil until golden.

On each of 4 plates, serve 2 pieces of chicken with its sauce, 1 egg, 1 potato, and 2 lettuce leaves topped with cucumber strips and mint dressing. Serve with boiled rice.   *Serves 4*   **MESH BOYJOONAUTH**

# Crispy Chicken and Seafood Fritters

## Cantonese-Style

*Although crispy fritters may sound prosaic enough, they recall to a Chinese cook many happy meanings – scenic beauty, pagodas, tea ceremonies, classic dances – in short, they recall a land where poets have always found inspiration while eating and drinking rice wines. Pictured on page 105.*

| FOR THE FRITTERS | 100 g (3½ oz) ham, chopped |
|---|---|
| 100 g (3½ oz) each lean chicken, peeled prawn | 1 × 500 g (1 lb) pig's caul or edible seaweed bag or paper |
| tails, canned water chestnuts, white fish, and | 100 g (3½ oz) bamboo shoots, cut into thin strips |
| white mushrooms, sliced at an angle into | |
| diamond shapes (for texture) | FOR THE BATTER |
| 2 egg whites | 4 egg whites |
| salt and pepper | 100 g (3½ oz) cornflour |
| 2 tbs saké (rice wine) or sherry | 3 tbs water |
| 1 tbs cornflour | soya oil for deep-frying |
| 1 tbs soya oil | |
| ½ tsp sugar | TO GARNISH |
| ½ tsp salt | few sprigs of thyme |
| 7 g (¼ oz) coriander leaves, roughly chopped | few lavender flowers |

*M*ix together all the fritter ingredients, except the caul and bamboo shoots, to make a sticky dough. Divide the dough into 12 balls. Flatten each ball and give it the shape of a leg of chicken. Divide the pig's caul or seaweed paper into 12 triangular pieces roughly 5 cm (2 inches) long and 5 mm (¼ inch) wide, and place on a pastry board dusted with cornflour. Place on top of each one a shaped leg. Top it with a few strips of bamboo shoot and reshape it like a small leg of chicken.

Prepare a sort of batter paste with the egg whites, half the cornflour, and the water. Pass each 'leg' in the remaining cornflour, then in the batter. Deep-fry for 3 minutes at 180°C (350°F) and then drain. Reheat the oil to 190°C (375°F) and fry again to give a second browning for 2–3 minutes. Drain well.

On a platter place a fancy doily and on it arrange the 12 miniature legs. Decorate with fresh sprigs of thyme and lavender flowers.     *Serves 4*                                                    HUI PUI-WING

# CHINESE CHICKEN WITH WILD RICE AND STUFFED PANCAKES

*Pictured on page 105.*

| 4 chicken breasts, skinned and boned | salt and pepper |
|---|---|

| FOR THE STUFFING | FOR THE VEGETABLE GARNISH |
|---|---|
| 4 tbs soya oil | 4 leeks, whites only |
| 1 onion, chopped | 4 thin pancakes, 13 cm (5 inches) in diameter |
| 125 g (4 oz) wild rice | 40 g (1½ oz) each carrot, turnip, potato, and |
| 300 ml (½ pint) chicken stock | courgette, cut into small balls |
| 20 g (¾ oz) tofu, chopped | 40 g (1½ oz) celery, diced |
| 1 egg, beaten | 40 g (1½ oz) small peas |
| salt and pepper to taste | 15 g (½ oz) soya margarine |
| | salt and pepper |

| FOR THE SAUCE | |
|---|---|
| 250 ml (8 fl oz) chicken stock | TO GARNISH |
| 125 g (4 oz) soft tofu | 2 tbs soya oil |
| 1 tsp chopped chervil | 20 small morels |
| juice of ½ lemon | 1 bunch watercress |

To make the stuffing, heat 2 tbs of the soya oil and fry the onion and wild rice for 1 minute. Cover with the stock and cook gently for 40 minutes. Drain. Blend in the tofu and season to taste. Cool, then bind with the beaten egg. Remove the under-fillets from the chicken breasts. Place the breasts and under-fillets between 2 sheets of waxed paper and polythene and pound slightly to make them thin. On each breast, place a spoonful of the rice mixture. Cover with an under-fillet. Roll each chicken breast into a cone shape. Wrap each one in well-oiled aluminium foil. To make the sauce, boil the chicken stock to reduce it by half, and whisk in a little soft tofu. Season to taste, then add the chervil and lemon juice. Place the chicken breasts in a shallow tray and cover with the sauce. Simmer for 12 minutes. Remove from the pan. Unwrap and discard the foil. Heat 2 tbs of the soya oil and brown the breasts for 5 minutes in the pan. Remove. Divide each breast into 6 slices, cut at an angle. Blanch the leeks, refresh, and drain. Dice the leeks, and spoon some onto each pancake. Cup the pancakes like a purse. Blanch the remaining vegetables for 30 seconds. Season and blend in a little soya margarine. Heat 2 tbs soya oil and stir-fry the morels for 1 minute. Remove and drain. On each of 4 plates, pour a pool of sauce, over which arrange the 6 pieces of each breast, overlapping, and beside the pool spoon some of the vegetable mixture and place 1 pancake parcel. Decorate with 5 cooked morels and a sprig of watercress.     *Serves 4*                                                                CHAN CHI-HUNG

# CHICKEN ST GERAN SUPRÊME

| | |
|---|---|
| 2 chicken breasts, skinned | 200 ml ( 7 fl oz ) chicken stock |
| salt, pepper, and curry powder | 5 tbs cream |
| 3 tbs soya oil | salt and pepper to taste |

| FOR THE CURRY SAUCE | FOR THE PICKLED VEGETABLES |
|---|---|
| 4 tbs soya oil | 50 g ( 2 oz ) each cabbage, beans, carrots, and |
| 2 spring onions, chopped | celery, cut into thin strips |
| 1 clove garlic, chopped | 4 tbs soya oil |
| 1 tsp turmeric | 1 clove garlic, chopped |
| 25 g ( 1 oz ) curry powder | 7 g ( ¼ oz ) each mustard seeds, chopped ginger, and turmeric |
| 2 tomatoes, skinned, de-seeded, and chopped | 1 small onion, cut into strips |
| 7 g ( ¼ oz ) ginger root, chopped | ½ tsp salt |

Rub the chicken breasts with the seasoning and curry powder. Heat the oil and shallow-fry the chicken for 12 minutes, until cooked. Slice the breasts thinly.

To make the curry sauce, heat the oil in a pan and stir-fry the onion and garlic until soft. Add the spices and cook for 30 seconds. Then add the tomatoes, ginger, and chicken stock. Boil for 25 minutes, then blend in the cream. Season with salt and pepper. Strain the sauce.

For the *achard de legumes,* or pickled vegetables, blanch the vegetables for 30 seconds and refresh in iced water. Drain well. Heat the oil and stir-fry the onion and garlic for 1 minute. Add the spices and cook for 1 more minute. Remove from the stove and mix the blanched vegetables with these spicy condiments. Chill.

Arrange the chicken slices on 2 plates in overlapping rosettes. Pour a pool of curry sauce around them, and in the centre arrange the vegetable pickle.     *Serves 2*                                    **BARRY ANDREWS**

# CHICKEN WITH PINEAPPLE AND SAFFRON RICE

| | |
|---|---|
| 1 kg ( 2 lb ) chicken, skinned, boned, and | 1 clove garlic, chopped |
| cut into small slices or cubes | 2 tbs soya oil |
| 150 g ( 5 oz ) shallots, chopped | 150 g ( 5 oz ) basmati rice |
| 15 g ( ½ oz ) ginger, peeled and chopped | 150 ml ( ¼ pint ) water or chicken stock |
| 25 g ( 1 oz ) coconut paste | 5 tbs milk |
| 100 g ( 3½ oz ) desiccated coconut, toasted | ¼ tsp each cinnamon, cloves, and star anise |
| 7 g ( ¼ oz ) tamarind, sliced | 3 strands saffron |
| 4 slices fresh pineapple | salt to taste |
| salt and pepper to taste | |
| | TO GARNISH |
| FOR THE SAFFRON RICE | a few spring onions |
| 25 g ( 1 oz ) onion, chopped | 4 radishes |
| 7 g ( ¼ oz ) ginger, chopped | 4 mooli |

Put all ingredients, except the chicken, pineapple, and seasoning, in a pot. Add 2 cups of water and boil for 12 minutes. Add the chicken and simmer for 20 minutes. Season to taste. Lastly add the pineapple slices to the sauce in a fan shape.

To prepare the rice, blend the onion, ginger, and garlic together in a liquidiser with half the soya oil, half the rice, half the stock or water, and half the milk. Heat the remaining oil and cook the liquidised ingredients for 2 minutes. Add all the spices, the remaining water or stock, and milk. Sprinkle the rice into the boiling liquid. Flavour with saffron. Cook slowly, covered, for 15 minutes. Season with salt to taste.

Serve the chicken and rice separately in individual bowls. Garnish the rice with spring onions, radishes, mooli, and other crudités.     *Serves 4*                    MRS UNGKU SHIRIN AHMAD

# CHICKEN CREOLE RISOTTO

| |
|---|
| 2 tbs soya oil |
| 125 g (4 oz) each of: onion, tomato, celery, green pepper, all diced |
| 500 g (1 lb) raw chicken meat without skin or bones, cubed |
| 150 g (5 oz) long-grain rice |
| 600 ml (1 pint) chicken stock |
| 50 g (2 oz) cheese, grated |
| a few sprigs of basil |
| a little salt and pepper |

In a shallow pan, heat the oil. Stir-fry all the vegetables for 5 minutes. Add the chicken and rice and cook for 5 minutes more. Stir in the stock and add the seasoning. Cook for 20 minutes, until the liquid has evaporated. Mix in the cheese.

Place on 1 dish. Garnish with basil.     *Serves 4*                                    **JEREMIE GARLICK**

# CHICKEN TERRINE WITH GARLIC

| | |
|---|---|
| 4 heads garlic | salt and pepper to taste |
| 500 g (1 lb) lean chicken, skinned, boned, and minced | |
| 2 eggs, beaten | TO GARNISH |
| 300 ml (½ pint) whipping cream | green and red chicory leaves |
| 7 g (¼ oz) soya margarine or oil | stems of fresh garlic |

Heat the oven to Gas Mark 6/200°C/400°F, and roast the heads of garlic for 30 minutes, until soft. Peel the garlic and blend it into the minced raw chicken in a bowl. Add the eggs, and chill on ice for 1 hour. Gradually blend the cream into the mixture. Season to taste.

Cut 2 squares of foil and grease them liberally with soya margarine or oil. Divide the mixture in two. Moisten hands with water and shape each portion into a sausage-shaped roll. Wrap the foil tightly around each portion, twisting the 2 ends of the foil to keep the mixture free from contact with steam. Place the 2 rolls in a steamer and cook for 20 minutes like a steamed pudding. Carefully remove the parcels from the steamer and cool.

On individual plates arrange slices of the mixture, overlapping, in an attractive geometric pattern. Decorate with green and red chicory leaves and stems of fresh garlic.     *Serves 4*     **FRANCISCO RUBIO SANCHEZ**

# *Chicken Satay with Peanut Sauce*

| | FOR THE PEANUT SAUCE |
|---|---|
| 1 kg (2 lb) chicken meat, cut into strips 2 cm (¾ inch) long and 1 cm (½ inch) thick | 250 g (8 oz) peanuts, toasted and ground |
| 2 onions, sliced | 100 g (3½ oz) onion, chopped |
| 7 g (¼ oz) root ginger, peeled | 100 g (3½ oz) lemon grass |
| 7 g (¼ oz) galangal, peeled | 1 clove garlic, chopped |
| 1 clove garlic, peeled | 25 g (1 oz) tamarind |
| 100 g (3½ oz) lemon grass | 50 g (2 oz) dried chillies |
| 7 g (¼ oz) each cumin, coriander, aniseed, and turmeric | 5 tbs soya oil |
| 50 g (2 oz) sugar or honey | salt to taste |
| 2 tbs soya oil | |

*L*iquidise in a blender the onion, ginger, galangal, garlic and lemon grass. Add all the dry spices and sugar. Mix well, and soak the chicken in this marinade for 5 hours. Weave the mixture on wooden satay sticks. Brush with soya oil, and charcoal-grill or deep-fry for 2 minutes.

To make the peanut sauce, liquidise all the ingredients, and add enough water to make it pourable.

Serve the satay and the sauce separately, so that the chicken can be dipped in the sauce as desired.

*Serves 4*                                                     MRS UNGKU SHIRIN AHMAD

# CHICKEN AND HAM FRICASSÉE WITH RICE

| | |
|---|---|
| 3 tbs soya oil | 2 tbs double cream or sour cream |
| 1 medium onion, chopped | 250 g (8 oz) white mushrooms, sliced |
| 100 g (3½ oz) cooked ham, diced | juice of 1 lemon |
| 250 g (8 oz) cooked chicken, diced | a little salt and pepper |
| 1 tsp curry powder | a pinch of chilli powder |
| ½ tbs plain flour | 1 green chilli, de-seeded and cut into strips |
| 300 ml (½ pint) chicken stock | |

Heat the oil in a shallow pan and stir-fry the onion until soft but not brown. Add the ham, chicken, and curry powder and simmer for 5 minutes. Sprinkle in the flour and stir well. Add the stock and cream. After 5 minutes add the mushrooms, and simmer for 10 minutes.

Season to taste with salt, pepper, and chilli powder. Lastly, add the lemon juice.

Divide the mixture between 4 plates, placing it to the side of each. Serve with boiled rice. Decorate the rice with strips of chilli.     *Serves 4*                                                            JEAN CONIL

# SOUTHERN FRIED CHICKEN

| | |
|---|---|
| 4 chicken portions, about 450 g (1 lb) in all | FOR THE SAUCE |
| 2 tbs plain flour mixed with ½ tsp salt and | 1 tbs soya oil and 1 tbs melted butter, mixed |
| a pinch of black pepper | 1 level tbs plain flour |
| 300 ml (½ pint) soya oil | 150 ml (5 fl oz) single cream, plus extra if required |
| 2 eggs, beaten | a few drops of Tabasco |
| 325 g (11 oz) 3-minute-cook canned rice | a little salt |
| 2 tbs chervil leaves | |
| 1 tsp paprika | |

Rub the chicken pieces in the seasoned flour. Shake off the surplus. Heat the oil in a deep-fryer until it reaches 180°C/350°F. Dip the chicken pieces in beaten egg and deep-fry them for 8–10 minutes until golden brown. Drain them well.

To make the sauce, heat the oil and butter mixture and the flour. Cook for 30 seconds, then gradually add the cream, stirring all the time. Simmer for 10 minutes. Season and strain. If the sauce is too thick, add a little extra cream. Season with Tabasco and salt to taste. Boil the rice according to the instructions on the packet. Drain.

Arrange a bed of rice on 4 plates and put a piece of fried chicken on top of each. Decorate with chervil leaves and paprika. Serve the sauce separately.     *Serves 4*                                                      **DAVID FELLOWES**

## *B*REAST OF *C*HICKEN *O*RIENTAL

| | |
|---|---|
| 4 chicken breasts | 2 shallots, chopped |
| 2 tbs soya oil | 1 clove garlic, chopped |
| | 1 small piece ginger, chopped |
| FOR THE STUFFING | 15 g ( ½ oz) candlenut, chopped |
| 4 tbs soya margarine | 1 tsp ground turmeric |
| 2 cloves garlic, chopped | 2 leaves each lemon grass and salam leaves or |
| 7 g ( ¼ oz) ginger, chopped | parsley, chopped |
| 1 tsp ground turmeric | 300 ml ( ½ pint) thick coconut milk |
| 150 g (5 oz) shallots, chopped | 150 ml ( ¼ pint) chicken stock |
| 7 g ( ¼ oz) candlenut, ground | salt and pepper to taste |
| 2 lemon grass leaves, chopped | |
| 1 egg white | TO GARNISH |
| | 12 mangetouts |
| FOR THE SAUCE | a few chilli flowers |
| 2 tbs soya oil | |

*S*kin the chicken breasts and scrape the breast bone a little to form a 'handle' for easy eating. Remove the under-fillets and mince them for stuffing. Place the breasts between 2 sheets of well-oiled polythene, and flatten them gently with a wooden mallet to thin escalopes.

Combine all the stuffing ingredients, including the minced under-fillets, into a stiff paste in a bowl. Spread this mixture over the inside of each breast. Roll up tightly and freeze for 20 minutes. Season on the outside. Heat 2 tbs soya oil and shallow-fry, covered, for 15 minutes. Keep warm.

To make the sauce, heat the oil in a pan and sauté all the vegetables and herbs for 4 minutes. Stir in the coconut milk and the chicken stock. Boil for 15 minutes. Season to taste and strain. The sauce should be reduced in volume by half.

Pour a pool of sauce on each of 4 plates. Slice each breast into 8 or 9 pieces overlapping each other. Decorate with the mangetouts and chilli flowers.     *Serves 4*                                          **WAYAN MALIASTRA**

# Turkey Kebabs with Peanut Marinade

| |
|---|
| 500 g ( 1 lb ) boneless turkey breast |
| 3 tbs crunchy peanut butter |
| 1 tsp orange peel, grated finely |
| 3 tbs fresh orange juice |
| 1 tsp paprika |
| 2 tsp Worcestershire sauce |
| 1 red pepper |

Cut the turkey meat into 2.5 cm (1-inch) cubes. Mix together the peanut butter, orange peel and juice, paprika, and Worcestershire sauce. Add the turkey and stir well until it is evenly coated. Marinate for 1 hour.

Cut the pepper into 2.5 cm (1-inch) pieces. Thread onto skewers alternately with the meat. Cook under a moderate grill or on a barbecue for 8–10 minutes, turning several times until evenly cooked. Serve hot with salad and toasted pitta bread or rice.     *Serves 4*                                    **WILLIAM UNDERWOOD**

# Pan-Fried Foie Gras with Caper Sauce

| |
|---|
| 4 × 75 g ( 3 oz ) goose or duck livers, trimmed, washed and pat-dried |
| 3 tbs soya oil |
| 4 tsp sherry vinegar |
| 200 ml ( 7 fl oz ) strong chicken stock |
| 100 ml ( 3½ fl oz ) single cream |
| 4 tbs capers |
| salt and black pepper to taste |
| kaiware ( spice sprouts ) or mustard leaves, to decorate |

Cut the liver into slices. Heat the oil and fry gently for a few minutes at a low heat. Discard the oil and remove the liver. Keep it warm while completing the sauce. In the same pan add vinegar and reduce to a third. Blend in the chicken stock and boil again to reduce by half. At this stage add the cream and capers. Season to taste. Cool the sauce slightly.

Pour a pool of sauce on each of 4 plates. Arrange some liver in the middle of each plate. Decorate with spice sprouts or mustard leaves.     *Serves 4*                                    **PATRICK LANNES**

# Alabama Peanut Chicken

2 chicken breasts, skinned and boned

salt and cayenne pepper to taste

1 large egg, beaten

125 g (4 oz) roasted peanuts, crushed

2 tbs unsalted butter

1 tbs soya oil

1 clove garlic, crushed

2 tbs lemon juice

2 tbs white wine

1 tbs chopped parsley

Flatten the chicken breasts gently with the side of a knife. Season with cayenne pepper and salt to taste. Coat the chicken breasts in the egg and then completely in the peanuts. Refrigerate for 30 minutes. Melt 1 tbs of the butter with the oil in a frying pan and sauté the chicken until golden brown on each side. Place on a heated serving dish. Add the remaining butter to the pan and cook the garlic. Add the lemon juice and white wine to the pan and deglaze. Pour this sauce over the chicken and sprinkle over some parsley. Serve with a seasonal salad or vegetables.    *Serves 2*                                    **WILLIAM UNDERWOOD**

# Parcel of Pheasant Breast with Citrus Sausage in Blackcurrant Sauce

| | |
|---|---|
| 4 pheasant breasts, skinned | FOR THE |
| 3 tbs soya oil | CITRUS SAUSAGE |
| 150 ml (¼ pint) game gravy | 1 grapefruit, segmented and pith removed |
| 100 ml (3½ fl oz) blackcurrant juice | 1 lemon, segmented |
| juice of ½ lemon | 50 g (2 oz) ground almonds |
| juice of 2 grapefruit | 2 tbs game gravy |
| juice of 1 orange | 1 egg white, beaten stiffly |
| salt and black pepper to taste | 1 tsp orange liqueur |
| | 15 g (½ oz) honey |
| FOR THE FILLING | 1 sausage skin, about 20 cm (8 inches) long |
| 50 g (2 oz) cream cheese | |
| 4 orange segments, diced | TO GARNISH |
| 1 tbs chopped mint leaves, plus 2 whole leaves | 250 g (8 oz) mixed carrots, cauliflower, |
| 1 tsp snipped chives | and broccoli |
| juice of ½ lemon | sprigs of herbs and chives |
| 4 spinach leaves, blanched | orange and grapefruit segments |
| 4 lamb's or pig's cauls, or pieces of transparent rice paper | a sprig of redcurrants |

Place the pheasant breasts between 2 oiled polythene sheets and flatten them as thin as possible without damaging the flesh. To prepare the filling, cream the cheese in a bowl, and add the orange segments, mint, chives, and lemon juice. Divide the mixture into 4 balls and shape them like cigars. Wrap them in the spinach leaves. Then place 1 parcel in each flattened breast of pheasant. Roll each breast into a cigar shape to hold the filling. Now decorate by placing a segment of orange and 2 mint leaves on one side. Wrap each breast in a caul or transparent rice paper so that the orange and mint leaves can be seen.

To prepare the citrus sausage, liquidise the citrus fruit with the ground almonds, and game gravy, orange liqueur and honey. Fold in the beaten egg white. Place the mixture in a piping bag fitted with a plain nozzle and fill the synthetic sausage skin. Twist to make 4 separate sausages.

Heat the oil in a sauté pan and shallow-fry the pheasant breasts gently for 12 minutes, turning from time to time until done. Remove and keep warm. Shallow-fry the sausages over a low heat for 6 minutes. Remove from the pan and keep warm. Discard the used oil. In the same pan, add the fruit juices, gravy, and seasoning. Boil the liquid to reduce it to a concentrated sauce.

Boil the vegetables separately in salted water for a few minutes. Mash the carrots, cauliflower, and broccoli and shape them with spoons. Cut the remaining vegetables into strips and blend them with the herbs.

On each of 2 large plates, place 1 cooked breast of pheasant and a spoonful of vegetable and herb mixture, and the orange and grapefruit segments, over which you arrange the citrus sausage. Pour a pool of sauce around the pheasant, leaving space on one side of the plate for the purées, carrots, broccoli and cauliflower. Arrange a sprig of redcurrants on top of each breast as the final touch.     *Serves 2*     **ANTONIO MANCINI**

# *Peanut Raisin Chicken*

| |
|---|
| 2 tbs olive oil |
| 1.5–1.75 kg (3–4 lb) chicken, cut into 4–8 pieces |
| 1 onion, sliced |
| 3 cloves garlic, crushed |
| 1 tbs sesame seeds |
| ¼ tsp ground cinnamon |
| ¼ tsp ground cloves |
| ¼ tsp coriander seeds, toasted and crushed |
| 2 tsp chilli powder |
| 450 ml (¾ pint) chicken stock |
| 3 tbs smooth peanut butter |
| 25 g (1 oz) Californian raisins |
| 100 g (3½ oz) plain chocolate |
| salt and pepper to taste |
| a few sprigs of watercress, to decorate |

Heat the oil in a large pan. Brown the chicken pieces, and remove when done. Add the onion, and sauté until light brown. Add the garlic, sesame seeds, cinnamon, cloves, coriander, and chilli powder, and cook on moderate heat for 3 minutes. Add the chicken stock and simmer for 5 minutes, stirring occasionally.

Pour the stock mixture into a liquidiser with the rest of the ingredients and process until smooth. Return the sauce to the pan and add the chicken. Cover and simmer for about 30 minutes, until the chicken is tender.

Transfer the chicken to a serving dish. Beat the sauce until smooth and pour over the chicken. Garnish with watercress, if liked.     *Serves 4*     **WILLIAM UNDERWOOD**

# *G*UINEA *F*OWL WITH *K*UMQUATS *J*ERUSALEM

| | |
|---|---|
| 5 tbs soya oil | 12 kumquat pieces, cut into wedges |
| 4 guinea fowl breasts | salt and coarse black pepper to taste |
| 1 carrot, chopped | 2 tbs orange liqueur |
| 1 onion, chopped | 25 g (1 oz) unsalted butter or 1 tbs vegetable oil (optional) |
| 1 sprig thyme | |
| 150 ml (¼ pint) red wine | TO GARNISH |
| 8 mint leaves, chopped | 1 bunch fresh mint |
| 1 tbs honey or sugar | 50 g (2 oz) peanuts, toasted |

*H*eat 4 tbs of the oil in a sauté pan. Brown the breasts of guinea fowl for 10–12 minutes. Season. Remove and keep warm. In the same oil, fry the guinea fowl bones, carrot, onion, and thyme. After 5 minutes, add the red wine and a cup of water. Then add the chopped mint and boil for 30 minutes. Strain.

Reheat the stock, add the honey or sugar, and poach the kumquat pieces for 2 minutes. Then remove carefully. Boil the liquor until reduced by a third in volume. Strain again, and add the liqueur. Check the seasoning, then emulsify the sauce with the remaining 1 tbs of soya oil (a non-kosher version of this dish might use unsalted butter instead).

Slice the breasts, and fan out the slices on 4 plates. Spoon the sauce on the side. Arrange the kumquat pieces and garnish with fresh mint leaves and toasted peanuts.     *Serves 4*     **OLARC CASYNS**

# Colorado Bean and Duck Casserole

## with Chillies

| |
|---|
| 6 tbs soya oil |
| 500 g ( 1 lb ) lean duck meat, cubed |
| 250 g ( 8 oz ) lean pork, cubed |
| 150 g ( 5 oz ) onion, chopped |
| 2 cloves garlic, chopped |
| 1.2 litres ( 2 pints ) water |
| 2 green chillies, de-seeded and chopped |
| 1 red chilli, de-seeded and chopped |
| 1 sweet red pepper, de-seeded and chopped |
| 1 tbs tomato purée |
| 2 tsp cumin seeds |
| 2 tsp oregano |
| 1 tsp salt |
| 500 g ( 1 lb ) baked beans |
| fresh oregano or mint leaves, chopped, to decorate |

Heat 3 tbs of the oil and sauté the meat for 5 minutes until brown. Remove the meat and, in the same fat, brown the onion for 1 minute and the garlic for 5 seconds. Discard any surplus oil and return the meat to the pan. Cover with 1 litre (1¾ pints) of the water. Bring to the boil and skim as necessary.

Meanwhile, pound the chillies and pepper to a paste. Add the tomato purée, cumin seeds, oregano, and the rest of the water. In a pan, cook this paste for 5 minutes to improve the flavour. Stir the paste into the duck stew. Simmer the casserole for 45 minutes to 1 hour. Remove any fat from the sauce. Mix in the baked beans and the salt.

Pour the mixture into four 150 ml (¼-pint) earthenware dishes. Sprinkle with fresh chopped oregano or mint leaves, and serve.     *Serves 4*                                    JAMES E. COHEN

# BREAST OF WILD DUCK EN SOUFFLÉ

| | |
|---|---|
| 4 wild duck breasts, skinned and chilled | 3 egg whites |
| 150 g ( 5 oz ) rhubarb, divided into 8 short sticks | salt, nutmeg, and cayenne pepper to taste |
| 2 tbs maple syrup, melted | |
| salt and pepper | FOR THE SAUCE |
| 500 g ( 1 lb ) puff pastry | 2 tbs soya oil |
| 1 egg yolk | 2 shallots, chopped |
| | 150 ml ( ¼ pint ) red wine |
| FOR THE SOUFFLÉ | 100 g ( 3½ oz ) carrot purée |
| 4 duck under-fillets, minced | 100 g ( 3½ oz ) tomato pulp, chopped |
| 4 duck legs, meat only, minced | 1 tbs snipped chives |
| 4 egg yolks | 25 g ( 1 oz ) butter or 1 tbs cream |
| 250 ml ( 8 fl oz ) double cream | salt and pepper to taste |

To prepare the soufflé mixture, blend the minced duck meat with the egg yolks in a bowl. Gradually add the cream. Beat well and chill for 15 minutes. In a separate bowl, beat the egg whites until stiff and blend gently with the duck mixture. Season to taste.

Heat the oven to Gas Mark 6/200°C/400°F. Grease a baking tray with soya oil and place the chilled breasts on it. Arrange 2 rhubarb sticks on each breast and brush with melted syrup. Heap the soufflé mixture on each one. Shape it smoothly into a dome with a palette knife.

Roll 4 ovals of puff pastry, and cut in a lattice pattern to cover the breasts, or use strips and criss-cross them on each breast. Brush with the egg yolk. Bake for 25 minutes, until golden-brown.

To make the sauce, heat the oil and shallow-fry the shallots for 1 minute. Add the red wine and boil for 10 minutes. At this stage blend in the carrot purée and season to taste. Add the chopped tomato and the snipped chives. Thin down the sauce with a little cream or whisk in a little butter to emulsify it.

Arrange a duck pastry on each of 4 plates and pour on a cordon of sauce.     *Serves 4*     **DAVID EVANS**

Top: *Baked Seafood Parfait Kenmare with Avocado Sauce* (*page 58*), below: *Chicken Ciara Maria Supreme* (*page 85*)

Top left: *Lobster in Fish Jelly* (*page 55*), top right: *Sole Fillets in Saffron Sauce* (*page 42*), below left: *Salmon Roll Stuffed with Pomfret and Chive Mousse* (*page 48*), below right: *Steamed Food Osaka* (*page 82*)

Top: *Chinese Chicken with Wild Rice and Stuffed Pancakes (page 89)*, below: *Crispy Chicken and Seafood Fritters Cantonese-style (page 88)*

Top: *Golden Pigeons with Melon (page 111)*, below: *Quail Breasts and Truffle Salad (page 110)*

# Oriental Pigeon Breasts with Rice and Pawpaw

| | |
|---|---|
| 16 pigeon breasts | 25 g ( 1 oz ) tomato pulp, chopped |
| a little soya oil | 15 g ( ½ oz ) ginger, chopped |
| 50 g ( 2 oz ) sugar | 1 red chilli, de-seeded and chopped |
| 3 tbs wine vinegar | 40 g ( 1 ½ oz ) shallots, chopped |
| 1 bay leaf | 1 tbs lemon grass |
| salt and pepper to taste | ( 3 ½ fl oz ) saké ( rice wine ) or sherry |
| 1 ripe pawpaw, peeled and cut into wedges | |
| 1 bunch watercress, to decorate | FOR THE SAUCE |
| | 3 tbs soya oil |
| FOR THE | 2 shallots, chopped |
| MARINADE | 150 g ( 5 oz ) tomatoes, peeled, de-seeded, and cubed |
| 2 cloves garlic, chopped | salt and pepper to taste |

Skin the pigeon breasts and remove the wing bones. In a bowl, place the marinade ingredients. Soak the breasts in this mixture overnight, turning them from time to time. Remove the pigeon breasts when ready to cook. Wipe them dry and brush with soya oil. Season to taste, and grill or shallow-fry for about 8 minutes, until done.

To make the sauce, heat the soya oil and shallow-fry the shallots and tomatoes. Add the remaining marinade mixture and cook for 4 minutes. Check the seasoning. The mixture should not be too mushy.

Mix together the sugar, wine vinegar, and seasoning, and marinate the pawpaw for 20 minutes in this mixture.

Place 4 small breasts of pigeon on each plate and among them a spoonful of rice. In the centre, arrange a spoon of tomato sauce and top it with diced pawpaw, which may also be served as a side dish. Decorate with watercress leaves. *Serves 4*

**ANTON WUERSCH**

# Duck Tour d' Argent, Normandy-Style

| |
|---|
| 1 × 2.75 kg (6 lb) oven-ready Barbary (green-neck) duck, preferably free-range |
| 3 tbs soya oil |
| 2 shallots, chopped |
| 3 tbs port wine |
| 3 tbs duck gravy |
| juice of ¼ lemon |
| juice of ¼ orange |
| 3 tbs double cream |
| 25 g (1 oz) foie gras or duck liver, minced |
| 3 tbs brandy |
| salt, pepper, and pinch of cayenne pepper |
| orange segments or black cherries, stoned, to decorate |

Heat the oven to Gas Mark 7/220°C/425°F. Pour oil over the duck. Season with salt and pepper inside and out, and roast in the oven for 18–20 minutes. Remove both the breasts and the legs. Continue cooking the legs only for 10 minutes. Place the breasts on a flat dish and keep hot while making the Rouennaise sauce.

In a small saucepan, boil the chopped shallots with the port wine and duck gravy for 5 minutes. Add the lemon and orange juice and seasoning. Boil for 5 minutes. Blend in the cream and minced liver. Simmer without boiling. Remove the roasted legs from the oven, which should be well cooked by now, and slice the meat off the bone.

On 4 plates, pour a pool of the liver sauce. Heat the brandy, set it alight and pour it over the cooked duck meat at the last moment. Then place a portion of breast and leg meat on each plate over the sauce. Decorate with segments of orange or black cherries.    *Serves 4*                                    **MANUEL MARTINEZ**

# Poached Guinea Fowl

| | |
|---|---|
| 4 × 200 g (7 oz) guinea fowl | 20 g (¾ oz) fresh truffle, cut into strips |
| 3 onions | 6 white button mushrooms, cut into strips |
| 3 medium carrots | salt and pepper to taste |
| 4 sticks celery | fresh chervil, to decorate |
| fresh parsley | |
| fresh tarragon | FOR THE NOODLES |
| 200 g (7 oz) unsalted butter or margarine, softened | 250 g (8 oz) flour |
| 200 g (7 oz) flour | 2 eggs |
| 6 litres (11 pints) white stock | 3 egg yolks |
| 4 artichokes | 1 tsp oil |
| juice of 2 lemons | salt to taste |
| 300 ml (1 pint) cream | |

Remove the feathers and feet from the birds, and ensure that the cavities are free from blood and intestines. Finely dice 2 onions, 2 carrots, and 3 sticks celery. Season inside and outside the birds, and fill with the diced vegetables and some of the parsley and tarragon, then truss the birds. Mix the softened butter with the flour to form a paste. Take 4 napkins, each 20 cm (8 inches) square and spread this paste evenly over the centre 15 cm (6 inches) of the napkins. Place a bird on each napkin. Then roll and tie the ends securely so that the birds are totally enclosed.

Place the remaining carrot, onion, celery, parsley, and tarragon into the stock and bring to the boil. Add the birds, cover, and cook for approximately 20 minutes. Remove the birds from the napkins and scrape the flour-and-butter paste off the napkins. Whisk this paste into the stock to thicken it into a sauce. Place the guinea fowl into a serving dish and cover to keep warm. Cook the whole artichokes in boiling salted water with the lemon juice for 20–30 minutes, until the bottoms are soft. Refresh in iced water and drain. Remove all the leaves and the choke from the base, and discard them, and cut the base into fine strips. To make the noodles, place the flour on a table and make a well in the centre. Add the remaining ingredients and mix well. When mixed, knead for 3–4 minutes. Leave the dough to rest for 10 minutes. Roll out and cut into strips 3 mm (⅛ inch) thick, either by hand or on a pasta machine, and then leave for 10 minutes before cooking in simmering salted water. The noodles take very little time to cook, so do not leave unattended.

Dip the noodles into hot salted water for 30 seconds if fresh, 2–3 minutes if dry, then drain them. Place in a pan over a medium heat and add the artichoke, half the cream, strips of truffle and mushroom, and seasoning to taste. Mix together gently so as not to break the noodles. Correct the seasoning of the sauce and add the remaining cream. Pass the sauce over the guinea fowl and garnish with chervil. Serve the noodles in a dish apart, also garnished with chervil.   *Serves 4*   **KEVIN CAPE**

# Quail Breasts and Truffle Salad

*Pictured on page 106.*

| | |
|---|---|
| 6 quails | **FOR THE VINAIGRETTE** |
| 50 g (2 oz) chanterelle mushrooms | 3 tbs soya oil |
| | 1 tbs saké vinegar |
| **FOR THE SAUCE** | 1 tbs chopped mixed fresh herbs |
| 5 tbs soya oil | (including parsley and tarragon) |
| 50 g (2 oz) wild mushrooms, stems only | 2 spring onions, chopped |
| 15 g (½ oz) truffle peel | salt and pepper to taste |
| 1 shallot, chopped | |
| 3 leaves fresh tarragon | **TO GARNISH** |
| 3 tbs truffle juice | 1 curly lettuce, separated and cleaned |
| 100 ml (3½ fl oz) water | 24 asparagus tips, blanched for 20 seconds |
| 3 tbs saké (rice wine) | 1 whole canned truffle, sliced into 12 pieces |
| 1 tsp cornflour | 4 oak leaves |
| 1 tbs soya sauce | 4 yellow courgettes, sliced and scalded 15 seconds only |
| salt and pepper | 2 tomatoes, skinned, de-seeded, and diced |

Cut and remove all the quail breasts. Season and place on a plate, ready to be used at the last moment.

To make the sauce, heat 2 tbs of the oil in a pan and fry the legs and bones of the quails for 12 minutes, until cooked. Remove the legs. Scrape off the meat, to add, chopped, to the salad. Add the mushroom stems, truffle peel, shallot, tarragon leaves, and the truffle juice. Cook for 5 minutes, then add the water and wine. Boil and reduce in volume by a third. Strain the stock and thicken it slightly with the cornflour, mixed with a little water. Cook for 4 minutes. Season, add the soya sauce, and strain again.

In a wok, heat the remaining oil and fry the breasts of quail for 7 minutes, turning. Season. Remove the breasts, then sauté the chanterelles for 30 seconds only. Remove and drain.

Mix all the vinaigrette ingredients together in a bowl. Cut the lettuce leaves into small pieces, and cut the asparagus tips slantways.

On each of 4 plates, place 3 pools of truffle sauce. Put a slice of truffle over the pool and place 1 breast on each truffle. Among the truffles arrange, in heaps, some curly lettuce and oak leaves with cooked chanterelle mushrooms cut into smaller pieces, and the chopped leg meat. Sprinkle with a little dressing. In the centre, arrange an island of sliced courgettes, overlapping in a circle. Place a spoonful of diced tomato and, over it, in a floral pattern, arrange 6 asparagus tips     *Serves 4*     **PATRICK LIN**

# Golden Pigeons with Melon

*Pictured on page 106.*

| | |
|---|---|
| 2 × 500 g ( 1 lb ) young pigeons, trussed and seasoned inside and out | 1 medium, ribbed cantaloup melon, peeled |
| 500 ml ( 18 fl oz ) soya oil, for deep-frying plus 2 tbs | FOR THE MARINADE AND SAUCE |
| 4 pieces ginger root, chopped | 250 ml ( 8 fl oz ) light soya sauce |
| 4 shallots, chopped | 250 ml ( 8 fl oz ) dark soya sauce |
| 250 ml ( 8 fl oz ) strong game stock | 250 ml ( 8 fl oz ) melon juice or pulp and liquid in purée |
| 1 tsp cornflour | salt and pepper to taste |
| | 2 bunches flowering chives, to decorate |

Mix together the marinade ingredients. Coat the pigeons in the mixture, turn often, and marinate for 3 hours. Drain the birds and pat dry. Heat the oil for deep-frying and fry the pigeons, covered, for 8–10 minutes until golden.

In a wok, heat 2 tbs oil and stir-fry the ginger and shallots for 30 seconds. Add 250 ml (8 fl oz) of the marinade liquid and the game stock. Boil for 15 minutes, then thicken with the cornflour mixed with cold water in a bowl. Cook for 4 minutes to obtain consistency and clarity. Season the sauce and strain it. Slice the melon, then cut it into triangular pieces. Immerse the pieces for 20 seconds in the hot sauce and remove.

Halve the pigeons, and remove cartilage of breast bones. Pour the sauce onto a dish. Arrange the 4 pieces of pigeon with 6 triangular pieces of melon on each side. Decorate with two bunches of flowering chives.    *Serves 4*                                                **YIP KWAI-SING**

# PARTRIDGE STUFFED WITH
# FOIE GRAS AND TRUFFLES

| | |
|---|---|
| 4 plump partridges, trussed | 1 bouquet garni |
| 75 g (3 oz) pure foie gras | 3 tbs game stock |
| 1 small truffle, diced | salt and black pepper to taste |
| 1 egg, beaten | |
| 2 tbs breadcrumbs | TO GARNISH |
| 250 ml (8 fl oz) red or white port wine | 16 button onions, fried |
| 4 rashers back bacon, rinded and minced | 16 new potatoes, boiled |
| 4 tbs soya oil | 4 slices of toast, buttered |
| 1 tbs butter | 1 bunch watercress |

Heat the oven to Gas Mark 7/220°C/425°F. Bone each partridge, starting from the wishbone and peeling the skin and flesh as the bone is scraped free. When finished, the partridges should be like deflated balloons.

In a bowl, combine the foie gras, diced truffle, egg, and breadcrumbs. Add 1 tbs of the port wine and the minced bacon. Fill the partridges with this mixture to reconstitute them to their original shapes. Brush over with 2 tbs of the soya oil. Season to taste. Place in a metal casserole with the remaining soya oil, butter, and bouquet garni. Roast in the oven for 20 minutes, basting the birds with the port wine and game stock. Remove the birds and keep warm. Transfer the liquid to a small pan and boil down to reduce it by half. Strain to remove fat.

Serve each partridge on hot buttered toast, with 2 potatoes and 4 baby onions each. Decorate with a bunch of watercress. Serve the gravy separately. *Serves 4* **ANTONIO ABEL GUERRERO**

# PIGEON BREASTS ON A BED OF BEAN SPROUTS AND ENDIVE IN TWO SAUCES

| | |
|---|---|
| 4 × 500 g (1 lb) tender pigeons | salt and pepper to taste |
| 3 tbs soya oil | |
| | **FOR THE** |
| **FOR THE STOCK** | **GINGER SAUCE** |
| 1 clove garlic, chopped | 2 tbs soya oil |
| 1 bouquet garni | 15 g (½ oz) ginger, peeled and chopped |
| 1 small onion, sliced | 1 clove garlic |
| 1 carrot, sliced | 100 ml (3½ fl oz) single cream |
| 500 ml (18 fl oz) water | salt and pepper to taste |
| 100 ml (3½ fl oz) white wine | |
| | **TO GARNISH** |
| **FOR THE** | 2 tbs mixed soya oil and butter |
| **RED-PEPPER SAUCE** | 175 g (6 oz) Belgian endives, cut into slices lengthways |
| 1 red pepper, de-seeded and diced | 175 g (6 oz) bean sprouts, washed and drained |
| 100 ml (3½ fl oz) single cream | 1 yellow pepper, de-seeded and cut into strips 1 cm (½ inch) long |

*B*one the pigeons and remove the skins from the breasts and bones. Season and brush with 1 tbs of the oil. Put to one side. To prepare the stock, heat the remaining oil and fry the pigeon bones and skins with the garlic, bouquet garni, onion, and carrot for 5 minutes. Add the water and wine. Boil gently for 45 minutes. Strain. Heat the oven to Gas Mark 7/220°C/425°F, and roast the breasts for 10 minutes, medium rare.

To make the red-pepper sauce, liquidise the red pepper and boil with 100 ml (3½ fl oz) of the pigeon stock. Reduce by half, add the cream, and reduce by half again. Season to taste.

To make the ginger sauce, heat the oil and sauté the ginger and garlic. Add 100 ml (3½ fl oz) of the pigeon stock and reduce by half. Stir in the cream and boil for 3 minutes. Strain. Season to taste. Heat the butter and the soya oil, and sauté the endives for 6 minutes. Add the bean sprouts and yellow pepper. Cook for 2 minutes until soft. Season and put to one side.

On each of 4 plates, place a pigeon breast. Pour a little of each sauce side by side for contrast. Arrange the vegetables artistically.    *Serves 4*    **KURT BINGGELI**

# GRILLED DUCK ON PEPPERY COULIS

| | |
|---|---|
| 2 large duck breasts | 100 ml ( 3½ fl oz ) red vinegar |
| 4 tbs soya oil | 10 pickled pink peppercorns |
| 25 g ( 1 oz ) butter | 200 ml ( 7 fl oz ) fresh pineapple juice |
| salt and pepper | a little sugar |
| | 250 g ( 8 oz ) fresh pineapple chunks |
| FOR THE LIME SAUCE | |
| 150 ml ( ¼ pint ) white wine vinegar | TO GARNISH |
| 100 g ( 3½ oz ) brown sugar | thin peel of 1 lime |
| 150 ml ( ¼ pint ) lime juice | thin peel of ½ orange |
| 1 litre ( 1¾ pints ) duck or chicken stock | 125 g ( 4 oz ) sugar |
| salt and pepper to taste | 5 tbs water |
| | 4 cherry tomatoes, peeled |
| FOR THE PINEAPPLE SAUCE | 8 potato croquettes, deep-fried |
| 100 ml ( 3½ fl oz ) white vinegar | 4 sprigs broccoli, boiled |

Brush the duck breasts with the oil and butter. Season, and grill slowly for 12 minutes, basting from time to time. When cooked, keep warm.

To make the lime sauce, boil the vinegar and brown sugar until the mixture caramelises. Add the lime juice and boil for 3 minutes. Then stir in the stock and simmer for 15 minutes. Season to taste.

To make the pineapple sauce, boil the white and red vinegars with the peppercorns, pineapple juice, and sugar for 15 minutes, to a syrupy consistency. Add the pineapple chunks and cook for 10 minutes more. Blanch the peel for 6 minutes and drain. Reboil with the sugar and 5 tbs water until the rinds are dried and candied. Boil the broccoli for 5 minutes. Scald the cherry tomatoes and skin them. Cook potato croquettes in deep-frying oil.

On each of 2 plates, pour a little of the lime sauce. Arrange some of the pineapple syrup, 1 cherry tomato, 2 potato croquettes, and 1 broccoli sprig. Slice the breasts into 8 small pieces. Place 4 on each plate, overlapping each other, pour over the pineapple-chunk syrup and sprinkle with the candied peel.

*Serves 2*

**JEAN-CLAUDE WEIBEL**

# Chicken Parcels with Broccoli Spears

| | |
|---|---|
| 300 ml ( ½ pint) soya oil | ½ tsp salt |
| 150 g ( 5 oz) lean chicken meat, diced | |
| 75 g ( 3 oz) black or field mushrooms, diced | FOR THE SAUCE |
| 125 g ( 4 oz) bamboo shoots, diced | 150 ml ( ¼ pint) chicken stock |
| 75 g ( 3 oz) water chestnuts, chopped | 1 tbs soya sauce |
| 1 tsp cornflour | 1 tsp cornflour |
| 2 egg whites | 3 tbs water |
| 8 spring onions, blanched | pinch cumin |
| salt and pepper to taste | pinch aniseed |
| | pinch sugar or 1 tsp honey |
| FOR THE PANCAKES | salt and pepper to taste |
| 6 egg whites | |
| 3 tbs water | TO GARNISH |
| 100 g ( 3½ oz) cornflour | 8 small broccoli spears, boiled 5 minutes |
| 100 g ( 3½ oz) self-raising flour | 50 g ( 2 oz) smoked lumpfish roe |

Heat 4 tbs of the oil in a wok and shallow-fry the chicken, mushrooms, bamboo shoots, and water chestnuts for 4 minutes. Sprinkle with the cornflour and seasoning, and toss for 1 minute more. Remove from the heat and cool. Blend in the 2 egg whites, and divide the mixture into 8 balls, well compressed by hand.

To prepare the pancakes, beat the 6 egg whites, flour, cornflour, and water to a smooth batter. Add the salt. Rest for 12 minutes. Heat a little oil in a 13 cm (5-inch) diameter pancake pan. Cook 8 thin pancakes as transparent as possible. Cool the pancakes and wrap each one round a chicken ball in a purse-like shape. Knot the loose ends with threads of spring onion. Heat the remaining soya oil and deep-fry the chicken purses until golden.

To make the sauce, boil the chicken stock until reduced in volume by half. Add the soya sauce and the cornflour, mixed with the water, to thicken. Season to taste.

Pour a little sauce on each of 4 plates. Arrange 2 broccoli spears and 2 chicken parcels around. Sprinkle some lumpfish roe over the chicken.     *Serves 4*     **LAI KAM LUN MAN WAH**

# Roast Barbary Duckling Breast in Italian Red Wine with a Garnish of Cabbage Rolls

| | |
|---|---|
| 4 × 250 g ( 8 oz ) Barbary duck breasts, skinned and boned | 3 egg yolks |
| 8 duckling hearts | 125 ml ( 4 fl oz ) water |
| 8 duck livers, well cleaned | salt to taste |
| 2 tbs soya oil | |
| salt and pepper to taste | FOR THE SAUCE |
| | 3 tbs soya oil |
| FOR THE | 50 g ( 2 oz ) mixed carrot, onion, celery, and leek |
| CABBAGE ROLLS | 1 tbs tomato purée |
| 3 tbs soya oil | 300 ml ( ½ pint ) Tignannello red wine |
| 50 g ( 2 oz ) streaky bacon, rinded and chopped | 100 ml ( 3½ fl oz ) water or stock |
| 50 g ( 2 oz ) onion, chopped | 3 black peppercorns, crushed |
| 250 g ( 8 oz ) green cabbage, shredded | 1 sprig thyme |
| 300 g ( 10 oz ) durum flour | salt to taste |

To make the cabbage noodle rolls, heat 2 tbs of the oil in a pan and stir-fry the bacon and onion for 2 minutes. Add the shredded cabbage and cook, covered, for 6 minutes, until tender. Put aside to cool. In a bowl, blend the flour, egg yolks, water, remaining oil, and a little salt. Knead to a dough. Divide the dough into 3 balls and roll them out as thinly as possible. Spread the cabbage filling on top of each layer of dough and roll up. Wrap the rolls in a wet cloth and tie both ends tightly. Boil in salted water for 8 minutes.

To make the sauce, heat the oil and sauté the bones and skins of the ducks. Add the vegetable mixture, and cook for 3 minutes more. Blend in the tomato purée, wine, and water or stock. Add the peppercorns. Boil for 20 minutes, to reduce by half its original volume. Strain and season to taste.

Heat the oven to Gas Mark 7/220°C/425°F. Brush the duck breasts with oil and season. Roast in the oven for 8 minutes. Heat a little oil in a pan and fry the livers and hearts.

Slice the duck breasts and noodle parcels. Arrange on 4 plates with a little sauce and the hearts and livers by the side. *Serves 4*                                      JEAN MICHEL HARDOUIN-ATLAN

# *M*EAT *D*ISHES

## PORK

Pigs were kept for food in the Middle Eastern countries about 9,000 years ago. The Chinese were keeping domesticated pigs 4,000 years later. The taste for pork spread through the Greek and Roman cultures to all the countries of the West, where skilled butchers perfected the art of curing meat with saltpetre (potassium nitrate), and the industry of charcuterie was born. Pigs were a staple of the peasant diet in Europe, including Britain and Ireland, and have remained popular ever since. Pork is the cheapest meat available today.

All cuts of pork can be roasted, and many cuts are suitable for grilling and frying. The flavour of cured and smoked gammon and bacon is an essential part of delicious country soups, including the many varieties of Italian minestrone.

## MUTTON AND LAMB

The inhabitants of all Arab and Middle Eastern countries have made lamb their national dish. The British are the largest eaters of lamb within the EEC and produce 50 per cent of the EEC's sheep; there are 50 recorded pure breeds of sheep and 300 cross-bred types in Britain alone.

Sheep grazing near the sea produce meat with a special saline quality which gourmets prefer. The type of lamb most sought by butchers for sale to consumers is a lean-fleshed type weighing around 17–20 kg (40–50 lb). The meat of lambs over one year old is called mutton. Mutton comes from a large carcass and needs careful hanging to ensure flavour and tenderness.

Lamb, like all meat, is an important source of protein, iron, B group vitamins, phosphorus, and other essential nutrients. Lamb is best roasted or grilled. Mutton can also be roasted but it provides cooks with a basic item for stews. Boiled mutton with caper sauce has been a favourite luncheon dish for a long time. Stock for lamb dishes can be made from scrag-end and neck cuts. The bones and meat are browned in the oven for brown gravies and pre-blanched and boiled for clear velouté sauces, as used in veal dishes. Like bacon, mutton can be pickled with saltpetre.

## THE FATTED CALF

A typical calf which is intended for veal, is fattened on a diet of reconstituted milk powder after weaning, which has controlled additives of fat, minerals, and vitamins. It is ready for slaughter at 13–20 weeks.

Grazing calves cannot be rated as first-class veal as the meat tends to be pinkish. Normally veal from grazing calves is used for pies and stews. The best quality veal comes from the Netherlands, the country which has the most improved feeding methods. For escalopes and fine joints, Dutch veal is what chefs recommend.

The cushion and undercushion cuts from legs are best for escalopes and for the fine joints known as *noix* and *sous-noix*. For the finer, sautéed dishes, the loin and fillets are used. Shoulder, belly, and other cuts are used for stews, blanquettes, and pies. The shins and knuckles of veal are best for producing tasty stocks from which the finest meat gravy is made. Veal is easy to digest and the offal is also used as food, particularly the liver and sweetbreads. Veal kidneys are also highly regarded.

## BEEF

In medieval Britain, beef was salted down towards the end of the year to preserve it for winter consumption. It was customary to 'corn' meat, that is, either to coat it with 'corns' (kernels of dry salt) or to soak it for several days in a flavoured brine containing saltpetre. Salting, drying, and smoking were then the only ways of preserving meat so that it could be kept throughout the winter.

As for the roast beef of old England, the best cuts are wing rib, fore rib, and sirloin. Remember the recipe for Yorkshire pudding to serve with roast beef: the formula is 1-2-5: one egg, two ounces of flour, five fluid ounces of milk; which makes enough for two portions. Be sure to use bread flour for a well-risen pudding.

The most luxurious joint is the whole fillet, which is enough to serve ten portions. When cooked in pastry it is called *fillet de boeuf Wellington* and has a coating of minced mushrooms (*duxelle*) and a rich Madeira or truffle sauce. For a quick dainty snack, sauté beef steaks. The fillet, sirloin, and lean part of rib cuts can be used in various forms, from kebabs to strips of Stroganoff or Tetraky, from tournedos to *filet mignon*.

## VENISON DISHES

Roast venison is lean and rather low in calories: 198 per 100 g (3½ oz). It needs basting with fat to improve flavour. The meat should be dark and close grained. It is lighter in younger animals.

Venison is a generic term, covering all animals of the families and sub-families of deer and antelopes. The Canadians have caribou; the Africans, antelopes; the Scandinavians, reindeer; and the French and Spaniards, chamois in the mountains. There is extensive farming of deer in Scotland, which exports much venison to the Continent. The meat will become more popular as it becomes cheaper because of increased production.

All recipes suitable for beef and mutton may be adapted for venison, but the cooking times have to be adjusted. The meat used to be kept by marination in wine and vinegar when refrigeration was non-existent. Mild marinades do not tenderise venison, but they do enhance its flavour. The meat is like a sponge, absorbing the liquid. A little oil should be poured over the marinade to keep air out.

# Basic Bacon Stock

| |
|---|
| 1 × 1 kg (2 lb) unsmoked bacon knuckle |
| 1.5 litres (2½ pints) water |
| 1 onion, studded with 3 cloves |
| 1 leek |
| 1 carrot |
| 1 parsnip |
| 1 stick of celery |
| 1 bouquet garni |
| 6 peppercorns, crushed |

De-salt the bacon knuckle in running water for 2 hours, or overnight, if very salty. Place it in a pan of water. Gently bring it to the boil and simmer for 1 hour. Remove the scum as it rises. Add the peeled, uncut vegetables, the bouquet garni, and the peppercorns. Continue to simmer for another hour. Strain the broth, which is now tasty enough to be used for stock or cabbage soups. The knuckle can be boned and the rind removed. The meat can then be used as a garnish for soups or a filling for ravioli.         JEAN CONIL

# Thai Pork and Vermicelli Royal Platter

| | |
|---|---|
| 500 g (1 lb) rice vermicelli | 75 g (3 oz) sugar |
| 300 ml (½ pint) soya oil | 5 tbs vinegar |
| 450 g (15 oz) neck or shoulder of pork, all fat removed | 100 ml (3½ fl oz) bacon stock |
| 225 g (7½ oz) shrimps, peeled | 175 g (6 oz) bean sprouts |
| 75 g (3 oz) tofu (soya curd) cubes | 20 chive strands, snipped |
| 100 g (3½ oz) salted soya beans, soaked overnight and half-boiled | a dash of lime juice |
| 5 eggs | 4 spring onions, chopped |
| 15 g (½ oz) shallots, chopped | 15 g (½ oz) citrus peel, crystallised |
| 3 cloves garlic, chopped | a little salt and pepper |
| 1 red chilli, de-seeded and sliced | |

Soak the rice vermicelli in cold water to soften it; then drain it and pat it dry over a colander. After heating 250 ml (8 fl oz) of oil in a deep-fryer, deep-fry the vermicelli for 45 seconds until crisp. Drain it well on an absorbent towel. Cut the pork, shrimps, and tofu into strips. Roughly cut the soya beans.

Beat the eggs and fry them as a flat omelette. Cut the omelette into strips. Heat the remaining soya oil in a sauté pan and stir-fry the shallot, garlic and chilli until light brown. Add the pork, shrimps, and tofu. Stir-fry and blend together the sugar, vinegar and bacon stock and cook until syrupy. Combine all the cooked ingredients except the vermicelli.

On the side of 8 plates, arrange the fried vermicelli in heaps. Arrange the pork mixture in the centre. Arrange the omelette mixture on top. Put the bean sprouts on the side of the plates and season to taste. Sprinkle with chives and lime juice, and sprinkle over the spring onions and citrus peel.

*Serves 8*

KHUNYING PRASANSOOK TUNTIVEJAKUL

# Smoked Pork Sausages with Mustard Sauce

| | MUSTARD SAUCE |
|---|---|
| 225 g (7½ oz) potatoes, sliced | |
| 150 g (5 oz) carrots | 100 ml (3½ fl oz) single cream |
| 50 g (2 oz) butter | 4 tsp made mustard |
| 25 g (1 oz) soya margarine | 25 g (1 oz) soya margarine, melted |
| 225 g (7½ oz) green cabbage leaves | 150 ml (½ pint) bacon stock |
| 450 g (15 oz) smoked pork sausages (frankfurter type) | a little salt and pepper |
| 1 tsp mustard seeds, toasted | |
| 1 tbs fresh coriander or chervil, chopped | |
| a little salt and black pepper | |

Cook and purée the potatoes and carrots. Season, and blend them with the margarine and half the butter until smooth. Keep hot. Boil the cabbage leaves in salted water for 7 minutes. Drain and roll each leaf into a ball. Melt the rest of the butter. Brush the leaves with melted butter and set aside. Wrap the sausages in muslin and heat them in hot water for 15 minutes.

For the mustard sauce, boil the cream and whisk in the made mustard, the melted soya margarine and the bacon stock. Season to taste. Strain and keep warm. Shape the puréed vegetables into quenelles with two spoons.

On 2 plates, pour a little mustard sauce to one side. Place 2 quenelles of vegetable purée and a hot cabbage ball brushed with butter on each plate. Slice the sausages slantwise and place them in alternate rows over the sauce. Sprinkle them with toasted mustard seeds and decorate with leaves of coriander or chervil.

*Serves 2*                                                                                    **SIMON TRAYNOR**

# Spring Rolls

| | |
|---|---|
| 450 g ( 15 oz ) pork, minced | 1 tbs soya sauce |
| 450 g ( 15 oz ) prawns, peeled and chopped | 1 tsp sugar or honey |
| 1 red pepper, de-seeded and chopped | salt and pepper to taste |
| 8 shallots, chopped | |
| 100 g ( 3½ oz ) mushrooms, chopped | FOR THE DOUGH |
| 1 × 3 cm ( 1-inch ) piece of ginger, peeled and chopped | ½ cup water |
| 250 g ( 8 oz ) water chestnuts, cooked and chopped | 2 tbs cornflour |
| 100 g ( 3½ oz ) green cabbage, | 1 × 455 g ( 1 lb ) packet spring roll wrappers |
| thinly shredded or chopped | or noodle paste |
| 2 tbs chopped parsley or coriander | 500 ml ( 18 fl oz ) soya oil for deep-frying |
| 3 tbs saké ( rice wine ) | |

For the filling put all the prepared ingredients into a bowl. Add the saké, soya sauce, sugar, salt, and pepper. Mix well.

For the dough, prepare a paste with the water and cornflour in a small bowl. Divide the filling mixture into about 25 × 50 g ( 2 oz ) balls. Wrap each one with a spring roll wrapper or thin noodle paste cut into oblongs 8 cm ( 3 inches ) long. The paste should be no more than 4 mm ( ⅙ inch ) thick. After filling, roll all the squares into cylindrical shapes. Brush the edges with cornflour paste to seal the ends. Heat the oil to 180°C/350°F and deep-fry for 4 minutes. Serve with the sauce of your choice (see page 65).     *Makes 25 spring rolls*  **JEAN CONIL**

# Steamed Pork Buns

| FOR THE SOYA DOUGH | 1 garlic clove, chopped |
|---|---|
| 3 cups plain bread flour and 1 tbs baking powder, or | 2 tbs soya oil |
| 450 g ( 15 oz ) self-raising flour | ½ cup water |
| 1 tsp salt | 1 tbs parsley, chopped |
| 60 g ( 2½ oz ) soya margarine | 1 tbs soya sauce |
| 125 ml ( 4 fl oz ) water, tepid | 1 tbs pineapple or lime juice |
| 1 tsp plain vinegar | 3 tsp cornflour |
| a little soya oil | 4 shallots, or spring onions, chopped |
| | 250 g ( 8 oz ) lean pork, minced |
| FOR THE PORK FILLING | 1 egg, beaten |
| 3 cm ( 1-inch ) piece of ginger, peeled and chopped | |

For the filling, place all the ingredients in a bowl and blend them well. Leave for 20 minutes.

To make the soya dough, sift the plain flour and baking powder (or self-raising flour) and salt in a bowl. Rub in the soya margarine with fingers to form a crumble. Blend with water, vinegar and oil to form a dough. Knead a little. Cover the dough with plastic food wrap and allow it to stand for 20 minutes. Knead again until it is smooth.

Cut the dough into 12 balls. Roll each ball into a circle of 10 cm (4-inch) diameter. Put 1 tbs of filling in the centre of each round. Press the edges of the dough together. Take the two ends of each, bring them up, fold them over to look like a purse and twist them firmly to seal the bun. Cut 12 pieces of greaseproof paper into squares. Brush one side with soya oil. On each piece of oiled paper, place a bun upside down, so that the smooth side is uppermost.

Stack the buns in single layers in wooden sieves or steaming racks. Choose a saucepan slightly smaller than the diameter of the sieves or racks and fill it ⅔ full with hot water. Place the buns in the sieves or racks inside. Alternatively, use an ordinary steamer with 3 racks. Put the lid on top and steam for 25 minutes. To serve, use sauces of your choice and serve with green cabbage or broad beans.     *Makes 12 buns; serves 4*     **JEAN CONIL**

Note: For prawn dumplings, the filling and dough are the same except that you use 125 g (4 oz) minced raw fish and 125 g (4 oz) chopped, peeled prawns instead of pork.

# Pork Medallions Danablu

| | |
|---|---|
| 100 ml (3½ fl oz) soya oil | 100 ml (3½ fl oz) bacon or pork stock |
| 25 g (1 oz) butter | 1 tbs potato flour |
| 250 g (8 oz) pork fillet, cut into 12 thick slices | 5 tbs water |
| 25 g (1 oz) shallots, chopped | 100 ml (3½ fl oz) double cream |
| 3 tomatoes, skinned, de-seeded, and chopped | 50 g (2 oz) Danish blue cheese, crumbled |
| 4 pieces of fresh sage | juice of ½ lemon, and its zest |
| a little salt and pepper | a little salt and black pepper |
| | 250 g (8 oz) green cabbage, with ribs removed |
| FOR THE SAUCE | |
| 3 tbs dry white wine | |

Heat the oil and butter in a sauté pan and quickly fry the pork medallions for 2 minutes on each side. Remove and place in an earthenware dish. In the same pan, stir-fry the shallots for 1 minute until tender. Add the chopped tomatoes. Cook for 5 minutes until thick. Add the chopped sage leaves. Season to taste. Cover the pork with this tomato mixture.

To make the sauce, boil the wine and stock for 15 minutes until the volume is reduced by half. In a bowl, blend the potato flour with the water, and thicken the sauce with this mixture. Boil for 4 minutes. Season to taste. Whisk to make the mixture smooth. Strain. Blend in the cream and the cheese. Simmer but do not boil. After 5 minutes, add the juice and zest. Check the seasoning and adjust if necessary. Strain again. Boil the cabbage in salted water for 8 minutes. Drain well.

Place 2 cabbage leaves on each plate with 3 medallions of pork. Coat with cheese sauce. Serve a mixture of boiled root vegetables separately.    *Serves 4*                                    JENS P. KOLBECK

# Lamb Loin with Globe Artichokes and Tomato Coulis

| | |
|---|---|
| 500 g (1 lb) lamb loin, boneless | 250 g (8 oz) tomatoes, skinned, de-seeded, and chopped |
| 3½ tbs soya and olive oil (mixed) | 1 tbs mixed fresh herbs (basil, thyme, parsley), chopped |
| 1 carrot, sliced | salt and pepper |
| 1 large onion, sliced | |
| salt and pepper | FOR THE GARNISH |
| | 6 tbs oil |
| FOR THE SAUCE | 250 g (8 oz) potatoes, peeled and sliced |
| 1 sprig of rosemary | 4 baby globe artichokes (all edible leaves) or |
| 300 ml (½ pint) lamb stock | use canned artichokes |
| 150 ml (¼ pint) water | 4 tbs butter |
| 3 tbs red port wine | 150 g (5 oz) white of leeks, cut into thin strips |
| 2 tbs soya oil | 4 sprigs rosemary |
| 1 shallot, chopped | |

Season the loin with salt and pepper. Heat the oils in a pan and shallow-fry the loin for 6 minutes all round to seal the juice in. Transfer the meat to a small roasting tray, resting it on a trivet of lamb bones and sliced carrot and onion. This will help to flavour the gravy. Roast for 12 minutes. Remove the meat and set aside.

Place the roasting tray on the stove. Discard the surplus fat, but keep the bones and vegetables. Add a sprig of rosemary, the lamb stock, the water, and the port. Boil for 20 minutes. Season and strain. Add the juice which has exuded from the meat during the period of rest.

Heat the oil and sauté the shallot for 1 minute. Add the tomatoes and cook until thick for about 10 minutes. Season to taste and add the mixed herbs. Blend in the gravy, boil for 8 minutes, and strain.

To make the garnish, heat 4 tbs of the oil and sauté the potatoes until cooked. Boil the baby artichokes for 12 minutes. Drain and cut each artichoke into 4 pieces. Sauté in the remaining oil and the butter. Cook strips of leeks in the oil and butter for 30 seconds. Drain well.

Pour some sauce onto 4 plates. Over the sauce on each plate, arrange 6 thin slices of meat in a 3-piece pattern, overlapping each other. Fill 1 corner of the triangle with 3 slices of fried potatoes, and fill each of the other 2 corners with 2 pieces of artichoke. Sprinkle the centre with fried leek strips, and place a small sprig of rosemary over the meat. *Serves 4* **SERGIO MEI**

# Lamb Fillet stuffed with Chicken, with Potato Pancakes

| | |
|---|---|
| 350 g (12 oz) lamb loin, boneless | **FOR THE** |
| 12 dried morels, soaked overnight in water | **CHIVE SAUCE** |
| 4 tbs soya oil | 2 tbs soya oil |
| 12 large spinach leaves, blanched 10 seconds, | 1 shallot, chopped |
| refreshed and pat dried | 1 tsp flour |
| | 3 tbs chicken stock |
| **FOR THE STUFFING** | 100 ml (3½ fl oz) single cream |
| 250 g (8 oz) lean chicken, minced | 5 strands chives, chopped |
| 100 ml (3½ fl oz) single cream | |
| 1 egg white | **FOR THE** |
| 15 g (½ oz) truffle, diced | **POTATO PANCAKES** |
| salt and pepper | 100 g (4 oz) potato, peeled and mashed to a pulp |
| | 10 g (½ oz) flour |
| **FOR THE PORT WINE SAUCE** | 1 egg, beaten |
| 3 tbs red port wine | 3 tbs milk or cream |
| juice of ½ orange | a pinch of salt |
| 1 pinch of ginger, ground or fresh | 4 tbs soya oil |
| 2 shallots, chopped | |
| 150 ml (½ pint) lamb gravy | **TO GARNISH** |
| 1 tsp redcurrant jelly | 12 small sprigs of broccoli, cooked 3 minutes |
| 1 tsp cornflour mixed with 5 tbs water (optional) | 1 large tomato, skinned, de-seeded and pulped |
| salt and pepper | a few strands of chives, chopped |

First prepare the chicken stuffing for the lamb. In a bowl, blend the minced chicken with the cream, egg white, diced truffle, and seasoning. Chill the mixture in a freezer for 10 minutes to firm it. Trim the loin of lamb. Remove the fat and skin. Using a large skewer or larding needle, make a hole of 2 cm (¾-inch) diameter in the middle of the fillet. Enlarge it. Fill this cavity with chicken stuffing, using a piping bag. To make the port wine sauce, blend together the port wine, orange juice, ginger, and shallots, and boil for 12 minutes. Add the lamb gravy and redcurrant jelly. Season to taste. If required, thicken it with a little cornflour and water. Boil for 4 minutes to clear, and strain.

To make the chive sauce, heat the oil in a pan and shallow-fry the shallot for 2 minutes without browning. Stir in the flour to make the mixture into a roux. Cook for 1 minute and then blend in the chicken stock. Stir in the cream. Boil for 5 minutes more and strain. Reheat and add the chopped chives. To make the potato pancakes, combine the potato pulp and the other ingredients listed, except the oil, in a bowl, to form a smooth batter. Heat half the oil in a large frying pan and drop in 6 spoons of mixture, 1 per pancake. Cook on each side for 1 minute. Remove. With a pastry-cutter, round each one to 4 cm (1½ inches) in diameter. Repeat with 6 more spoons of mixture.

Heat the oven to Gas Mark 7/220°C/425°F. Heat the soya oil in a roasting tray and brown the lamb for 6 minutes. Then roast the lamb for 20 minutes (until slightly pink); longer if liked well done. Remove it from the pan. Slice the fillet into pieces 2 cm (¾ inch) thick. Wrap the pieces in spinach leaves. Sauté the soaked morels in soya oil for 2 minutes and remove. Blanch the broccoli florets.

Make sure all the items are hot before serving them. On each of 4 plates, pour a small pool of chive sauce. Spoon the port wine sauce onto 3 spots, touching the chive sauce. Over the port wine sauce, place 3 slices of lamb. Between each piece of lamb place a small round of potato and on top of it a sprig of broccoli. In the centre of the plate put 3 halves of the morels and, dead in the bull's eye of this circle, place a spoon of tomato pulp. Sprinkle a few chopped chives over the tomato.     *Serves 4*          LIN MAN-SANG

# $\mathcal{L}$AMB $\mathcal{S}$ARLADAISE

| | |
|---|---|
| 3 best ends of lamb, 1 kg (2 lb) each, | and sliced thinly (reserve trimmings or a few |
| skinned and boned completely | slices to add to stock for sauce) |
| (only the 'eye' of the meat, or loin part, is used) | 150 ml (8 fl oz) concentrated lamb stock |
| 1 tbs each chives, basil, and tarragon, chopped and mixed | 2 tbs meat glaze |
| 6 pig cauls or Chinese rice paper for wrapping | 1.5 kg (3½ lb) potatoes, cut with cylindrical |
| 8 tbs butter | cutter, then sliced 4 mm (⅙ inch) thick |
| 8 tbs soya oil | 1 bunch watercress |
| 1 large fresh truffle, brushed, washed, pat dried, | a little salt and pepper |

$\mathcal{S}$eason the loins of lamb. Sprinkle with the herbs and wrap in a pig's caul or in Chinese rice paper. Heat 2 tbs butter and 2 tbs oil in a sauté pan and shallow-fry the lamb loins for 8–10 minutes, turning them for even cooking. They are perhaps best slightly pink, but it is up to individual taste. After taking the meat out onto a dish, remove surplus fat from the pan. Slice the meat 5 mm (½ inch) thick.

To make the sauce, add the truffle trimmings or peels and the lamb stock to the meat glaze. Boil down in volume by half to a gravy. Season to taste and strain. Heat the remaining oil and butter and shallow-fry the potatoes and truffle in a frying pan until they are well coloured and cooked through. Season to taste. Drain off the fat. Add the juice to the gravy.

Form a rosette by alternating slices of lamb, potato, and truffle. Pour on a ribbon of gravy, and decorate with a small sprig of watercress in the centre.     *Serves 6*          CHRISTIAN CONSTANT

# PRIME BEST END JOINT OF LAMB IN SESAME SEED COATING, WITH STUFFED COURGETTE FLOWERS

| | |
|---|---|
| 600 g ( 1 ¼ lb ) best end of lamb cutlet joint, chined and | TO GARNISH |
| skinned, in one piece as a small joint | 2 courgettes |
| 2 tbs soya oil | 1 tbs soya oil |
| 1 garlic clove | 1 shallot, chopped |
| 1 sprig of rosemary | 2 tbs tomato, diced |
| 50 g ( 2 oz ) sesame seeds | 1 tbs chopped basil |
| 250 ml ( 8 fl oz ) lamb gravy | 8 courgette flowers |
| a little salt and pepper | 10 g truffles |

Heat the oven to Gas Mark 7/220°C/425°F. Season the lamb with pepper, and roast in soya oil with the garlic and rosemary for 30–40 minutes. Remove, season it with salt, and allow it to stand. Roll the meat in sesame seeds. Chop the courgettes and stew them in the oil with the shallot and tomato. Add the basil, and stuff the courgette flowers with the mixture. Bake them in the oven for about 5 minutes.

Place the sliced lamb on 4 plates. Arrange 2 stuffed courgette flowers on each portion. Pour the gravy on top and garnish with truffle slices.    *Serves 4*                                                    **WOLFGANG GROBAUER**

# DOUBLE NEW ZEALAND CHOPS WITH MIXED PEPPERS AND SABAYON SAUCE

| | |
|---|---|
| 6 tbs soya oil | FOR THE |
| 2 tbs butter | SAUCE |
| 3 medium peppers of different colours, split and cut into small cubes | 3 egg yolks |
| 2 shallots, chopped | 3 garlic cloves, peeled and chopped |
| 4 double New Zealand lamb chops, trimmed | 125 ml ( 4 fl oz ) white wine, warmed |
| 4 mint leaves | 125 ml ( 4 fl oz ) lamb stock, warmed |
| a little salt and pepper | a little salt and pepper |

*P*ut the egg yolks and garlic in a food blender and mix until frothy for 2 minutes. Transfer the mixture to a double boiler and add the wine and stock. Cook for 8 minutes until the mixture thickens like a custard, whisking all the time to prevent curdling. Keep the temperature below boiling point. Season the sauce.

Heat 2 tbs oil with the butter and sauté the peppers and shallots for 5 minutes until soft. Season to taste.

Season the lamb chops and brush them with soya oil. Grill or pan-fry them to taste – rare, medium, or well done.

On 4 plates, spoon the pepper mixture on one side and place the chops in the middle. Pour a little of the sauce on the other side. Decorate with mint leaves.      *Serves 4*      NEL McINNES

# Noisettes of New Zealand Loin with Pumpkin Mousseline

| | |
|---|---|
| 12 boneless lamb loins, trimmed and rounded | FOR THE MARSALA SAUCE |
| 4 tbs soya oil | 600 ml (1 pint) lamb stock, made from bones |
| a little salt and pepper | 50 ml (2 fl oz) dry Marsala wine |
| | 100 g (4 oz) morels, washed and drained |
| FOR THE | 100 g (4 oz) lamb sweetbreads, trimmed, blanched, and diced |
| PUMPKIN MOUSSELINE | juice of ½ lemon |
| 50 g (2 oz) soya margarine | 2 tbs butter |
| 250 g (8 oz) fresh pumpkin pulp, diced | a little salt and pepper |
| 150 g (5 oz) raw chicken breast, without skin or bone | |
| 50 g (2 oz) curd cheese | TO GARNISH |
| 2 egg whites | 4 fresh mint leaves |
| a little salt and pepper | 4 tomato roses, made from outer part of fruit |

*G*rease 4 × 150 ml (¼ pint) metal moulds with soya margarine. Heat the oven to Gas Mark 4/180°C/350°F. In a food processor purée the pumpkin pulp, chicken, cheese, and egg whites. Pass the mixture through a sieve. Season to taste. Fill the moulds with the mixture and place them in a deep tray half filled with water. Cover the moulds with foil. Bake for 18 minutes. Boil the lamb stock to reduce it by a third. Add the Marsala, morels, and sweetbreads. Simmer for 12 minutes. Season to taste. Finish the sauce with the lemon juice and a little butter whisked in at the last moment. Season the lamb noisettes on both sides. Brush with soya oil and pan-fry for 2 minutes on each side. On 4 plates place 1 pumpkin mousseline and a little pool of the sauce. Garnish with sweetbread pieces and morels drained from the sauce. Serve 3 lamb noisettes per portion. Add mint leaves and tomato roses for decoration.

*Serves 4*

HENNIE SILLEMAN

# Lamb Loin with
# Rosemary Sauce Andalusian-style

| | |
|---|---|
| 2 best end loins of lamb, boned and skinned | 1 small yellow and 1 red pepper, |
| 3 tbs soya oil | split, de-seeded and chopped |
| salt and pepper to taste | 1 small aubergine, sliced, |
| | soaked in water for 10 minutes, and diced |
| FOR THE ROSEMARY SAUCE | 1 courgette, diced |
| 3 tbs dry sherry | 1 large tomato, skinned, de-seeded, and diced |
| 1 tbs sherry vinegar | 1 sprig of rosemary |
| 1 sprig of rosemary | juice of 1 lemon |
| 1 tbs meat extract | salt and pepper to taste |
| 15 g (½ oz) butter | |
| | TO GARNISH |
| FOR THE PEPPER SAUCE | mixture of red and green curly chicory leaves |
| 3 tbs soya oil | |

Prepare the lamb loin and divide it into 4 × 200 g (7 oz) portions. Reserve 4 rib bones for decoration. Season the lamb. Heat the oil in a pan and sear the meat all round quickly to brown it on the outside. Cook for 2–3 minutes on each side to keep the meat juicy and pinkish, longer if required well done. Remove the meat and keep it warm while preparing the sauce.

To make the rosemary sauce, remove some of the oil from the pan in which the meat has been cooked. Boil this for 30 seconds, add the sherry and vinegar, and boil to reduce by half. Then add a sprig of rosemary and the meat extract. Boil for 2 minutes and whisk in a little butter to emulsify and flavour the sauce. Season to taste.

To make the pepper sauce garnish (known as pistou), heat the soya oil and sauté all the chopped vegetables for 2 minutes. Add a little rosemary. Season to taste and, lastly, add lemon juice.

On 4 plates, pour a pool of the pepper sauce (pistou). Arrange each piece of cooked lamb by carving it fanwise without separating the slices. Place each piece on a plate over the chopped vegetable sauce. Pour a ribbon of the rosemary sauce over the meat. To decorate, arrange a small heap of assorted red and green chicory leaves to the side of the meat. Insert one rib bone into the thicker side of the meat, to hold all the slices together.  *Serves 4*                                                 **JAVIER BASELGA**

# Fillet of Lamb 'Orient Express'

| | |
|---|---|
| 600 g ( 1 ¼ lb ) lamb fillet in one piece | 4 tbs brandy |
| 4 tbs soya oil | 50 g ( 2 oz ) carrots, diced |
| 300 ml ( ½ pint ) lamb stock | 50 g ( 2 oz ) onions, sliced thickly |
| 40 g ( 1 ½ oz ) redcurrant jelly | 1 bouquet garni |
| salt and pepper to taste | 2 tbs soya oil |
| 50 g ( 2 oz ) unsalted butter | |
| | TO GARNISH |
| FOR THE MARINADE | 225 g ( 7 ½ oz ) sprigs fresh redcurrants |
| 250 ml ( 8 fl oz ) red wine | a few mint leaves |

Remove the outer skin of the lamb fillet. Place the lamb in a long shallow dish. Cover it with wine and brandy and add the vegetables and bouquet garni. The lamb must be immersed completely. Sprinkle with oil. Refrigerate for 24 hours.

Strain the marinade mixture, retain the liquid for sauce, and pat the vegetables dry. Heat 2 tbs oil in a sauté pan and fry the vegetables for 5 minutes without browning them. Add half the marinade liquid and boil to reduce it in volume by half. Now add the lamb stock and the remaining marinade liquid. Boil until reduced by half again. Strain the sauce. Blend in the redcurrant jelly and season to taste. At the last minute, whisk in the butter to emulsify the reduced gravy.

Heat the remaining oil in a sauté pan, shallow-fry the fillet to seal it, and then cook it evenly for 8–10 minutes. Do not overcook it.

Carve the fillet into small slices. On each of 4 plates, pour a pool of sauce and arrange the slices overlapping each other. Garnish the centres with fresh redcurrants and mint leaves.     *Serves 4*     **CHRISTIAN BODIGUEL**

# *L*AMB *R*OLL WITH *F*RESH *D*ATES AND *A*LMONDS

| | |
|---|---|
| 4 lean lamb escalopes | 1 shallot, chopped |
| 4 tbs soya oil | 1 garlic clove, chopped |
| | 1 tbs tomato purée |
| FOR THE STUFFING | 150 ml (¼ pint) red wine |
| 250 g (8 oz) dried dates, stoned | 150 ml (¼ pint) lamb stock, well reduced, as gravy |
| 150 g (5 oz) skinned almonds | 1 tsp honey |
| 2 egg whites | 1 tsp water |
| | 1 sprig fresh mint, chopped |
| FOR THE | salt and pepper to taste |
| TUNISIAN WINE SAUCE | a little ground chilli and |
| 2 tbs soya oil | ground cumin |

*P*lace the lamb escalopes on a board. Fill the dates with almonds, keeping aside 8 dates for decoration. Brush the lamb with the beaten egg whites. Put some dates in the centre of each escalope and roll them up. Tie them with string. Heat the soya oil and shallow-fry the escalopes until brown. Cook gently for 15 minutes with a lid over the pan. Remove, untie, and slice thickly.

To make the sauce, heat the oil and shallow-fry the shallot and the garlic for 2 minutes. Add the tomato purée, wine, and lamb stock. Boil for 15 minutes. Season with salt, pepper, ground chilli, and ground cumin. Add honey, water, and chopped mint. Boil for 2 minutes. Add the juice from the meat.

Pour a pool of sauce on one side of each plate. Arrange 3 slices of meat over the sauce. Decorate with sliced stuffed dates. Serve with 2 baby carrots, a handful of French beans, 2 turned turnips, and a boiled spring onion.    *Serves 4*

**HAMADI KAROUI**

# *Moroccan Couscous with Mutton and Vegetables*

| | |
|---|---|
| 1 double best end of mutton, | 2 red peppers cut into 6 pieces |
| or 1 loin and 1 kg (2 lb) shoulder | 6 baby carrots |
| 3 litres (5½ pints) lamb stock, plus a little extra | 1 aubergine |
| veal bones, blanched | 200 g (7 oz) button onions |
| 1 onion, chopped | 150 g (5 oz) white cabbage, cut into pieces |
| a pinch of saffron threads | 2 fresh chillies |
| 250 g (8 oz) packet couscous | 120 g (4 oz) broad beans, fresh or frozen |
| 3 turnips, peeled and quartered | 1 bunch coriander |
| 200 g (7 oz) pumpkins | 75 g (3 oz) soya oil |
| 4 baby courgettes | salt and fresh ground pepper to taste |

Put the trimmed best end of mutton into the bottom half of a steamer (or use a sieve or colander over a pan of boiling water) with the stock, veal bones, onion, and saffron. Bring to the boil, skim, and simmer for 20 minutes.

Soak the couscous according to the instructions on the packet for approximately 15 minutes.

Put the rest of the vegetables in the steamer to cook, bearing in mind the cooking times for each one. Add the coriander and season to taste. Put the couscous into the upper part of the steamer and place on the pot. Seal and cook gently until the couscous starts steaming and becomes swollen (approximately 10 minutes). Then remove, pour into a kasas (earthenware dish), add the oil, and mix well. Arrange the couscous attractively on the plate with the meat and vegetables, moisten with plenty of stock, and serve immediately.

*Serves 6*

**MOHAMED DAHO**

# Lamb Constantia

| 1 pair best ends of lamb (cutlet joints), 1 kg (2 lb), | FOR THE PINOTAGE SAUCE |
|---|---|
| chined, trimmed, skinned, with only shortened ribs left | (the name is derived from a strong wine |
| | similar to port or sherry and sold as |
| FOR THE HERB CRUST | Pinot des Charentes) |
| 3 tsp made mustard | 350 ml (12 fl oz) rich lamb stock |
| 3 tbs soya margarine or oil, plus extra for | 350 ml (12 fl oz) Pinot wine or port |
| sprinkling over lamb | 1 sprig of rosemary |
| 225 g (7½ oz) white breadcrumbs | 2 tbs sherry vinegar |
| 225 g (7½ oz) sultanas and mixed candied peels | 1 tbs redcurrant jelly |
| 1 tsp mixed dried herbs (with rosemary) | 1 tsp made mustard |
| 2 tbs parsley, chopped | 3 tbs orange juice concentrate |
| 1 egg, beaten, and 2 tbs water | salt, pepper, and |
| a little salt and pepper | ground ginger to season |

Heat the oven to Gas Mark 6/200°C/400°F. Put the loin of lamb, facing upwards, on a board. In a bowl, mix all the herb crust ingredients except the egg and the seasoning into a spreadable paste. Add the beaten egg to make the mixture more sticky. Season to taste. Spread this mixture evenly over the white fat of the loin. Place the lamb in a pan on a trivet of bones and sprinkle it with a little oil. Roast in the oven on the medium shelf for 45 minutes.

Boil all the sauce ingredients except the seasoning together for 25 minutes, reducing the liquid by half. Strain. Season to taste.

Cut the lamb joints into cutlets, 1 rib per cutlet. Arrange 2 on each plate with a pool of sauce. Suggested accompaniments are stuffed tomatoes, button mushrooms, olive-shaped carrots, small stuffed yellow squashes, and artichoke bottoms stuffed with chopped tomato. *Serves 4* **BILL GALLAGHER**

# MARINATED LAMB WITH VEGETABLES

| | |
|---|---|
| 450 g (1 lb) leg of lamb, | 1 bouquet garni, including rosemary and mint |
| cut into lean 3 cm (1-inch) cubes | 1 tbs wine vinegar |
| 3 tbs soya oil | 6 peppercorns, crushed |
| 3 tomatoes, skinned, de-seeded, and chopped | |
| 1 tsp cornflour | TO GARNISH |
| 4 tbs water | 10 olive-shaped marrow pieces |
| salt, pepper, and ground cinnamon to taste | 10 small carrots |
| | 10 plum-sized, barrel-shaped potatoes |
| FOR THE | 100 ml (3½ fl oz) soya oil |
| MARINADE | 25 g (1 oz) butter |
| 350 ml (12 fl oz) red wine | a few sprigs of parsley, chopped |
| 2 tbs soya oil | a few sprigs of mint |
| 1 tsp coriander seeds | |

Combine the ingredients for the marinade. Marinate the meat for 6 hours. Drain and reserve the liquid.

Heat the oven to Gas Mark 6/200°C/400°F. Pat the meat dry with a cloth. Heat the oil in a pan and shallow-fry the meat for 6 minutes until golden brown. Drain well over a colander. Place the meat in a casserole dish and cover it with the marinade and the chopped tomatoes. Braise it in the oven for 40 minutes.

Drain the sauce into a saucepan. Thicken it with the cornflour, mixed with the water. Boil for 4 minutes. Season with salt, pepper, and cinnamon to taste. During the cooking of the lamb, boil, separately, the marrow pieces for 1 minute and carrots for 4 minutes. Cook the potatoes in oil and butter for 10–12 minutes, until golden.

Serve in individual shallow plates. Place the meat and sauce on the plates and arrange the vegetables artistically on top. Sprinkle with chopped parsley and fresh mint.     *Serves 4*     **YANNIS KOULOUROS**

# Lamb Loin with Chestnut Stuffing

| | |
|---|---|
| 4 boneless racks of New Zealand lamb | 2 eggs, beaten |
| 450 g ( 1 lb ) puff pastry | 50 g ( 2 oz ) chestnut purée |
| 4 tbs soya oil for greasing and oiling | 25 g ( 1 oz ) white breadcrumbs |
| 1 egg yolk, beaten | 1 large pinch of dried rosemary |
| 2 tbs sesame seeds or caraway seeds | a little salt and pepper |
| 450 g ( 1 lb ) assorted baby root vegetables, broad beans and mangetout | |
| a little salt and pepper | FOR THE SAUCE |
| | 3 mint leaves, chopped |
| STUFFING | 125 ml ( 4 fl oz ) mayonnaise |
| 25 g ( 1 oz ) cooked ham, minced | 150 ml water |

Trim the lamb racks of all fat and sinews, leaving only the eye of the meat. Make a hollow cavity in the length of the meat.

Prepare the stuffing by blending the ham, beaten eggs, chestnut purée, and breadcrumbs. Add the rosemary and season to taste. Place the stuffing in a forcing bag and pipe it into the cavity of each rack of lamb. Put a cocktail stick through each end and set aside.

Heat the oven to Gas Mark 6/200°C/400°F.

Roll out the puff pastry and cut it into narrow strips. Make pastry horns by wrapping well-oiled metal horn moulds with overlapping strips of pastry. Brush them all over with egg yolk and sprinkle them with either sesame or caraway seeds. Bake for 15 minutes until golden. Cool and remove the cornets of pastry from the moulds.

Cook the baby vegetables for a few minutes only to keep them crunchy. Brush the lamb with soya oil and season to taste. Roast for 25 minutes to keep it pink but cooked through.

Blend the fresh chopped mint with mayonnaise made with soya oil. Make a gravy in the usual way, by adding a little water to the roasting tray after the meat has been cooked. Reduce the gravy to concentrate the flavour. Strain and season.

On 4 plates arrange 5 thin slices of lamb. Fill the pastry horns with some of the vegetables. Arrange the remaining root vegetables to look like overflowing cornucopias. Pour over a little gravy. Garnish each plate with a few mangetout in a row. Serve the mint mayonnaise separately or inside the pastry horns.

*Serves 4*

NEL McINNES

# Lamb with Aubergine Custard Pudding

| | |
|---|---|
| 2 best ends of lamb, boned, with skin removed | 1 aubergine, diced |
| (keep bone and skin for stock) | 1 garlic clove, chopped |
| 600 ml (1 pint) water | ½ red and ½ green pepper, de-seeded and chopped |
| 150 g (5 oz) raw minced chicken, skinless | 6 small tomatoes, skinned, de-seeded, and chopped |
| 150 ml (¼ pint) double cream mixed with 1 egg white | 6 eggs, beaten |
| 4 tbs soya oil | salt and pepper to taste |
| a little salt and pepper | |
| 1 tbs chopped parsley | FOR THE SAUCE |
| | 150 ml (¼ pint) red port wine |
| FOR THE | 2 tbs double cream |
| BAVAROIS MIXTURE | juice of ½ lemon |
| 4 tbs soya oil, plus extra for greasing | |
| 1 large onion, chopped | TO GARNISH |
| 1 courgette, diced | a sprig of coriander, or chervil |

Make a stock with the lamb trimmings, bones, and water. Boil for 30 minutes and strain. Retain some of the fat of the fillets for wrapping. Lay the fillets on a board.

Heat the oven to Gas Mark 7/220°C/425°F. In a bowl, blend the minced chicken with the cream and egg white. Season to taste and add the parsley. Spread this mixture on top of the fillets. Wrap them with the fat trimmings, and tie them with string. Heat the oil in a pan and brown the fillets for 8 minutes. Finish the cooking in the oven. Remove after 15 minutes and keep warm. Keep the meat juice for the sauce.

To make the bavarois, heat the soya oil in a shallow pan and stir-fry the onion for 5 minutes. Add the courgette, aubergine, and garlic and cook for 4 minutes more. Sauté the red and green peppers separately. Retain half for layer topping; add the rest to the mixture, along with half the chopped tomatoes. Cook the mixture to a purée, liquidise, and cool it. Mix the remaining diced peppers and chopped tomatoes together to use for the topping later on. In a bowl, break 6 eggs and blend them with 1 litre (1¾ pints) of the vegetable purée. Season to taste. Fill 6 well-greased 150 ml (¼ pint) basins with the mixture and place a spoonful of cooked pepper on top of each. Bake for 40 minutes. Remove and keep warm.

To make the sauce, pour 150 ml (¼ pint) mixture of meat juice and well-reduced lamb stock into a saucepan with the port. Boil for 12 minutes. Add the cream and the lemon juice. Season to taste.

Pour a pool of gravy onto 4 plates. Turn a vegetable bavarois onto each plate and add 3 thinly carved slices of meat. Decorate the top of the bavarois with the chopped tomato and pepper mixture. Decorate with a sprig of chervil or coriander. *Serves 6*

**BRUCE BUCHAN**

# Veal Poached in Consommé

| | |
|---|---|
| 1 litre ( 1¾ pints ) veal stock | 4 large radishes |
| 600 g ( 1¼ lb ) veal fillet, skinned | a little salt |

| FOR THE | FOR THE |
|---|---|
| CLARIFICATION MIXTURE | MINT AND |
| 50 g ( 2 oz ) each carrots, celery, leeks, and onions, | TOMATO MAYONNAISE |
| all finely chopped | 2 egg yolks |
| 150 g ( 5 oz ) raw, lean minced veal or beef | 1 tsp made yellow French mustard |
| ( use same meat for all kinds of consommé ) | 300 ml ( ½ pint ) soya oil |
| 2 egg whites | 6 fresh mint leaves, chopped |
| | 1 tomato, pulped and chopped |
| TO GARNISH | 1 dash of chilli sauce |
| 8 baby turnips | 1 tsp honey |
| 8 baby carrots | 1 tsp sherry vinegar |
| 4 small leeks | 1 tbs yogurt |
| 4 small sticks celery | a little salt and pepper |

Place all the ingredients for clarification in a bowl and mix them well. Add the cold veal stock. Transfer to a pan and bring to the boil very gently. Simmer for 35 minutes. Strain through a muslin cloth into another pan. This clarification mixture can be used for any meat consommé.

Tie the veal with string and place it in the hot consommé. Simmer it for about 20 minutes until it is cooked (it should be bloodless throughout). Meanwhile, cook the garnish vegetables separately in salted water: turnips, 5 minutes; carrots, 8 minutes; leeks, 7 minutes; celery, 9 minutes; radishes, 2 minutes. Drain well.

To make the mayonnaise, mix together the egg yolks, mustard, salt, and pepper in a bowl. Gradually pour in the oil in a small trickle until it begins to thicken, and then add the whole amount. Blend in the mint, tomato, chilli sauce, honey, and vinegar. Check the taste. Add the yogurt last.

Pour a little mayonnaise on one side of each plate. Arrange the slices of veal and the vegetables neatly around the mayonnaise. Any consommé left over can be used for gravies or clear soups.

Note that beef cooked in this way is known in France and Switzerland as *fondue de veau* or *fondue de boeuf bourguignonne*. For beef, the cooking time is only 10 minutes, as beef is usually preferred underdone.     *Serves 6*                                                        **EËRO MÄKELÄ**

Top: *Beef Fillet Shoppenhanger with Mulberries* (*page 145*), below: *Beef Fillet la Villette* (*page 149*)

*Seafood Kebab Princess Anne (page 41), with (in clockwise order)*
*Israeli Hazeret Sauce (page 169), Creole Sauce (page 170), Jamaican Pawpaw Sauce (page 171), Chinese Watermelon*
*Salad Dressing (page 168), Green Mexican Sauce (page 173), and Almond and Lime Sauce (page 174)*

*Kebab of Veal Epicure (page 143), with (in clockwise order)*
*Hong Kong Lime Sauce (page 168), Basic Curry Sauce (page 167), Satay Sauce (page 172), Pumpkin Sauce (page 170),*
*Chilli Plum Sauce (page 166), and Tunisian Charmoula Sauce with Raisins (page 171)*

Top: *Tuna-filled New Zealand Kiwi fruit (page 47)*, below: *Fried Chicken Drumsticks on Oriental Salad in Chilli Lime Dressing (page 162)*

# Kebab of Veal Epicure

*Pictured on back cover and page 141.*

| | |
|---|---|
| 500 g (1 lb) veal fillets, cut in 2 cm (1-inch) cubes | 1 medium onion, segmented |
| 1 veal kidney, cleaned and cut in slices | 5 tbs soya oil |
| 1 red pepper, split, de-seeded | 1 tbs mixed crushed mustard and peppercorn seeds |
| and cut in 4 cm (2-inch) squares | salt to taste |
| 8 medium firm mushrooms | |

*I*mpale on 4 skewers the meat and kidney with the peppers, mushroom caps and layers of onion. Brush with oil and sprinkle with the crushed seeds and peppercorns. Grill for 8 minutes. Serve with an assortment of sauces and salads of your choice.　*Serves 4*　　　　　　　　　　　　　　　　**JEAN CONIL**

# Veal Chima Gibraltar

| | FOR THE PILAFF |
|---|---|
| 30 g (½ oz) breadcrumbs | |
| 100 g (3½ oz) cheese, grated | 3 tbs soya oil |
| 1 garlic clove, chopped | 1 shallot, chopped |
| 1 tsp marjoram and thyme, mixed | 25 g (1 oz) red peppers, diced |
| 4 × 150 g (5 oz) escalopes from veal topside | 350 g (12 oz) rice |
| 50 g (2 oz) plain flour, seasoned with a pinch of salt | 4 strands of saffron |
| 2 eggs, beaten | 25 g (1 oz) green peas |
| 6 tbs soya oil | 750 ml (1¼ pints) chicken stock |
| 4 sprigs of thyme | salt and pepper to taste |

*C*ombine the breadcrumbs, grated cheese, garlic, and herbs in a bowl. Coat the veal escalopes in seasoned flour, then in beaten eggs, and finally in the breadcrumb mixture. Heat 4 tbs oil in a pan and shallow-fry the escalopes for 3 minutes on each side. Drain them well and keep them warm. Heat the oven to Gas Mark 6/200°C/400°F. Heat the soya oil and shallow-fry the shallot for 1 minute. Then add the pepper and cook for a further minute. Add the rice, saffron, and peas, and finally stir in the chicken stock and a little salt and pepper. Bring to the boil for 4 minutes and transfer the mixture to a pie dish. Cook in the oven for 20 minutes, covered with paper or a lid. Grease a dariole mould, fill it with hot cooked rice, press, and turn it out onto a plate. Repeat this operation on 3 more plates. Arrange the cooked escalopes on the plates and garnish.　*Serves 4*　　　　**J.J. SOLLIER**

# $\mathcal{A}$SIAN $\mathcal{B}$EEF $\mathcal{B}$ARBECUE

| | |
|---|---|
| 1 kg (2 lb) tenderloin of beef, trimmed and | 2 tbs dark soya sauce |
| cut into thin slices | 150 ml (¼ pint) water or beef stock |
| 3 tbs soya oil | 2 tsp fresh ginger, peeled and chopped |
| 100 ml (3½ fl oz) beef stock | 3 tbs onions, chopped |
| 1 tsp cornflour | 2 chilli peppers (1 red and 1 green) |
| 4 tbs water | split, de-seeded, and chopped |
| 3 tbs saké (rice wine) or sherry | 6 peppercorns |
| a few chives or spring onions, chopped | |
| a little salt | TO GARNISH |
| | 6 spring onions, cut into brushes |
| FOR THE MARINADE | 6 chillies, cut into flowers |
| 3 tbs light soya sauce | 1 tbs sesame seeds, toasted |

$\mathscr{C}$ombine all the marinade ingredients. Place the marinade and the meat in a large earthenware bowl. Mix well and leave for 4 hours under refrigeration. Remove the meat, drain it in a colander, and pat dry. Heat the oil and stir-fry the meat until it is tender (5–6 minutes). Boil the marinade for 10 minutes with the beef stock. Thicken it with cornflour mixed with water. Cook for about 4 minutes until it is of the right consistency. Strain the sauce.

Divide the sauce between two pans. To one, add the saké or sherry. To the other, add chopped chives or spring onions. Reheat each sauce and season with salt to taste. You can, if you wish, flavour the sherry sauce with pineapple juice and the other sauce with tomato ketchup.

On 6 Asian-style platters, place some meat strips. Decorate with spring onion brushes, chillies cut into floral patterns and sesame seeds. Serve 1 small basin of each sauce with each portion for guests to dip their beef in as they eat. Serve with boiled rice in separate bowls. *Serves 6* **PETER TOBLER**

# Beef Fillet Shoppenhanger with Mulberries

*Pictured on page 139.*

| | |
|---|---|
| 4 × 175 g (6 oz) middle-cut fillets of beef, trimmed, 1 cm (½ inch) thick | a pinch of cinnamon |
| 2 tbs soya oil and butter, mixed | TO GARNISH |
| a little salt, pepper, and ground cinnamon | 16 asparagus tips, trimmed |
| | 100 g (4 oz) girolles (wild mushrooms) |
| FOR THE SAUCE | 2 tbs melted butter |
| 2 tbs soya oil | 50 g (2 oz) fresh, uncooked mulberries or |
| 1 shallot, chopped | blackberries for decoration |
| 125 g (4 oz) mulberries or blackberries | 100 g (4 oz) celeriac, peeled, diced, and |
| 1 tsp sugar or honey | blanched until tender |
| 150 ml (3½ fl oz) brown sauce, well reduced | a few sprigs of fresh coriander, chopped |

Prepare the sauce first. Heat the soya oil in a pan and shallow-fry the shallot for 2 minutes without browning. Add the mulberries or blackberries and sugar or honey and cook until the mixture is like a jammy purée. Dilute it with the brown sauce. Boil for 5 minutes. Season and strain. Add a pinch of cinnamon to enhance the mulberry flavour.

In another pan, heat just enough oil and butter and pan-fry the seasoned steaks according to taste – rare, medium, or well-done. Remove the steaks and keep them warm. Discard the surplus oil and add the sauce to absorb the meat juice. Boil for 3 minutes and strain again.

Cook the asparagus tips separately. Boil them for 5 minutes only, making sure they remain crunchy, and refresh. Toss the girolles in melted butter and cook them for 1 minute. Drain.

Place a ribbon of sauce on one side of each plate. Arrange a fillet steak on this pool of sauce. Surround with fresh asparagus, girolles, and a few raw mulberries or blackberries. On top of each steak, place a spoon of diced celeriac. Sprinkle on a little chopped coriander leaf. *Serves 4* **ROBERT WEBSTER**

# Beef Steak and Fruit Casserole

| | |
|---|---|
| 3 tsp soya oil | 300 ml ( ½ pint ) beef stock |
| 650 g ( 1 lb ) lean topside beef cut into small cubes | 250 g ( 8 oz ) mixed dried fruits ( apricots, |
| 1 garlic clove, chopped | peaches, pears ), soaked in water for 6 hours |
| 1 medium onion, diced | 1 heaped tbs cornflour |
| 1 medium carrot, peeled and diced | 6 tbs water |
| 150 ml ( 5 fl oz ) red wine | a little salt and pepper |

Heat the oil in a shallow pan and sauté the beef, garlic, onion, and carrot for 5 minutes. Add the wine and stock. Bring to the boil and simmer, covered, for 1 hour.

Add the soaked fruit and cook for another 30 minutes.

Blend the cornflour and water, and add to the liquid. Stir and simmer for 5 minutes. Check the seasoning. Serve with boiled rice or new potatoes.     *Serves 4–6*

JEAN CONIL

# Sliced Beef Carpaccio with Herb Cream and Beluga Caviar

| | |
|---|---|
| 450 g ( 1 lb ) tenderloin beef fillet, | F O R   T H E |
| trimmed and skinned | S O U R   C R E A M   S A U C E |
| | 3 tbs sour cream |
| F O R   T H E | 1 tbs mixed fresh herbs ( chives, basil, and tarragon ), chopped |
| B A L S A M I C O   M A R I N A D E | a little salt and pepper |
| 3 tbs balsamico vinegar | |
| 1 tbs each olive, grape seed, and soya oil | T O   G A R N I S H |
| 1 tbs vermouth, dry or sweet | 4 tsp beluga caviar |
| a little salt and coarsely ground black pepper | a few sprigs of fresh dill or chervil |

Wrap the trimmed tenderloin in clean cloth and freeze it for 3 hours. Combine the marinade ingredients in a bowl. Blend together the sour cream and herbs in another bowl with salt and pepper to taste. Take the meat from the freezer, unwrap it, and cut it into paper-thin slices while the meat is still frozen hard.

Arrange 6 thin slices per portion on 4 × 24 cm (10-inch) dinner plates. Overlap the slices neatly. Rest the meat for 3 minutes before serving to thaw it out. Brush the beef slices with the marinade and decorate the centres with a spoonful or two of the cream sauce. Top each portion with 1 tsp of caviar and garnish with the fresh herb leaves.     *Serves 4*                                                     JEAN MICHEL HARDOUIN-ATLAN

# CREOLE GRILLADES

| |
|---|
| 3 tbs soya oil |
| 450 g (1 lb) beef sirloin, cut in 5 cm (2-inch) squares |
| 1 small onion, chopped |
| 1 large tomato, skinned, de-seeded, and chopped |
| 1 tsp tomato purée |
| 2 garlic cloves, chopped |
| 100 ml (4 fl oz) beef stock |
| 2 tsp cornflour, blended with a little cold stock |
| 250 g (8 oz) long-grain rice, cooked |
| 1 tsp chopped mint or oregano |
| a little salt and pepper |

Heat the oil in a pan. Shallow-fry the steaks for 1 or 2 minutes. Remove and keep hot. In the same pan, in what is left of the oil, shallow-fry the onion until it is soft (2 minutes), then add the chopped tomato, tomato purée, and garlic. Simmer for 2 minutes. Stir in the stock and boil for 6 minutes. Thicken with cornflour paste, then cook for 4 minutes to clear the starch. Season to taste.

On 4 plates arrange a bed of cooked hot rice and 2 small pieces of steak. Coat the meat with the Creole sauce. Sprinkle a little chopped mint or oregano on top.     *Serves 4*                                JEREMIE GARLICK

# Filet Mignon Maltaise

| | |
|---|---|
| 3 tbs soya oil | 1 garlic clove, chopped |
| 2 small beef fillets, cut into pieces about | 2 large tomatoes, skinned, |
| 125 g (4 oz) each and ½ cm (¼ inch) thick | de-seeded, and chopped |
| | 1 tsp tomato purée |
| FOR THE MALTAISE SAUCE | salt and pepper |
| 2 egg yolks | |
| 1 tsp made yellow mustard | FOR THE |
| 2 tbs blood orange juice | VEGETABLE GARNISH |
| 1 tbs wine vinegar | 2 tsp chopped parsley |
| 150 ml (¼ pint) soya oil | 6 button mushrooms |
| 2 tbs cream | 4 baby carrots, shaped |
| a little salt | 4 potatoes, shaped like barrels |
| pinch black pepper, crushed | and roasted |
| | 8 french kidney beans |
| FOR THE TOMATO FONDU | (all vegetables blanched separately and |
| 1 small onion or 2 shallots, chopped | reheated in soya oil) |

As the meat only takes a few minutes to cook, prepare the Maltaise sauce first. In a bowl over a saucepan of boiling water, whisk together the egg yolks, made mustard, and orange juice for about 6 minutes until the mixture begins to thicken. Then add the salt, pepper, and wine vinegar. Gradually, away from the heat, pour in the soya oil in a small trickle to emulsify the sauce and thicken it. Lastly, blend in the cream. This sauce can be served tepid but not hot.

Heat 3 tbs oil in a pan and quickly fry the steaks for 4–5 minutes until done. Remove and keep them hot. Discard the excess oil and in the same pan fry the onion or shallots and garlic for 1 minute. Then add the tomatoes and tomato purée and cook until the mixture is thick. Season to taste.

On 2 plates pour a pool of the Maltaise sauce. Add the meat and cover it with a spoon of tomato fondu. Decorate with chopped parsley. On each plate arrange 3 mushrooms, 2 carrots, 2 roasted potatoes, and a small bunch of french beans. *Serves 2* 　　　　　MARTIN BAUMANN

# BEEF FILLET LA VILLETTE

*Pictured on page 139.*

| | |
|---|---|
| 2 tbs soya oil and 1 tbs butter | 20 g (¾ oz) beef marrow |
| 250 g (8 oz) tenderloin beef steak, 2 cm (¾ inch) thick | 50 g (2 oz) Sainte-Maure goat cheese, |
| | cut into cubes or crumbled |
| FOR THE SAUCE | 10 g (½ oz) bread croûtons |
| 3 tbs port wine | 1 tsp snipped chives |
| 3 tbs red wine | a little salt and pepper |
| 1 shallot, chopped | |
| 1 sprig of fresh thyme | FOR THE |
| 3 tbs brown sauce | VEGETABLE GARNISH |
| 3 tbs double cream | 2 baby carrots, with green leaves attached (cut short) |
| | 1 baby turnip with green leaves attached |
| FOR THE CHEESE GARNISH | 1 wild mushroom |
| 2 tbs soya oil and 1 tbs butter | 1 courgette |
| 1 shallot, chopped | a few fresh chives, snipped |
| 1 sprig of fresh thyme | 1 small bunch of bean sprouts |

Heat the oil and butter and pan-fry the tenderloin until it is cooked to taste – rare, medium, or well done. Remove when it is cooked and keep it hot. Discard the excess fat, and to the same pan add the port wine, red wine, shallot, and sprig of thyme. Boil for 3 minutes and then add the brown sauce. Boil for 5 minutes, stir in the cream, and boil briskly for 2 minutes more. Strain the sauce.

To make the cheese garnish, heat the oil and butter in another pan. Stir-fry the shallot, the thyme, the beef marrow cut into small pieces, the goat cheese, the croûtons, and the chives. Season to taste.

To make the vegetable garnish, boil the carrots and turnip separately, keeping them slightly crunchy. Refresh and reheat. Stir-fry the mushroom for 30 seconds. Blanch the courgette for 1 minute and cut it fanwise without separation.

Pour a little strained sauce onto a plate. Arrange the fillet in the centre, and top the meat with the cooked cheese mixture. Sprinkle with a few fresh chives. Garnish with the courgette, carrots, turnip, bunch of raw bean sprouts, and mushroom.     *Serves 1*                                        MICHEL ADDON

# *S*TRIPS OF *B*EEF AND *S*CALLOPS *N*ORFOLK

| |
|---|
| 250 g ( 8 oz) queen scallops, shelled and cleaned |
| 1 × 500 g ( 1 lb) fillet of beef, cut 2 cm ( ¾ inch) long and ½ cm ( ¼ inch) thick |
| 1 tbs flour, seasoned with salt and pepper |
| 2 tbs soya oil and butter, mixed |
| 150 ml ( ¼ pint) white wine |
| 1 medium onion, chopped |
| 4 strands of saffron |
| 25 g ( 1 oz) peppercorns, crushed |
| 150 ml ( ¼ pint) double cream |
| 225 g ( 7½ oz) pilaff rice |
| 4 boiled crayfish ( écrevisses) |
| 1 bunch of dill |

*R*ub the scallops and beef strips in seasoned flour and shake off the surplus over a sieve. Heat the oil and butter in a pan and stir-fry the mixture of beef and scallops for 5 minutes. Remove and drain off the fat. To the same pan, add the wine, onion, and saffron. Boil until reduced in volume by half. Add the crushed peppercorns and the cream, and cook until the mixture is as thick as a custard (the mixture should coat the back of a spoon). Reheat the beef and scallops in the sauce without boiling.

On 4 plates, place the beef mixture. Garnish each plate with pilaff rice, moulded if you wish, a crayfish and a sprig of dill.  *Serves 4*  **DAVID LODGE**

# Loin Steak of Venison

| | |
|---|---|
| 4 venison loin steaks, skinned and trimmed, | 1 carrot, sliced |
| total weight about 1 kg ( 2 lb ) | 2 sticks of celery, sliced |
| 300 ml ( ½ pint ) red port wine | 1 onion, sliced |
| 1 carrot, finely chopped | 1 garlic clove |
| 1 leek, white only, chopped | 4 juniper berries |
| 1 stick of celery, chopped | 560 ml ( 1 pint ) meat stock |
| 6 juniper berries | 1 tbs tomato purée |
| 6 peppercorns, crushed | a little butter or cream ( optional ) |
| 1 garlic clove | 1 tsp cornflour |
| 4 bay leaves | 2 tsp water |
| 1 bouquet garni | a little salt and pepper |
| 1 tsp sugar | |
| 1 tbs wine vinegar | TO DECORATE |
| 1 beetroot, cooked, sliced | 50 g ( 2 oz ) sugar |
| 4 tbs soya oil | 2 tbs water |
| | 25 g ( 1 oz ) sesame seeds |
| FOR THE SAUCE | 2 large ripe pears, best-quality Comice |
| 4 tbs soya oil | iced water for cooling |
| 350 g ( 12 oz ) venison bones and skins or | 12 juniper berries |
| breast parts cut into small pieces | 8 fresh bay leaves |

Place the meat in a stainless steel or earthenware pot. Cover it with port wine, and add the chopped vegetables, juniper berries, peppercorns, garlic, bay leaves, bouquet garni, and sugar. Add the vinegar and a beetroot. Marinate for 3 days, turning the meat each day. Cover with cling film throughout. To make the sauce, heat the oil with the bones, meat trimmings, carrot, celery, onion, and garlic. Add the juniper berries. Cover these ingredients with meat stock and tomato purée. Boil this game stock for 1 hour and strain. Boil the marinade until it is reduced in volume by one-third. Add the game stock and boil for 20 minutes. Season to taste. The sauce can be emulsified with a little butter or cream, or thickened with cornflour and water, which are mixed together and added when the mixture is boiling. To cook the venison steaks, heat the oil in a pan and fry the steaks until done then keep warm. To make the caramelised pears, heat the sugar and water until the mixture becomes golden. Add the sesame seeds and the halved pears. Cook for 30 seconds and remove into a bowl of iced water. The pears will harden quickly. Remove them immediately. Cut each steak into 3 slices laterally. Pour a pool of sauce on each of 4 plates. On each plate arrange the meat and a half pear. Decorate each with a few juniper berries and fresh bay leaves. *Serves 4*   **MARTYN EMSEN**

# Paillard of Venison with Poivrade Sauce

| | FOR THE POIVRADE SAUCE |
|---|---|
| 4 × 250 g (8 oz) venison steaks (from loin) | |
| | 150 ml (¼ pint) soya oil |
| FOR THE | 75 g (3 oz) marinade vegetables, well-drained |
| MARINADE | 300 ml (½ pint) marinade liquid |
| 2 tbs soya oil | 150 ml (¼ pint) game stock |
| 300 ml (½ pint) red wine | 2 tbs soya oil and 2 tbs butter, mixed |
| 1 tbs cognac | a little salt |
| 1 small onion, sliced | 4 peppercorns, crushed |
| 1 carrot, sliced | 1 tbs cognac |
| 6 juniper berries | |
| 4 peppercorns, crushed | TO GARNISH |
| 1 garlic clove, chopped | 4 poached pears, cut into halves |
| 1 tsp sugar | 50 g (2 oz) redcurrant jelly |
| 1 bouquet garni | 12 mint or watercress leaves for decoration |

Combine the marinade ingredients in an earthenware dish. Soak the steaks for 2 hours and turn them over twice during this time.

To prepare the sauce, heat the oil and shallow-fry the marinade vegetables for 5 minutes. Remove the surplus oil, and stir in the marinade liquid and game stock. Boil for 15 minutes. Season and strain. Pat the marinaded steaks dry. Sprinkle crushed peppercorns over each. Season with salt. Heat the mixed oil and butter in a pan. Shallow-fry the steaks for 2–3 minutes. Remove them from the pan and discard the surplus fat from the pan. Add the cognac, set alight, and pour in the poivrade sauce. Reduce it to coating consistency.

Place the cooked steaks on 4 plates. Coat them with sauce. On each plate, arrange a half pear, cavity upward. Fill each pear with 2 tsp redcurrant jelly. Decorate with mint or watercress leaves.    *Serves 4*

ERWIN BOTTNER

# 𝒮ALADS

𝒜lmost all foods can be eaten in salad form. Perhaps salads began when the Romans first sprinkled a pinch of salt over a carrot or wild dandelion. After all, it is from the Latin word for salt (*sal*) that the word 'salad' is derived. The Romans had numerous tasty sauces made from ingredients such as anchovies and other smoked or salted fish. They had learned to press oil from olives and obtained vinegar by exposing wines to air. Their lemon groves provided lemon juice, another good dressing.

Today, the creation of contrasts in salads has converted what used to be a side dish into a main dish. By adding a garnish of salad leaves to hot food – be it fish, meat, poultry, game, or eggs – the modern chef has given the salad a new dimension as a main entrée. Alternatively it can be a luxurious starter, incorporating lobster, scampi, smoked salmon, or wild feathered game.

In classic cuisine, salads are identified by names. Today nouvelle cuisine chefs list the ingredients of a salad in its title. This ends the mystique for many gourmets, but it does help the rest of us to know what we have to look forward to. A salad called 'Aida' or 'Carmen' inevitably is less exciting today than it was when such references were readily understood. The old system does, of course, save a lot of time in writing out the menu.

# ℋOT 𝒯URKEY 𝒮ALAD WITH ℬEAN 𝒮PROUTS, 𝒫INEAPPLE, AND 𝒫EPPERS

| 150 g (5 oz) raw turkey meat from breast, | 4 radicchio leaves |
|---|---|
| cut into thin strips | 50 g (2 oz) bean sprouts |
| 2 tbs plain flour, seasoned with | 50 g (2 oz) red and green peppers, cut into thin strips |
| a pinch of salt and of pepper | 75 g (3 oz) fresh pineapple, cut into small slices |
| 5 tbs soya oil | 4 tbs sour cream |
| | juice of 1 lime |
| T O   G A R N I S H | 1 tsp sesame seeds, toasted |
| 8 Webb's lettuce leaves | a little salt and pepper |

ℛub the turkey strips in the seasoned flour. Shake the surplus off over a sieve. Heat the oil in a wok and stir-fry the meat for 6 minutes until done. Remove and drain.

Arrange on 4 plates the salad leaves and bean sprouts, with the strips of pepper and the pineapple slices. Just before serving, sprinkle a little sour cream over the hot turkey. Mix the lime juice with salt and pepper and put 2 spoonfuls of this mixture on each plate. Sprinkle with toasted sesame seeds.     *Serves 4*     **JEAN CONIL**

# CRUNCHY PEANUT SALAD

| | |
|---|---|
| 50 g ( 2 oz ) sweetcorn, cooked | 4 tbs soya oil |
| 50 g ( 2 oz ) peanuts, toasted | juice of 1 lemon |
| 50 g ( 2 oz ) spring onions, chopped or cut into chunks | 1 tsp made mustard |
| 175 g ( 6 oz ) bean sprouts | 1 tbs chopped parsley |
| 50 g ( 2 oz ) raw button mushrooms, washed and sliced | zest of 1 lemon |
| 8 radishes, sliced | a little salt and pepper |
| 1 small gherkin, sliced | |
| | TO GARNISH |
| FOR THE DRESSING | 1 curly-leaved lettuce |
| 50 g ( 2 oz ) peanuts | |

Liquidise the dressing ingredients in a blender. Combine the salad ingredients in a bowl and toss with half the dressing. On 4 plates, arrange a bed of curly lettuce leaves and cover with tossed salad. *Serves 4*

JOHN ASH

# NEW POTATO SALAD WITH STAR-FRUIT DRESSING

*No other tuber vegetable salad is tastier than hot new potato salad, flavoured with fragrant star-fruit dressing. Originally from Ecuador but now imported from New Zealand and also grown in the Channel Islands, the star-fruit is a five-sided fruit known also as a babaco. It is well known in tropical and Oriental countries and is beginning to appear in restaurants. The star-fruit is rich in vitamin C, and its flavour makes it an ideal salad garnish.*

| | |
|---|---|
| 1 kg ( 2 lb ) new potatoes | 50 g ( 2 oz ) star-fruit pulp |
| | a little salt and pepper |
| FOR THE DRESSING | |
| 1 tsp made Dijon mustard | TO GARNISH |
| 2 egg yolks | 12 curly lettuce leaves, washed and drained |
| 150 ml ( ¼ pint ) soya oil | 1 large star-fruit, sliced |
| 1 shallot, chopped | 1 tbs chopped parsley |
| 1 tsp cider vinegar | 2 tbs snipped chives |

Boil the potatoes for 20 minutes in their skins. Peel, and slice or dice them while still hot.

Prepare the dressing in the same way as ordinary mayonnaise. Put the made mustard, egg yolks, salt, and pepper in a bowl. Gradually drip in the oil while whisking in one direction to emulsify the sauce. When thick, add the shallot, vinegar, and star-fruit pulp. Place the hot potato mixture in the bowl and toss in the sauce.

On each of 6 plates, arrange 2 lettuce leaves with a helping of the hot new potato salad. Decorate the tops with star-fruit slices and sprinkle with parsley and snipped chives.     *Serves 6*     **JEAN CONIL**

# *Salad Alia*

| | |
|---|---|
| 2 cos lettuces | a few sprigs of mild thyme or a few chives |
| 4 large fresh dill cucumbers | 5 tbs plain yogurt |
| 4 button onions | a pinch of salt |
| 2 blood oranges | |
| 100 g (3½ oz) black olives, preserved in spices and herbs | FOR THE DRESSING |
| 4 dates, quartered | 4 radishes, finely chopped |
| 10 g (½ oz) seedless grapes, halved | 5 tbs groundnut oil |
| | 1 dried chilli pepper, lightly crushed |
| FOR THE | 10 g (½ oz) fresh coriander, chopped |
| FLAVOURED CREAMY CHEESE | juice of 1 lemon |
| 2 litres (3½ pints) milk | a little salt and pepper |

To make the cheese, boil the milk with the thyme or chives. Then transfer it into an earthenware dish and leave it to cool. Stir in the yogurt and salt. Cover it with a clean towel and keep it in a warm place to ferment for at least 10 hours. Store in the refrigerator. When it is chilled, pour it into a fine sieve lined with muslin and leave to drain. Remove the muslin containing the cheese, tie it securely and place it on a strainer over a bowl. Return it to the refrigerator to drain for a day before use.

Liquidise the dressing ingredients. Trim and wash the lettuces and tear them into rough pieces. Peel and slice the cucumbers, onions, and oranges. Arrange the salad on 4 plates. Top with the cheese. Garnish with olives, dates, and seedless grapes, and sprinkle with the dressing.     *Serves 4*     **MOHAMED DAHO**

# Green Lentils with Bacon, Rabbit, and Mushroom Salad

| | |
|---|---|
| 150 g (5 oz) lean back rabbit meat, cubed | 1 small sprig of fresh thyme or marjoram |
| 1 tbs flour, seasoned with a little salt and pepper | 1 tbs chopped chervil |
| 5 tbs soya oil | 1 tbs sour cream or yogurt |
| 1 small onion, chopped | a little salt and pepper |
| 1 garlic clove, chopped | |
| a little salt and black pepper | TO GARNISH |
| | 150 g (5 oz) cooked green lentils |
| FOR THE DRESSING | 2 endives, shredded |
| 3 tbs soya oil | 1 bunch of lamb's lettuce or dandelion leaves |
| 2 tbs sherry vinegar | 4 curly lettuce leaves |

Rub the rabbit meat in the seasoned flour. Shake off any surplus. Heat the oil in a frying pan and toss the meat for 4 minutes until cooked. Remove and keep warm. In the same oil, stir-fry the onion and garlic for 1 minute. Reheat the rabbit for a few seconds with the onion and garlic. Season with salt and black pepper.

Liquidise the dressing ingredients.

Put 2 spoonfuls of lentils with the salad leaves on each of 4 plates. Top with the cooked rabbit mixture just before serving the salads. Sprinkle a little dressing on each plate. *Serves 4* **JEAN CONIL**

# Creole Rice

| | |
|---|---|
| 3 tbs soya oil | 250 g (1½ lb) long-grain rice |
| 250 g (1½ lb) onions, chopped | 600 ml (1 pint) chicken stock |
| 1 red pepper, split, de-seeded, and cut in strips | 4 strands of saffron |
| 1 stick celery, diced | 1 small courgette, sliced |
| 1 aubergine, diced | a little salt |
| 1 green chilli pepper, split, de-seeded, and chopped | a few coriander leaves |
| 2 garlic cloves, crushed | |

*H*eat the oil in a shallow pan. Stir-fry all the vegetables except the courgette. Add the rice, chicken stock, and saffron. Boil for 20 minutes. Blanch the courgettes for 30 seconds in salted water. Remove and drain.

Arrange the ingredients on 4 plates. Decorate with courgettes and coriander leaves.     *Serves 4*     **JEAN CONIL**

# Stuffed Chicken Breasts with Green Salad in Walnut Dressing

| 2 chicken breasts | FOR THE DRESSING |
| --- | --- |
| (from free-range chickens) | 125 ml (4 fl oz) walnut oil |
| 100 g (4 oz) spinach leaves | 1 tbs fresh chopped mixed herbs |
| 80 g (3 oz) lobster meat | 1 shallot, chopped |
| 2 tbs soya margarine | 2 tbs raspberry vinegar |
| a little salt and pepper | a little salt and pepper |

| FOR THE SALAD | TO GARNISH |
| --- | --- |
| 200 g (8 oz) mixed green salad leaves: endive, | 1 tbs diced tomato |
| curly lettuce, radicchio, lamb's lettuce | 2 tbs fresh chopped mixed herbs |

*H*eat the oven to Gas Mark 7/220°C/425°F. Cut a pocket in each chicken breast, rub in the salt and pepper, and line the pockets with spinach leaves. Fill the pockets with lobster meat and close them. Season them again and roast the breasts, using soya margarine, for 20 minutes. Allow them to cool.

Wash and dry the green salad leaves. Mix the dressing ingredients in a bowl and use half to dress the salad.

To serve: on each of 4 plates, place a helping of green salad in the centre, and surround it with slices of chicken breast. Pour the remaining salad dressing over the salad portions. Garnish with tomato cubes and mixed herbs.     *Serves 4*     **WOLFGANG GROBAUER**

# Chicken Liver Salad and Mango with Soya Vinaigrette

| | |
|---|---|
| 1 ripe mango | 1 beef tomato, diced |
| 200 g (7 oz) chicken livers | 25 g (1 oz) cucumber, sliced |
| 75 g (3 oz) plain flour, seasoned with | |
| a little salt and pepper | FOR THE |
| 3 tbs soya oil | SOYA VINAIGRETTE DRESSING |
| | 5 tbs salad oil |
| FOR THE SALAD | 2 tbs soya oil |
| mixed leaves: oak leaves, radicchio, curly chicory, | 1 tsp Dijon mustard |
| wild chicory, endive, corn salad | 2 tbs sherry vinegar |
| 50 g (2 oz) pine kernels | juice of 1 lemon |
| a few leaves of chives, chopped | a pinch of salt and of ground pepper |

Liquidise all the dressing ingredients. Peel the mango and cut it into thin slices. Clean the chicken livers and remove the gall. Wash and pat them dry. Rub them in seasoned flour. Heat the oil and sauté the liver for 3–5 minutes. Remove and keep warm.

In the centre of 4 plates, arrange a nest of mixed salad leaves neatly. Put the liver and mango slices around it. Finally, sprinkle a little dressing on top and garnish with pine kernels, chives, tomato, and cucumber.
*Serves 4*
                                                                                    HUGH LANG

# Tomato, Onion, and Okra Salad

| | |
|---|---|
| 125 g (4 oz) 10-minute-cook | FOR THE SOYA DRESSING |
| long-grain rice | 2 tbs soya oil |
| 1 onion, chopped | 1 tbs red wine vinegar |
| 2 tomatoes, skinned, de-seeded, and chopped | 1 level tsp made Dijon mustard |
| 300 g (10 oz) fresh okra, trimmed | 1 small red chilli, de-seeded and chopped |
| a little salt | or a few drops of Tabasco |
| 2 sprigs of mint | a little salt and pepper |

*B*oil the rice according to the instructions on the packet. Drain and chill.

Liquidise the dressing ingredients.

Mix the onion, tomatoes, and cooked rice. Toss with the dressing. Meanwhile boil the okra for 10 minutes in salted water. Rinse it quickly and immerse it in iced water to bring back the green colour. Drain.

Either serve in individual bowls or in a large dish. Decorate the top with the cooked okra. Garnish with mint leaves.   *Serves 4–6*                                                        **DAVID FELLOWES**

# *T*IMBALE OF *A*UBERGINE ON A *B*ED OF *T*OMATO AND *P*EPPER *S*AUCE

| | |
|---|---|
| 3 firm young aubergines | 1 large red pepper, finely chopped |
| 4 shallots, finely chopped | 4 ripe tomatoes, blanched |
| 2 garlic cloves, crushed | 125 ml (4 fl oz) chicken stock |
| 3 tbs soya oil | 1 tbs coriander, chopped |
| 1 tsp ground cumin | 4 sprigs coriander |
| 1 dried chilli pepper | a little salt and pepper |
| 50 g (2 oz) flour | |

*H*eat the oven to Gas Mark 4/180°C/350°F. Peel and slice 2½ aubergines (save the rest for decoration); plunge in boiling salted water for 4–5 minutes. Transfer to a colander, squeeze, and leave to drain. Meanwhile, fry 2 shallots and the garlic in the oil. Increase the heat and add the aubergines. Season well with cumin, salt, pepper, and the chilli, sauté for 3 minutes and pass through a fine sieve. Pour the purée into a well-oiled dariole mould and keep it hot in a warm oven.

To make the sauce, fry the rest of the shallots and stir in the flour. Add the red pepper, tomato, and chicken stock, and reduce. Then season and liquidise, add the chopped coriander, and correct the seasoning. Unmould the purée into the centre of each plate and pour the sauce around. Decorate with the remaining aubergine, sliced and fried, and sprigs of coriander.

The mixture can be used as a filling for sandwiches and as a stuffing for meat and poultry dishes. It can be served hot or cold and can also be used as a dip.   *Serves 4*                              **MOHAMED DAHO**

# Lobster Salad Symphonika

| | |
|---|---|
| 1 × 750 g (1½ lb) lobster | 1 bunch of dill |
| 1 bouquet garni | 8 spring onions |
| 1 litre (1¾ pints) salted water | 4 tomatoes cut into roses (use outer part only) |
| | a little salt |
| **TO GARNISH** | |
| 4 asparagus spears, scraped lightly | **FOR THE DRESSING** |
| 1 tsp sugar | 3 tbs soya oil and olive oil, mixed |
| a few drops of lemon juice | 1 tsp Dijon mustard |
| 2 avocados | 2 tbs balsamico vinegar |
| mixture of salad leaves: curly lettuce, | juice of ½ lemon |
| radicchio, and endive | a little salt and pepper |

Boil the lobster with the bouquet garni in salted water for 8 minutes. Cool in iced water. Shell the lobster. Cut the tail into rounds and remove the meat from the claws. Boil the asparagus in water with a little salt, sugar, and lemon juice for 5 minutes. Refresh it in iced water and drain well. Liquidise the dressing ingredients. Marinate the lobster in the dressing for 5 minutes and then remove the lobster. Peel the avocados and cut them fanwise.

On each of 4 plates, arrange a nest of salad leaves on one side. Decorate with a few pieces of dill and with spring onions. Place 2 slices of lobster and one claw with a quarter of the avocado pieces on each plate. Put a tomato rose in the centre. Finally, sprinkle a little dressing over the salad leaves.
*Serves 4*

WALTER SUCHENTRUNK

# Octopus and Chick-pea Salad

| | |
|---|---|
| 125 g (4 oz) chick-peas, boiled until tender | **FOR THE** |
| 250 g (8 oz) piece of octopus, washed, and | **DRESSING** |
| beaten to soften the flesh | juice of 1 lemon |
| 4 large tomatoes, sliced laterally | 1 green chilli, chopped |
| 4 hard-boiled eggs | 3 tbs soya oil |
| 1 spring onion, chopped | 1 sprig of parsley, chopped |
| 1 green pepper, split, de-seeded, and chopped | 1 garlic clove, chopped |
| 16 black olives, stoned | 1 tsp made mustard |

Soak the chick-peas overnight and boil for 2 hours. Drain. Boil the octopus for 20 minutes until tender. Cut into slices and drain. Liquidise the dressing ingredients.

On each of 4 plates, arrange 4 pieces of tomato and 4 of egg. In the centre, place the chopped onion and pepper with the octopus slices. Decorate with black olives. Sprinkle half the dressing over the portions. Serve the remainder separately.    *Serves 4*                                              MOHAMED MECHECH

## SCOTCH SALMON SALAD WITH CELERIAC, APPLE, AND GRAPEFRUIT

| | |
|---|---|
| 1.5 kg (3½ lb) fresh Scottish salmon, filleted, | 2 tbs soya oil |
| with scraped skin attached | juice of 1 lime |
| 50 g (2 oz) coarse salt and 25 g (1 oz) castor sugar, mixed | a little salt and pepper |
| 12 peppercorns, crushed | |
| juice of 2 limes | TO GARNISH |
| 1 bunch of dill | 1 apple, cored and sliced into triangles, with peel on |
| | 1 grapefruit, segmented, with peel and pith removed |
| FOR THE DRESSING | 2 sticks of celery, thinly sliced |
| 100 ml (3½ fl oz) Arran mustard | 8 large lettuce leaves |
| 100 ml (3½ fl oz) sour cream | dill leaves for decoration |

The salmon is prepared raw like gravelax. Wash and pat the salmon fillets dry. Sprinkle the mixture of salt and sugar and the peppercorns over the flesh side of the 2 fillets. Place the first fillet skin downwards in a deep tray and sprinkle it with lime juice and dill leaves (which act as both preservative and flavouring). Cover with the other fillet, skin upwards like a sandwich. Leave to marinate for 48 hours under refrigeration. Baste from time to time with the liquid from the fish. To serve, carve, skin downwards, as if it were a side of smoked salmon.

Blend all the dressing ingredients together. Combine the apple, grapefruit, and celery, and toss in half of the dressing mixture. On each of 4 plates, arrange 2 lettuce leaves and on them place 2 spoons of the salad mixture. Put 1 slice of salmon beside the salad and decorate it with dill. Serve the remaining dressing separately.    *Serves 4*                                              RICHARD STURGEON

# Fried Chicken Drumsticks on Oriental Salad in Chilli Lime Dressing

*Pictured on page 142.*

| | |
|---|---|
| 20 chicken drumsticks | 1 tsp sugar |
| 300 ml (½ pint) soya oil | 1 tbs chopped coriander leaves |
| | 100 ml (3½ fl oz) water |
| FOR THE | (no salt is required as sauce is salty) |
| SPECIAL SPICE MIXTURE | |
| 1 tsp chopped garlic | FOR THE |
| 1 tsp ground turmeric | SALAD GARNISH |
| 1 tsp salt | 250 g (8 oz) assorted salad leaves: |
| 1 tsp ground chilli | radicchio, curly lettuce, watercress |
| 1 tsp ground coriander | or others according to availability |
| 250 g (8 oz) plain flour | 1 small cucumber, skin grooved with a fork |
| 250 g (8 oz) sesame seeds | 1 mango, peeled and sliced |
| | 8 small asparagus tips, |
| FOR THE | cooked so that they are crunchy |
| LIME DRESSING | 2 tomatoes, cut into wedges |
| 1 tsp Thai sauce or anchovy sauce | 2 hard-boiled eggs, halved |
| 1 green chilli, split, de-seeded, and chopped | 2 tbs bean sprouts or alfalfa sprouts |
| juice of 1 lime | 1 bunch of dill |

Mix all the spice mixture ingredients together thoroughly. Rub the chicken drumsticks in this dry mixture. Heat the oil in a shallow pan and deep-fry the drumsticks for 6 minutes until cooked through. Drain them well. Liquidise the dressing ingredients. Arrange on 4 plates an assortment of salad leaves. Decorate with sliced cucumber, mango, asparagus, tomato, and hard-boiled eggs. Sprinkle a little dressing over the garnish. Place 5 drumsticks per portion in a circle over the salad ingredients. Top with bean or alfalfa sprouts and dill leaves. *Serves 4*

**ANDREAS STALDER**

# Duck Strips with Vegetable Salad

| | |
|---|---|
| 250 g (8 oz) celeriac root, peeled, sliced and | FOR THE DRESSING |
| cut into strips 4 cm (1½ inches) long and matchstick thick | 3 tbs soya oil |
| 50 g (2 oz) each carrot and beetroot, | 1 tbs sherry vinegar |
| cut into strips | 1 tbs sour cream |
| 250 g (8 oz) breast of cooked duck, | ¼ tbs English mustard |
| cut into strips 4 cm (1½ inches) long and 6 cm (2½ inches) thick | 1 tsp redcurrant jelly |
| 2 tbs water | juice of ½ orange |
| 1 tbs white vinegar | a pinch of ground ginger |
| 4 large cos lettuce leaves | a little salt and pepper |

In a bowl, combine the vegetable strips with water and vinegar. Soak for 20 minutes and drain. In another bowl, blend together the duck meat and the vegetables.

Liquidise the dressing ingredients. Add the dressing to the mixture.

To serve, place 4 large cos lettuce leaves on each plate and top with the duck mixture.
*Serves 4*

KEITH STANLEY

# Chicken and Shrimp with Oriental Fruit Salad

| | |
|---|---|
| 150 g (5 oz) skinless breast of cooked chicken, sliced | 2 tbs peanuts |
| 150 g (5 oz) cooked shrimps, peeled and diced | 2 shallots, chopped |
| | 75 g (3 oz) green and red grapes, seeded |
| FOR THE | 75 g (3 oz) orange segments, skinless and thinly sliced |
| ORIENTAL FRUIT SALAD | 75 g (3 oz) dessert apples, cored and diced with peel on |
| 2 tbs lime juice | 75 g (3 oz) strawberries, halved |
| 1 tsp sugar and salt, mixed | 75 g (3 oz) lychees, stoned |
| 3 tbs soya oil | 75 g (3 oz) chestnuts, diced |
| 2 garlic cloves, sliced | |

To make the Oriental fruit salad, mix the lime juice, the salt and sugar, and blend with 2 tbs of the oil. Heat the remaining oil and stir-fry the garlic, peanuts, and shallots until golden. In a salad bowl, gently toss all the fruits, the chestnuts, and half the shrimps with the dressing. *Serves 4* CHALIE AMATYAKUL

# CELERIAC FRITTER ROLLS STUFFED WITH WILD MUSHROOMS

*Celeriac is a member of the celery family. Celery root can be used as an alternative in this recipe.*

| | |
|---|---|
| 2 medium-size celeriac | 4 strands of saffron |
| 500 ml ( 1 pint ) water | 1 egg, beaten |
| 1 tbs vinegar | a little salt and pepper |
| 1 egg yolk and 2 tbs water for egg wash | |
| 75 g ( 3 oz ) plain flour | TO GARNISH |
| 300 ml ( 2 pint ) soya oil | radicchio, curly lettuce, spinach, endive, and watercress leaves |

| FOR THE FILLING | FOR THE DRESSING |
|---|---|
| 3 tbs soya oil | 3 tbs soya oil |
| 2 shallots, chopped | 1 tbs yogurt |
| 1 garlic clove, chopped | 5 tbs pineapple juice |
| 450 g ( 15 oz ) assorted wild mushrooms | 15 g ( ½ oz ) fresh almonds, skinned |
| (ceps, giroles, chanterelles, field mushrooms), | 10 g ( ½ oz ) green olives, peeled |
| all washed, pat dried, and chopped coarsely | 1 tbs chopped parsley and mint leaves |
| 3 tbs breadcrumbs or nuts | a little salt and black pepper |
| 100 ml ( 3½ fl oz ) double cream | a pinch of chilli |

Scrub, wash, peel, and slice the celeriac, and immediately immerse it in cold water and vinegar to prevent it from browning. Prepare the stuffing while the celeriac is soaking. Heat the oil in a pan and stir-fry the shallots and garlic for 30 seconds. Add the mushrooms and cook for 4 minutes. Be sure to evaporate all the juices. When the mixture is dried, add the breadcrumbs or nuts. Season to taste and blend in the cream and saffron. Boil for 3 more minutes. Add the beaten egg and scramble the mixture to bind it. Remove from the heat and cool.

Pat all the celeriac slices dry. Use them like pastry rounds or pancakes: spread 3 slices overlapping each other to form a circle of 18 cm (7 inches) in diameter. Seal the circle with egg wash to glue the 3 slices together. Place 2 spoonfuls of the mushroom mixture on top, fold over, and wrap like a cylindrical parcel. Make 3 more parcels in the same way. Roll each in flour and the remaining egg wash. Heat the oil and deep-fry them for 1 minute until golden. Drain them well on kitchen paper.

Liquidise the dressing ingredients in a blender. Arrange a mixture of salad leaves on 4 plates. Place 1 roll on each. Serve the dressing separately. *Serves 4*      **JEAN CONIL**

# Ethnic and Modern Sauces

*L*ong before the great French sauces emerged in their ultimate perfection, the people of Eastern countries knew that their own fragrant plants were ideal for flavouring their foods. The plants that yield spices are the nucleus of all Oriental sauces. Soya is also much used in the East as the provider of protein and as an equivalent to dairy products.

## Chilli Vinaigrette

| |
|---|
| 3 tbs mirin (sweet rice wine) |
| 7 g (¼ oz) red chillies, de-seeded and chopped |
| 25 g (1 oz) each red, green, and yellow pepper, de-seeded and diced |
| 1 tbs soya sauce |
| 3 tbs soya oil |
| juice of 1 lime |
| 2 tbs rice vinegar |
| 1 clove garlic, chopped |
| 15 g (½ oz) fresh ginger, chopped |

*H*eat the sweet wine and set it alight. Add the chillies and peppers. Cool and then liquidise with the other ingredients. Add salt to taste.

## Wasabi Condiment

| | |
|---|---|
| 1½ tbs wasabi powder (dried Japanese horseradish) | 4 strands chives, chopped |
| 2 tbs rice vinegar | 1 tbs chopped ginger |
| 2 tbs soya oil | 2 cloves garlic, chopped |
| 3 spring onions, chopped | 300 g (10 oz) soya margarine |
| ½ bunch coriander or watercress, chopped | |

*S*oak the wasabi (horseradish) in the vinegar. Blend all ingredients together except the margarine, in a liquidiser. Add the soft margarine, and mix to a paste. Roll the paste into a cylindrical shape 2 cm (¾ inch) in diameter, and wrap it in greaseproof paper. Freeze. To use, cut into thick slices and serve with grilled or fresh fish, poultry, or meat. This is a tastier paste than parsley butter, which is used similarly.          **HOWARD BULKA**

# Chilli Plum Sauce

*Pictured on the back cover and page 141.*

| |
|---|
| 2 tbs soya oil |
| 1 garlic clove, finely chopped |
| 1 tsp fresh chopped ginger |
| 25 g (1 oz) onion, chopped |
| 250 g (8 oz) red or black plums, stoned |
| 300 ml (½ pint) water |
| 1 small chilli pepper, split, de-seeded, and chopped |
| 1 beef stock cube |
| 2 tsp cornflour and 4 tbs water, mixed in a cup for thickening |
| a little salt |

Heat the oil and stir-fry the garlic, ginger and onion for 30 seconds. Add the plums and cook for 5 minutes. Stir in the water, the chilli, and the crumbled stock cube. Boil for 10 minutes and strain through a fine sieve. Thicken by adding the cornflour mixture and boiling for 4 minutes. Season to taste with salt. Use hot or cold.

# Pork Sauce

| |
|---|
| 250 g (8 oz) red and green sweet peppers |
| 2 tbs soya oil |
| 125 g (4 oz) lean unsmoked bacon rashers, cut into thin strips |
| 1 tbs tomato purée |
| 300 ml (½ pint) water |
| 2 tbs sugar or honey |
| 1 tbs saké or sherry vinegar |
| 2 tsp cornflour and 4 tbs water, mixed in a cup for thickening |
| salt to taste |

Split the peppers, remove the seeds and cut into matchstick-thin strips. Heat the oil and stir-fry the peppers and the bacon strips for 3 minutes. Add the tomato purée, water, sugar or honey, and saké or vinegar, and boil for 5 minutes. Season with salt. Thicken the sauce with the cornflour mixture and cook for 4 more minutes. Serve with barbecued pork or spare ribs.

# Pekin Sweet and Sour Sauce

| |
|---|
| 100 g (3½ oz) syrup, sugar, or lime cordial |
| 100 ml (3½ fl oz) cider, rice vinegar, or sherry vinegar |
| 300 ml (½ pint) water, or vegetable or chicken stock |
| 2 tbs tomato purée |
| 1 tbs cornflour and 4 tbs water, mixed in a cup for thickening |
| a little salt |
| a pinch of pepper or chilli powder |

Boil the syrup, sugar or lime, cider or vinegar, and water or stock for 3 minutes. Dissolve the tomato purée in this mixture. Boil for 5 more minutes and thicken with the cornflour mixture until smooth and shiny. Season to taste. Note that lime cordial can be used instead of syrup or sugar.

# Basic Curry Sauce

*Pictured on the back cover and page 141.*

| |
|---|
| 1 tsp mustard seeds |
| 1 pinch cinnamon |
| 1 pinch fenugreek seed |
| 2.5 cm (1 inch) green ginger, chopped |
| 1 red chilli, de-seeded and chopped |
| 2 tbs soya oil |
| 1 medium onion, chopped |
| 1 garlic clove, crushed |
| 1 tbs tomato purée |
| 600 ml (1 pint) vegetable, fish, meat, or poultry stock, or water |
| a little salt |

Pound, chop, grate, or grind the first 5 ingredients before using them. Heat the oil and stir-fry the onion and garlic for 2 minutes on low heat. Sprinkle them with the aromatic spices. Cook for 30 seconds and then add the tomato purée and stock. Boil for 15 minutes, adjust the seasoning, and strain.

The sauce can be thickened with cornflour mixed with water, with roux, or with lentil flour or purée. It can be made more mellow by adding yogurt, or be given a fuller flavour by including grated fresh coconut. It can be made more acid by using lime, pineapple, or lemon juice. Western cooks add double cream for chicken or fish dishes.

# Hong Kong Lime Sauce

*Pictured on the back cover and page 141.*

| |
|---|
| 300 ml ( ½ pint ) chicken stock |
| 1 tsp ground turmeric |
| 1 tsp chopped green ginger |
| 2 tsp cornflour or rice starch, mixed with 4 tbs water in a cup for thickening |
| grated zest and juice of 1 lime |
| 2 tbs honey |
| 1 tbs sherry vinegar |
| a little salt and pepper |

Boil the chicken stock with the turmeric and ginger for 10 minutes. Thicken the sauce with the cornflour or rice starch mixture and cook for 4 minutes. Boil the grated lime zest with the honey and lime juice until it is almost dry: the zest will then be crystallised. Add it to the sauce, add the sherry vinegar, and season to taste. Soya sauce may be added for extra flavour.

# Chinese Watermelon Salad Dressing

*Pictured on the back cover and page 140.*

| |
|---|
| 150 g ( 5 oz ) red melon pulp |
| 1 tbs saké or sherry vinegar, plus extra if wished |
| 2 tbs soya oil |
| 1 small piece of ginger |
| a little salt and pepper |
| 1 tsp honey |
| juice of 1 orange |

Liquidise all the ingredients except the seasoning, which should be added afterwards to taste. The acidity can be increased with extra vinegar if wished.

Use for cold fish or salad vegetables.

# Israeli Hazeret Sauce

*Pictured on the back cover and page 140.*

| |
|---|
| 250 g (8 oz) baked or boiled beetroot, peeled and diced |
| 50 g (2 oz) fresh grated horseradish |
| 1 small shallot, chopped |
| 1 garlic clove, chopped |
| 100 ml (3½ fl oz) wine or fruit vinegar |
| a little salt and pepper |

Combine all the ingredients except the seasoning and liquidise. Add salt and pepper to taste. Dilute with either stock or yogurt, depending on the use. For kosher cookery, omit the yogurt; use cornflour instead to thicken the sauce slightly: add cornflour mixed with water and reboil the mixture for 5 minutes.

# Chinese Oyster Sauce

| |
|---|
| 2 tbs soya oil |
| 1 small shallot, chopped |
| 4 smoked oysters (or fresh oysters if available), chopped |
| 300 ml (½ pint) fish stock, or water |
| 3 tbs dry sherry |
| 1 tbs lemon juice |
| 1 tbs soya sauce |
| 2 tsp cornflour and 4 tbs water, mixed in a cup for thickening |
| a little salt and pepper |

Heat the oil and stir-fry the shallot and the oysters for 2 minutes. Stir in the fish stock or water, add the sherry, lemon juice, and soya sauce and boil for 12 minutes. Thicken with the cornflour mixture and boil for 4 minutes more. Season and strain.

# CREOLE SAUCE

*Pictured on the back cover and page 140.*

| | |
|---|---|
| 3 tbs soya oil | 4 tomatoes, skinned, de-seeded, and chopped |
| 1 medium onion, chopped | 300 ml ( ½ pint ) water or any stock |
| 2 garlic cloves, chopped | 1 tbs vinegar |
| 1 red pepper, de-seeded and chopped | seasoning to taste |
| 1 green chilli, de-seeded and chopped | |

Heat the oil and stir-fry all the vegetables for 4 minutes. Add the water or stock and vinegar and simmer for 20 minutes. Season to taste. Serve with poultry, fish, pasta, or rice dishes.

# PUMPKIN SAUCE

*Pictured on the back cover and page 141.*

| | |
|---|---|
| 2 tbs soya oil | 1 tsp ginger, chopped |
| 150 g ( 5 oz ) red pumpkin pulp | 1 tsp honey |
| 1 medium onion, chopped | juice of 1 lemon |
| 300 ml ( ½ pint ) stock or water or milk | a little salt and pepper |

Heat the oil and stir-fry the vegetables until soft. Add the water and spices and season to taste. Add the honey and lemon juice last. Serve with roast turkey or other poultry dishes.

# FERMENTED SOYA SAUCE

*Soya is made from toasted soya beans and wheat and is preserved in salt.*

| | |
|---|---|
| 225 g ( 7½ oz ) soya beans | 225 g ( 7½ oz ) malt syrup or honey |
| 50 g ( 2 oz ) peanuts, toasted | 10 g ( 1⅓ oz ) brewer's yeast |
| 2 litres ( 3½ pints ) water | 100 g ( 3½ oz ) salt |
| 225 g ( 7½ oz ) crushed wheat or millet | |

*S*oak the beans overnight in 4 times their volume of water. Drain them well. Bake them in the oven, preheated to Gas Mark 7/220°C/425°F, until golden brown. Add the peanuts. Grind the mixture with a rolling pin or pestle and mortar. Blend this mixture with the water. Liquidise. Add the crushed wheat or millet, the malt syrup or honey, and the yeast. Pour into a 4.5 litre (1-gallon) jar. Seal the top and keep at room temperature. Leave to ferment for 10 days.

Strain the mixture through a muslin cloth. Re-boil it for 5 minutes to evaporate the alcohol. Dissolve the salt in this mixture while it is boiling. Cool and bottle, corking the bottles tightly.

# Jamaican Pawpaw Sauce

*Pictured on the back cover and page 140.*

| |
|---|
| 1 large ripe pawpaw, peeled, de-seeded, and chopped |
| 300 ml ( ½ pint ) water |
| juice of 1 lime and 1 lemon |
| 1 tbs honey or syrup |
| 1 pinch of mixed spices |
| a little salt and pepper |

*B*oil all the ingredients except the seasoning for 5 minutes and liquidise to a purée. Adjust the seasoning.

Serve with roast duck or pork dishes.

# Tunisian Charmoula Sauce with Raisins

*Pictured on the back cover and page 141.*

| |
|---|
| 550 ml ( 19 fl oz ) soya oil |
| 500 g ( 1 lb ) onions, chopped |
| 1.5 kg ( 3½ lb ) seedless raisins |
| 50 g ( 2 oz ) harisa |
| 1 tsp salt |

*H*eat the oil in a frying-pan and shallow-fry the onion till soft. Add the raisins, harisa and salt. Cook for 10 minutes. Remove from the heat and cool. When cold, store in jars. This sauce can be used with fish, and it can be diluted to make a thinner sauce, if wished, with stock.

# Satay Sauce

*Pictured on the back cover and page 141.*

| | |
|---|---|
| 2 tbs soya oil | 1 tsp curry powder |
| 1 small onion, chopped | 1 tbs sweet sherry |
| 2 tbs soya sauce | 300 ml (½ pint) water or beef stock |
| 2 tbs toasted peanuts, ground | juice of ½ lime |
| (or use peanut butter) | 2 tsp cornflour and 4 tbs water, |
| 1 small chilli, de-seeded and chopped | mixed in a cup for thickening |
| 1 tbs tomato purée | a little salt |

Heat the oil and stir-fry the onion for 2 minutes until soft. Add all the remaining ingredients except the cornflour mixture and the salt. Boil for 15 minutes. Thicken with the cornflour mixture and boil to clear the starch for 4 minutes. Strain and adjust the seasoning.

# Cyprus Salad Dressing

| | |
|---|---|
| 100 ml (3½ fl oz) soya oil | 2 tbs chopped fresh mint, |
| mixed with 4 stoned green olives | or oregano and parsley |
| juice of 1 lemon and grated zest of ¼ lemon | a little salt and pepper |

Liquidise all the ingredients except the seasoning, which is added at the end according to taste.

# Turkish Hazelnut Sauce

| | |
|---|---|
| 3 tbs soya oil | 1 tbs water |
| 250 g (8 oz) hazelnuts, skinned | 5 tbs yogurt |
| 2 garlic cloves, chopped (optional) | 1 tbs wine vinegar |
| 150 g (5 oz) breadcrumbs | a little salt and pepper |

Heat the oil and fry the hazelnuts until golden. Add the garlic (if wanted) and fry for 1 minute. Blend in the breadcrumbs and cook for 30 seconds until crisp. Remove from heat and liquidise with the water and yogurt. Season to taste. Finally, add the vinegar. Lemon juice can be used instead of vinegar, and any other nuts can be used instead of hazelnuts. Serve with fish or vegetables.

## Green Mexican Sauce

*Pictured on the back cover and page 140.*

| |
|---|
| 1 green chilli, de-seeded |
| 1 small bunch of chives or spring onions, chopped |
| 2 garlic cloves, chopped |
| 4 spinach leaves, chopped |
| 3 mint leaves, chopped |
| 1 tbs sugar |
| 300 g ( 100 oz ) green tomatoes |
| a little salt |

Liquidise all the ingredients except the salt, which is added afterwards to taste. Use the sauce with meat or spread it on tortillas.

## Pineapple Sauce for Duck

| | |
|---|---|
| 2 tbs soya oil | a little salt |
| 1 small onion, chopped | 2 tbs sweet sherry |
| 1 garlic clove, chopped | 1 tbs sherry vinegar |
| 1 small piece of ginger, peeled and chopped | 1 tbs honey |
| 4 slices of fresh pineapple, chopped | 1 chicken stock cube |
| 300 ml ( ½ pint ) water | 2 tsp cornflour and 4 tbs water, mixed in a cup for thickening |
| 1 small green chilli, de-seeded and chopped | 1 tbs soya sauce |

Heat the soya oil in a pan and stir-fry the onion, garlic, and ginger for 3 minutes. Add the pineapple and water and cook for 10 minutes. Liquidise the sauce and reboil it. Add the chilli, salt, sherry, sherry vinegar, honey, and the stock cube. Boil for 4 minutes. Thicken the sauce with the cornflour mixture and cook for another 3–4 minutes until glossy. Lastly, add soya sauce to adjust the taste.

# ALMOND AND LIME SAUCE

*Pictured on the back cover and page 140.*

| | |
|---|---|
| 2 tbs soya oil | 4 strands of saffron |
| 1 medium onion, chopped | 100 g ( 3½ oz ) skinned almonds |
| 1 garlic clove, chopped | 150 ml ( ¼ pint ) water |
| 1 small piece of ginger, peeled and chopped | 1 × 100 ml ( 3½ fl oz ) carton of yogurt |
| 1 tsp toasted ground poppy seeds | juice of 2 limes or 1 lemon |
| 1 cardamom seed, crushed | a little salt and pepper |
| 2 tbs snipped chives | |

Heat the oil and stir-fry the onion, garlic, and ginger for 3 minutes. Add the poppy seeds, cardamom seed, chives, saffron, almonds, and water. Boil for 12 minutes and liquidise. Season to taste, and blend in the yogurt and lime or lemon juice. Strain the sauce.

Serve with lamb kebabs or with pawpaws and fried chicken livers.               CLAUDE ROMAGNOSI

# RED MEXICO TURKEY SAUCE

| | |
|---|---|
| 1 red pepper, split, de-seeded, and chopped | 2 tbs cornmeal, toasted, or crumbled tortillas |
| 1 red and 1 green chilli, de-seeded and chopped | 2 large tomatoes, skinned, de-seeded, |
| 1 sweet red onion, chopped | and chopped |
| 2 garlic cloves, chopped | 300 ml ( ½ pint ) water or chicken stock |
| 3 tbs soya oil | 1 tbs cocoa powder or 15 g ( ½ oz ) unsweetened |
| 1 pinch each of cinnamon, aniseed, and | chocolate, diluted in a little warm water |
| coriander seeds | a little salt |
| 100 g ( 3½ oz ) nibbed almonds | 50 g ( 2 oz ) seedless raisins or sultanas |

In a large sauté pan, stir-fry the pepper, chillies, onion, and garlic for 5 minutes in the oil. Add the spices, the almonds and the cornmeal or tortillas. Cook for 3 minutes and then add the tomatoes and the water or stock. Simmer for 4 minutes. Add the diluted cocoa or chocolate to the sauce. Season with salt to taste.

Serve with sautéd turkey escalopes or fried turkey strips. The dish may be garnished with seedless raisins or sultanas.

Top left: *Chestnut Mousse in a Biscuit Cup (page 198)*, top right: *Jerusalem Artichoke Ice Cream Cake (page 186)*, below left: *Apple Fritters with Caramel Sauce (page 193)*, *Gratin of Honey with Pine Kernels (page 184)*

*Biscuit Basket with Summer Fruit (page 187)*

# Jerusalem Raisin Sauce

| | |
|---|---|
| 3 tbs soya oil | a little salt, pepper, cinnamon, and ginger |
| 1 small onion, chopped | |
| 1 tbs honey | TO GARNISH |
| 300 ml (½ pint) meat stock | 125 g (4 oz) seedless raisins |
| 1 tbs wine or vinegar | |

Heat the oil and stir-fry the onion until soft. Add the honey and stock. Boil for 15 minutes and strain. Season to taste and garnish with raisins. Add the wine or vinegar last.

Serve with boiled beef or tongue.

# Turnip Sauce

| |
|---|
| 3 tbs soya oil |
| 1 onion, chopped |
| 500 g (1 lb) turnip, peeled and chopped |
| 600 ml (1 pint) chicken or white meat stock |
| 1 tbs sugar |
| juice and grated zest of 1 lemon |
| 5 tbs cream or yogurt |
| a little salt and pepper |

Heat the oil and stir-fry the onion and turnip, without browning, on low heat for 5 minutes. Add the stock, the sugar, and the lemon juice and zest, and boil for 12 minutes until tender. Liquidise the sauce. Strain it, reheat, and blend in the cream or yogurt. Season to taste.

Serve with poultry or wild fowl.

# Dominican Uncooked Tomato and Pepper Sauce

| | |
|---|---|
| 5 tbs soya oil | 1 green chilli, de-seeded and chopped |
| 2 tbs cider vinegar | 2 garlic cloves, chopped |
| 4 large tomatoes, skinned, de-seeded, and chopped | a little salt and pepper |
| 1 red or green pepper, split, de-seeded, and chopped | |

Combine all the ingredients in a bowl. Marinate for 2 hours. Serve as a dressing for roasted chicken, grilled fish, or meat.

# Chakah Afghanistan Yogurt Sauce

| |
|---|
| 300 ml (½ pint) yogurt |
| 2 tbs chopped fresh mint leaves |
| 1 small green chilli, de-seeded and chopped |
| 1 tbs chopped coriander leaves |
| a little salt |

Combine all the ingredients, adding the salt to taste at the end. Use with pasta or vegetables.

# Muscovite Sauce

| |
|---|
| 2 tbs soya oil |
| 1 tbs plain flour |
| 600 ml (1 pint) stock, strongly flavoured with onion |
| 1 bouquet garni, including fennel greens |
| 100 ml (3½ fl oz) sour cream |
| a little salt and pepper |

Heat the oil and cook the flour on low heat for 2 minutes until it is a pale colour. Add the stock gradually and the bouquet garni, and simmer the sauce for 20 minutes. Strain. Blend in the sour cream and season to taste. Strain the sauce again.

## Guacamole Sauce

| |
|---|
| 1 small onion, chopped |
| 1 large tomato, skinned, de-seeded, and chopped |
| 1 ripe avocado, peeled and stoned |
| 1 green chilli, de-seeded and chopped |
| juice of 1 lime and some grated zest |
| a little salt |

Liquidise all the ingredients and serve as a dressing. Alternatively, combine the first 4 ingredients and serve as an accompaniment to corn dishes or salads.

## Chilli Sauce

| |
|---|
| 1 fresh green chilli, de-seeded and finely chopped |
| 1 garlic clove, chopped |
| 1 medium red onion, chopped |
| 3 small sprigs of coriander or parsley, chopped |
| 2 tbs wine or fruit vinegar |
| 3 tbs soya oil |
| 3 tbs water |
| a little salt |
| a little sugar |
| a little tomato purée (optional) |

Liquidise all the ingredients except the salt and sugar, which are added afterwards to taste. The colour can be enriched by adding a little tomato purée.

# Tamari Sauce

| |
|---|
| 500 ml ( 18 fl oz ) vegetable stock |
| 3 tbs Tamari or yeast extract |
| 2 tbs soya oil |
| 1 tbs wholemeal flour |
| a little pepper |

Bring the vegetable stock to the boil and dissolve in it the Tamari or yeast extract. In a saucepan, heat the oil and cook the flour for 4 minutes until it is slightly brown. Gradually stir in the hot stock and cook for 15 minutes. Strain and add pepper according to taste.

# Tokyo Peanut Dressing

| |
|---|
| 2 tbs soya oil |
| 1 garlic clove, chopped |
| 100 g ( 3½ oz ) salted peanuts |
| 1 small red chilli, de-seeded and chopped |
| 1 small piece of ginger, peeled and chopped |
| 50 g ( 2 oz ) prawns, peeled |
| 300 ml ( ½ pint ) water, or any kind of stock |
| 1 tbs honey or sugar |
| juice and grated zest of 1 lime |

Heat the oil and stir-fry the garlic, peanuts, chilli, and ginger for 4 minutes. Add the prawns and after 1 minute stir in the water or stock. Add the honey or sugar and the lime juice and zest. Boil for 12 minutes and liquidise. Strain through a coarse sieve or conical strainer. Serve with vegetables, fish, or chicken.

# Sweet and Sour Desserts

Centuries before European cooks knew how to make ice cream or how to crystallise fruits, rose petal sherbets and chilled fruit beverages were appreciated at the courts of Chinese and Indian kings and emperors. All the princes of the Orient entertained with style, and bowls of the most exotic fruits were served fresh or candied with nuts. Fruits were also made into sweetmeats, fritters, halvas, and nougats.

Modern ethnic confectionery has become more sophisticated. There are now desserts with a rich protein content, such as pancakes filled with red kidney beans in avocado and pear syrup, coconut mousse served with guava fruit, and rice flour cakes. A new range of tropical sherbets, or sorbets as they are called today, is served in many international hotels.

In this, the last chapter, we invite you to sample the best of the new desserts. We also present a few of the old favourites in somewhat modified formats. Bear in mind, though, that over-indulgence in sugary sweets is not recommended. Sugar is converted to fat in your body unless you burn the calories as fast as you acquire them.

Here are a few preliminary notes on making ice cream and sorbet. Usually sorbets are textured with egg whites; another method is to use agar (seaweed gelatine). The factor that controls the texture in ices is the sugar content: with too little sugar, you will have a hard product like lollipop; with too much, your ice cream will not freeze. Usually the right proportion is 40–50 per cent sugar.

# Gaufres du Nord

| | |
|---|---|
| 2 tbs soya oil for greasing | 150 g (5 oz) soya margarine |
| 50 g (2 oz) icing sugar, flavoured with a vanilla pod | 1 egg white |
| | 100 g (3½ oz) caster sugar |
| FOR THE DOUGH | grated zest of ¼ lemon |
| 250 g (8 oz) self-raising flour | 1 pinch of salt |

Mix all the dough ingredients in a bowl to produce a soft dough firm enough to be rolled into a ball. Rest the dough for 30 minutes, then divide it into 8 balls. Grease a hot waffle iron with oil and place on it a small ball of dough. The machine will flatten it to the right shape. Cook for 2–3 minutes until golden on both sides. Remove and dust with vanilla-flavoured icing sugar. These are very popular with children.

*Serves 6*

**PIERRE CONIL**

# Malaysian Sweet Potato and Yam Pudding

| |
|---|
| 500 ml ( 18 fl oz ) cold water |
| 50 g ( 2 oz ) sago, rinsed in cold water |
| 600 ml ( 1 pint ) lukewarm water, plus extra water if required |
| 2 mature coconuts, grated |
| 500 g ( 1 lb ) yam, peeled and diced into 1 cm ( ½-inch ) cubes |
| 500 g ( 1 lb ) sweet potatoes, peeled and diced into 1 cm ( ½-inch ) cubes |
| 6 lengths of pandanus, mint or lemon mint leaves, tied into a knot |
| 125 g ( 4 oz ) fresh kidney beans, rinsed in cold water |
| 50 g ( 2 oz ) sugar or palm syrup to taste |
| 50 g ( 2 oz ) soya margarine |

In a small, deep pan, bring the cold water to the boil. Add the sago and bring it back to the boil while stirring so that the mixture does not stick. Cook for 15 minutes until soft. Set aside.

Add the lukewarm water to the grated coconut. Strain the milk after 15 minutes' soaking. Repeat this operation twice to extract the maximum flavour from the grated coconut. Set the coconut milk aside.

Place the diced yam, sweet potatoes, pandanus leaves, and the coconut milk in a pan. Bring to the boil. Simmer the ingredients until soft, and drain. Keep the liquid left over and cook the kidney beans in it for 20 minutes. Add extra water if the liquid evaporates too fast. Mix together the sago and the yam and potato mixture. Blend in the sugar or syrup and the soya margarine. Remove the pandanus leaves.

Serve heaped on small plates, together with slices of carambola (star-fruit) or mango.
*Serves 4*

SOO PENG WAH

# Bali Pumpkin Cake with Raisins

| | |
|---|---|
| 750 g ( 1½ lb ) pumpkin pulp, diced | 1 tsp ground cinnamon |
| 300 ml ( ½ pint ) water | |
| 5 eggs, beaten | FOR THE SWEET SHORT PASTRY |
| 50 g ( 2 oz ) maizena ( cornmeal ) | 450 g ( 15 oz ) soya margarine, softened, plus extra for greasing |
| 250 g ( 8 oz ) brown sugar | 250 g ( 8 oz ) icing sugar, sifted |
| 5 g ( ¼ oz ) salt | 750 g ( 1½ lb ) self-raising flour |
| 50 g ( 2 oz ) seedless raisins | 2 eggs, beaten |

*B*oil the pumpkin with the water until soft. Cool and place in a mixer. Add the beaten eggs, maizena, sugar, and salt. Heat the oven to Gas Mark 6/200°C/400°F. Cream the margarine and icing sugar until fluffy. Blend in the flour and finally add the eggs to make the mixture into a stiff dough. Take 50 g (2 oz) of this dough and blend it with the pumpkin filling. Now roll out the remaining dough on a floured board to 4 mm (¼-inch) thickness. Place on a greased shallow tray or flan tin. Sprinkle with the raisins and ground cinnamon and then add the pumpkin mixture. Bake for 45 minutes. Serve cold, with a custard sauce or ice cream.

*Serves 8*                                                                                      **PETER DAVIS**

## SOUFFLÉ WITH WILD STRAWBERRIES

| | |
|---|---|
| 150 ml (¼ pint) single cream | 2 tbs water |
| 25 g (1 oz) cornflour or fecula | 5 egg whites |
| 10 g (⅓ oz) gelatine leaves | |
| 5 egg yolks | FOR THE APRICOT COULIS |
| 50 g (2 oz) caster sugar | 150 g (5 oz) apricot pulp |
| 125 ml (4 fl oz) lemon juice, strained | 50 g (2 oz) sugar |
| a little soya oil, for greasing | 75 ml (3 fl oz) water |
| a little icing sugar, sifted | 1 small tea bag |
| | |
| FOR THE COOKED MERINGUE | TO GARNISH |
| 125 g (4 oz) caster sugar | 250 g (8 oz) wild strawberries |

*B*oil the cream, reserving a little. Thicken it with cornflour which has been mixed in a cup with the reserved cream. Cook for 5 minutes. Soak the gelatine in water. In a metal bowl, over a pan of hot water, whisk the egg yolks, sugar, and lemon juice for 5 minutes until smooth and creamy. Gradually add the thickened cream while it is still hot. Add the gelatine to the hot mixture, stirring it in gently.

To prepare the meringue, boil the sugar and water to a syrup until it reaches 120°C/225°F on a sugar thermometer. Allow the mixture to cool.

In a bowl, beat the egg whites. When the syrup has cooled to 80°C/180°F, gradually pour in the syrup. Now combine the custard and the meringue, stirring gently.

Place 4 small circular flan rings, well greased, on a tray lined with greased paper. Fill these rings to the brim with the mixture. Freeze for at least 4 hours. When ready to serve, remove from the freezer. Take off the rings and sprinkle each with icing sugar. Place each soufflé under a heated grill for a few seconds to colour it and then in a microwave oven on High for 1 minute to swell the soufflé. Boil the apricot pulp, sugar, and water for 4 minutes. Add the tea bag and leave it for 5 minutes before removing it. Liquidise the apricot mixture to a thin purée sauce. Pour a pool of apricot coulis onto each plate. Decorate with wild strawberries.

*Serves 4*                                                                                      **YVES THURIES**

# Lavender Ice Cream

| | |
|---|---|
| 1 tsp lavender flowers or seeds | a little soya oil, for greasing |
| 60 g ( 2½ oz ) caster sugar | |
| 250 ml ( 8 fl oz ) fresh full cream milk | TO GARNISH |
| 3 tbs double cream | 4 curved Langues de Chat (see page 186) |
| 3 egg yolks | several mint leaves |
| 25 g ( 1 oz ) granulated sugar | 4 sprigs fresh lavender flowers |

Grind the lavender flowers or seeds with the caster sugar. Blend the milk and cream together and bring to the boil. In a bowl, beat the egg yolks with the granulated sugar and lavender sugar until thick over a saucepan of hot water. When the mixture is thick, gradually pour the milk into the egg mixture. Strain the mixture. Line an oblong ice-cream mould with paper previously greased with oil. Fill with the mixture and freeze for 3 hours.

Arrange 1 Langue de Chat on each of 4 plates along with a slice of the ice cream. Decorate with mint leaves and a sprig of fresh lavender flowers.    *Serves 4*                                                      ROGER VERGÉ

# Gratin of Honey with Pine Kernels

*Pictured on page 175.*

| | |
|---|---|
| 4 egg yolks | FOR THE MERINGUE |
| 35 g ( 1½ oz ) granulated sugar | 4 egg whites |
| 90 ml ( 3 fl oz ) liquid honey | 35 g ( 1½ oz ) granulated sugar |
| 20 g ( ¾ oz ) cornflour | |
| juice of 1 lemon | TO GARNISH |
| 500 ml ( 18 fl oz ) single cream, brought to boiling point | 125 g ( 4 oz ) pine kernels, toasted |
| 2 gelatine leaves, soaked in cold water for 30 seconds and drained | a little icing sugar, sifted |
| a little soya oil, for greasing | 125 ml ( 4fl oz ) whipping cream |

In a bowl, whip the egg yolks and sugar for about 5 minutes until thick. Heat the honey till it is boiling hot, and pour over in a stream, beating all the time. Add the cornflour, lemon juice, and boiled cream. Reheat the mixture gently until it begins to thicken like a custard. Remove from heat and dissolve the soaked gelatine in this hot mixture.

In a separate bowl, whip the egg whites until thick for the meringue. Blend in the sugar gradually.

Combine the custard and meringue mixtures.

Grease four 8 cm (3-inch) rings and place them on a tray lined with greased paper. Fill the rings with the mixture. Freeze for 15 minutes. Remove the rings and transfer the ices onto 4 plates. Sprinkle each with pine kernels and dust with icing sugar. Glaze under a heated grill for a few seconds.

Decorate with rosettes of whipped cream.      *Serves 4*                                     **ROGER VERGÉ**

# CHEESE PUDDINGS WITH CLOUDBERRY SAUCE

*Pictured on page 34.*

| 2 egg yolks | FOR THE CLOUDBERRY SAUCE | |
|---|---|---|
| 75 g (3 oz) sugar | 250 g (8 oz) cloudberries | |
| 6 drops of vanilla essence | 50 g (2 oz) icing sugar | |
| 150 ml (¼ pint) milk | 5 tbs water | |
| 4 gelatine leaves, soaked in water 30 seconds (pat dry) | | |
| 250 g (8 oz) cream cheese | TO GARNISH | |
| 150 ml (¼ pint) whipping cream or soya margarine, whipped | 4 lemon grass leaves | |
| a little soya oil, for greasing | a few cloudberries | |

Whip the egg yolks, sugar, and vanilla in a bowl. Parboil the milk and gradually pour it into the egg mixture. Reheat and gently bring the mixture to boiling point, without exceeding it, while whisking. When the mixture coats the back of a spoon, it is thick enough. Remove it from the heat and dissolve the soaked gelatine in the mixture.

Cool the mixture and blend in the cream cheese. Finally fold in the whipped cream. Grease 4 individual moulds and fill them with the mixture. Set in the refrigerator for 1 hour.

To make the cloudberry sauce, liquidise the cloudberries with sugar and water and strain.

Pour a pool of sauce of 4 plates. Unmould the cheese puddings and place one on each plate. Decorate with lemon grass leaves and a few cloudberries.      *Serves 4*                         **EËRO MÄKELÄ**

# Jerusalem Artichoke Ice Cream Cake

*Pictured on page 175.*

| | |
|---|---|
| 250 g ( 8 oz ) jerusalem artichokes, peeled | 100 g ( 3½ oz ) icing sugar |
| 350 ml ( 12 fl oz ) milk | |
| 6 egg yolks | TO GARNISH |
| 85 g ( 3 oz ) glucose | zest of 1 lemon or lime, finely grated |
| 100 ml ( 3½ fl oz ) double cream or | 50 g ( 2 oz ) caster sugar |
| 100 g ( 3½ oz ) soya margarine, whipped | 2 tbs water |
| 6 drops vanilla, lemon, or orange essence; or | a few berries |
| 2 drops of each of the 3 flavours | a few mint or lemon grass leaves |
| a little soya oil for greasing | |

FOR THE BLUEBERRY OR

CRANBERRY SAUCE

450 g ( 15 oz ) berries

Wash, drain, and boil the artichokes in 100 ml (3½ fl oz) of the milk. When cooked, drain and mash. In a bowl, beat the egg yolks and glucose for 5 minutes until thick. Bring the remaining milk to the boil and gradually pour into the egg mixture while whisking briskly. Blend the artichoke purée with the egg mixture. Cool. Fold in the whipped cream or margarine. Add the flavouring essence. Freeze for 3 hours in an ice-cream machine or in a freezer, in 4 pudding basins lined with greased paper. Liquidise the sauce ingredients. Strain. Boil the lemon zest with the sugar and water until the water has evaporated. Leave to dry for a short while. Turn each ice cream out onto a plate. Decorate each with a ribbon of sauce and arrange a few berries and mint leaves on top. Sprinkle with the candied lemon rind.     *Serves 4*     **EËRO MÄKELÄ**

# Langues de Chat

| | |
|---|---|
| 100 g ( 3½ oz ) soya margarine | 125 g ( 4 oz ) cake ( low-gluten ) or plain flour |
| 2 drops each lemon and vanilla essence | 10 g ( ½ oz ) desiccated coconut |
| 1 drop almond essence | 2 tbs soya oil for greasing tin |
| 100 g ( 3½ oz ) icing sugar, sifted, plus a little extra for dusting | 1 small pinch of salt |
| 2 eggs, beaten | |

$\mathcal{W}$hip the margarine until it is fluffy. Add the essences and sugar and beat the mixture again until it is light. Beat in the eggs. When the mixture is fluffy again, blend in the flour, salt, and coconut. The mixture should have a dropping consistency so that it can be piped through a tube.

Heat the oven to Gas Mark 6/200°C/400°F. Oil a baking tin. Put the mixture into a piping bag with a plain nozzle 5 mm (½ inch) in diameter. Pipe langues 6 cm (2½ inches) long on the baking tin, spacing them at regular intervals to allow for spreading while baking. Bake for 5–6 minutes. Cool and detach the langues from the tin with a palette knife. The biscuits will harden on cooling.

Store the langues in an airtight tin. When you are ready to use them, dust them with icing sugar, if required.

*Makes 48 langues de chat*                                                    HUGH LANG

# $\mathcal{B}$ISCUIT $\mathcal{B}$ASKET WITH $\mathcal{S}$UMMER $\mathcal{F}$RUIT

$\mathcal{P}$ictured on page 176.

| FOR THE | 500 g (1 lb) assorted berries: red, white and blackcurrants, |
|---|---|
| BISCUIT MIXTURE | raspberries, wild strawberries, cleaned |
| 50 g (2 oz) soya margarine | |
| 50 g (2 oz) caster or icing sugar | FOR THE SAUCE |
| 2 egg whites | juice of 2 oranges |
| 50 g (2 oz) plain flour | 25 g (1 oz) caster sugar |
| 3 drops of vanilla essence | 1 tsp cornflour and 3 tbs water |
| soya oil, for greasing | 1 tbs Grand Marnier liqueur (optional) |

$\mathcal{H}$eat the oven to Gas Mark 6/200°C/400°F. Beat the margarine and sugar until fluffy. Add the egg whites gradually and lastly the flour. Flavour with the vanilla essence. Oil a baking tray and drop onto it 4 spoonfuls of the mixture; and with a palette knife spread each round to a circle of 10 cm (4 inches) in diameter, and of equal thickness. Bake in the oven for 4–6 minutes until the edges are light and golden. Carefully but quickly remove each round with a large palette knife. Brush 4 individual metal moulds with oil on the outside, stand them upside down and cover them with each round of biscuit mixture. Cool until the biscuit mixture is cold and set hard. When set, remove carefully.

To make the sauce, boil the orange juice and sugar for 2 minutes. Thicken with cornflour and cook for 3 minutes. Strain, then flavour with the liqueur.

Place the biscuit baskets on individual plates. Blend the fruit and fill each basket. Pour a little sauce over the top or serve it separately. The biscuit baskets are very brittle when baked. Handle them with care. Store in airtight tins.

*Serves 4–6*                                                    CHRISTOPHER CONIL

# *Star-fruit Sorbet with Two Sauces*

*Carambolas (star-fruit) are sour tropical fruit which are now grown in Jersey. When ripe, they are bright-yellow in colour, waxy-looking, and up to 10 cm (4 inches) long. With their delicious sweet-sour taste, carambolas lend themselves to various desserts such as mousses and sorbets. The pawpaw or papaya has a flavour reminiscent of mixed peach, melon, and strawberry. In shape it looks like a marrow. It can be split in two and eaten like an avocado, after removing the seeds. The green pawpaw can be cooked and used in pickles.*

| FOR THE SORBET | 2 tbs honey |
|---|---|
| 250 g (8 oz) granulated sugar | juice of 1 lime |
| 250 ml (8 fl oz) pulp and juice of star-fruit | |
| | TO DECORATE |
| FOR THE SAUCE | 150 g (5 oz) carton low-fat yogurt |
| 2 small, ripe pawpaws, 1 pulped and 1 peeled and sliced | a little jam |
| (reserve seeds for presentation) | |

*B*oil the sugar and the star-fruit pulp and juice for 5 minutes to produce a syrup. Cool, then freeze until snowy. Beat the mixture to break up the crystals. To make the pawpaw sauce, liquidise the fruit pulp with the honey and lime juice. Pour some yogurt in the centre of each of 4 plates. Garnish each with 3 slices of peeled star-fruit. In the middle of the slices place a scoop of sorbet. Surround with a ribbon of pawpaw sauce. Make a marble design with the point of a knife, pulling the yogurt over the pawpaw sauce in star points. A ribbon of liquidised pawpaw seeds with a little jam can be piped around the edge. Alternatively, use the seeds in another way.     *Serves 4*                                    **RALF WIEDMANN**

# *Pick-me-up*

| 250 g (8 oz) Mascarpone cheese or cream cheese |
|---|
| 250 ml (8 fl oz) whipped cream |
| 3 egg yolks |
| 125 g (4 oz) caster sugar |
| 4 drops of vanilla essence |
| 3 drops of lemon essence |
| 16 ladies fingers or 2 plain sponge fingers, cubed |
| 1 tsp concentrated fresh coffee (use instant) or, for better flavour, Tia Maria liqueur |
| 25 g (1 oz) chocolate, grated |
| 1 tsp cocoa powder |

*In* a bowl, soften the cheese with 3 tbs of the cream. Blend the egg yolks, sugar, and flavourings together and whisk briskly until fluffy. Lastly fold in the whipped cream.

Divide the ladies fingers or sponge fingers among 4 individual glass bowls. Soak them with the concentrated fresh coffee or Tia Maria. Top each bowl with cream mixture as for a trifle. Decorate with grated chocolate and dust with cocoa powder. Chill and serve when required.     *Serves 4*          **ANGELO TORRESIN**

# GRAPEFRUIT AND KIWIFRUIT JELLY MOULD

| | |
|---|---|
| 6 grapefruits | a few berries |
| 25 g (1 oz) gelatine, powdered | |
| 150 ml (¼ pint) grapefruit juice | FOR THE KIWIFRUIT SAUCE |
| 150 ml (¼ pint) champagne cider | 4 kiwifruit |
| zest of 1 lime, grated | 150 ml (¼ pint) sweet sparkling cider or wine |

*To* make the terrine, peel the grapefruit, removing also the white skin. Cutting into the fruit with a sharp knife, divide the segments. Pat them dry with a clean towel. In a small saucepan dissolve the gelatine in the grapefruit juice. Warm gently to boiling point but do not exceed it. Add the champagne cider. Arrange the segments on an oblong terrine. Pour in some jelly and chill the first layer. Repeat until the terrine is full, setting each layer in the same way.

To make the kiwifruit sauce, liquidise the sauce ingredients. Unmould the jelly and cut it into slices. Pour the sauce onto 4 plates and arrange a slice of fruit jelly on each one. Decorate with zest of lime and a few berries (whatever is in season).     *Serves 4*          **PASCAL DIRRINGER**

**Note: This recipe can be used in exactly the same way with other citrus fruits and with soft fruits.**

# Hope and Glory: Stuffed Pancake with Cheesecake Mixture

| FOR THE PANCAKES | FOR THE SAUCE |
|---|---|
| | 15 g ( ½ oz ) cornflour |
| 150 ml ( ¼ pint ) milk | 2 egg yolks |
| 1 egg, beaten | 1 tbs soya oil |
| 50 g ( 2 oz ) strong flour | 300 ml ( ½ pint ) milk |
| 1 tsp melted honey | 50 g ( 2 oz ) caster sugar |
| a pinch of salt | juice of ½ lime |
| 1 tbs soya oil | zest of 1 lemon, grated |
| | 15 g ( ½ oz ) chopped and peeled pistachios |
| FOR THE FILLING | 1 tsp anisette or other liqueur ( optional ) |
| 1 egg yolk | TO DECORATE |
| 100 g ( 5½ oz ) cream cheese | 25 g ( 1 oz ) dark chocolate, melted |
| 25 g ( 1 oz ) mixed candied fruits: | 50 g ( 2 oz ) assorted berries ( raspberries, strawberries, or others ) |
| cherry, citrus peel, pineapple | mint leaf or plain macaroons |
| 25 g ( 1 oz ) icing sugar | 50 g ( 2 oz ) choux pastry ( optional ) |
| 15 g ( ½ oz ) seedless raisins | see Lemon Profiteroles, page 192 |

Combine the first 5 pancake ingredients into a smooth batter. Rest the mixture for 12 minutes. Heat the oil in a pan and cook 4 pancakes until golden on both sides. Do not let them become too dry. Keep them warm.

To make the filling, mix the egg yolk and cream cheese in a bowl until light. Blend in the fruits and the sugar. Fill the pancakes with the mixture and roll them up. Dip a fork in the chocolate and wave it criss-cross fashion over the pancakes to form small threads for decoration.

To make the sauce, blend the cornflour, the egg yolks and the oil in a bowl. Boil the milk and gradually mix it into the egg mixture. Reboil for 3 minutes to cook the cornflour. Add the sugar, lime juice, lemon zest, and pistachios. 1 tbs of your favourite liqueur can be used to flavour this sauce.

Pour a pool of sauce on 4 plates. Decorate each with assorted fruits, a macaroon and choux flowers. Dust all the pancakes with icing sugar. Arrange 1 pancake on each plate.     *Serves 4*     **ANTONIO MANCINI**

# *B*LACKCURRANT *P*UDDING *C*HARLOTTE

| | |
|---|---|
| 250 g (8 oz) blackcurrants, liquidised | 150 g (5 oz) plain flour, plus extra for flouring baking tray |
| 4 gelatine leaves, soaked and melted | a little soya oil, for greasing |
| 250 ml (8 fl oz) double cream | 100 g (3½ oz) raspberry jam |

| FOR THE BISCUIT ROULE | FOR THE CRÈME ANGLAISE |
|---|---|
| | 275 ml (9 fl oz) milk |
| 6 eggs | 3 egg yolks |
| 150 g (5 oz) caster sugar | 65 g (2½ oz) sugar |

*H*eat the oven to Gas Mark 6/200°C/400°F. In a bowl, mix the eggs and sugar. Beat for 8 minutes until thick and fluffy. Add the sifted flour. Oil a flat baking tray and cover it with greaseproof paper, oiled and dusted with flour. Pour the biscuit mixture over. Bake for 6 minutes on the middle shelf. Cool. Spread the raspberry jam over the surface and roll it up tightly. Wrap it in foil and freeze for 1 hour in order to hold the roll in shape.

To make the crème anglaise, boil the milk in a pan. Mix the egg yolks and sugar until you have a smooth paste. Pour the milk over the yolks and return the mixture to the pan. Reheat and stir with a wooden spoon, cooking slowly until the custard coats the back of the spoon. Cool. Add the liquidised blackcurrants to the custard. Dissolve the gelatine in the hot mixture and allow to cool. When cold, fold in the whipped cream.

Line 4 individual ramekins with sliced sponge and fill with the blackcurrant mixture. Chill before serving, and remove from the ramekins onto plates to serve.     *Serves 4*                              MARC LEGROS

# Coupe Bambino

*This is a children's party sweet.*

| |
|---|
| 4 sponge fingers, diced |
| a little fruit syrup, for soaking sponge fingers |
| 100 ml (3½ fl oz) whipping cream, whipped |
| 100 g (3½ oz) each of 3 flavours of ice cream: pistachio, vanilla, and chocolate |
| 4 wafer cornets |
| 75 g (3 oz) chocolate smarties |
| 150 g (5 oz) fresh strawberries, halved |

Begin by placing diced sponge fingers, soaked in a little fruit syrup, in 4 glass bowls. Cover each with whipped cream. Now make 4 small clown figures with small balls of the different ice creams: make the bases of chocolate, followed by pistachio for the bodies, and smaller balls of vanilla for the heads. Top each with a cornet wafer for a hat. Decorate with smarties to imitate buttons, and eyes and noses. Surround each glass bowl with halved strawberries.     *Serves 4*     YANNIS KOULOUROS

# Lemon Profiteroles

| FOR THE CHOUX PASTRY | 25 g (1 oz) cornflour |
|---|---|
| 250 ml (8 fl oz) water | 2 egg yolks |
| 100 g (3½ oz) soya margarine | 1 tbs soya oil |
| 200 g (7 oz) strong flour | 3 drops lemon essence |
| 5 large eggs, beaten | juice of ½ lemon |
| a pinch of salt and sugar | |
| 1 tbs soya margarine for greasing | TO DECORATE |
| a little plain flour | 4 scoops |
| | a little icing sugar |
| FOR THE | 8 glacé cherries |
| CUSTARD FILLING | 4 crystallised lemon jelly sweets |
| 300 ml (½ pint) milk | 100 g (3½ oz) orange segments, peeled and sliced |
| | Apple, Peach and Lemon Sorbet (see page 196) |

*I*n a saucepan, boil the water and margarine until melted. Away from the heat, add the flour together with the salt and sugar to form a stiff dough. Reheat, stirring continuously. Once the dough is in a solid mass, remove it from the heat and cool. Add the beaten eggs gradually while beating the mixture to a soft, semi-fluid consistency. Heat the oven to Gas Mark 6/200°C/400°F. Grease a baking tray with the soya margarine. Dust over with a little flour. Using a 4 mm (½-inch) plain nozzle, pipe the mixture onto the tray, in blobs about the size of a walnut. Leave about 2 cm (1 inch) between them. Bake for 20 minutes. Cool on a wire tray.

To make the custard filling, boil the milk. In a bowl, mix the cornflour and egg yolks, and gradually stir in the milk. Blend in the oil and reheat until the mixture thickens under low heat. Stir constantly for 4 minutes. Cool the cream. Add lemon essence and juice.

Fill a plain piping bag and stuff the profiteroles with the filling through a slit in the side made with a knife. Dust all the profiteroles with a little icing sugar.

Arrange 3 or 4 profiteroles on each of 4 plates in a pyramid. Decorate with piped cream, glacé cherries, lemon jellies, and candied orange segments. Serve with a scoop each of lemon sorbet.
*Serves 4*                                                                                     MICHEL SIMIOLI

# *A*PPLE *F*RITTERS WITH *C*ARAMEL *S*AUCE

*P*ictured on page 175.

| 500 g (1 lb) cooking apples, cored, peeled and | 300 ml (½ pint) soya oil for deep-frying |
|---|---|
| cut in wedges | |
| 50 g (2 oz) caster sugar | FOR THE CARAMEL SAUCE |
| 1 tsp ground cinnamon | 50 g (2 oz) cubed sugar |
| | 1 tbs water |
| FOR THE BATTER | 100 ml (3½ fl oz) water |
| 2 eggs, beaten | 100 ml (3½ fl oz) corn syrup or maple syrup, or honey |
| 125 g (4 oz) plain flour, plus extra for flouring | 2 tsp cornflour mixed with 5 tbs cold water |
| 1 tsp salt | 3 drops of rose water essence or |
| 300 ml (½ pint) milk | any other flavour |

*S*prinkle the peeled apple pieces with sugar and cinnamon and leave to rest for 15 minutes. Prepare the batter by combining the ingredients to a smooth mixture. Strain and rest for 15 minutes. Heat the oil to 180°C/360°F in a deep frying-pan. Rub each apple piece in flour and dip them, one at a time, in the batter. Drain a little, then fry until golden for 3 minutes. Drain on absorbent paper.

To make the sauce, heat the cubed sugar with 1 tbs water in a copper or heavy-based pan. When it turns to a light caramel colour, remove from the heat and add 100 ml (3½ fl oz) water. Reboil until the sugar is melted again. Stir in the syrup or honey. Thicken with the paste of cornflour. Boil for 3 minutes to clear the starch, cool and flavour with the drops of rose water essence. Serve with the apple fritters.     *Serves 6*     JEAN CONIL

# $\mathcal{S}$TRAWBERRY $\mathcal{S}$OUFFLÉ $\mathcal{A}$CAPULCO

| | |
|---|---|
| a little soya oil, for greasing | 150 g (5 oz) caster sugar |
| | 100 g (3½ oz) strawberry purée, sieved |
| FOR THE | 150 ml (¼ pint) whipping cream, whipped |
| COOKED MERINGUE | |
| 300 g (10 oz) caster sugar | FOR THE SAUCE |
| 30 g (1 oz) glucose | 200 ml (7 fl oz) single cream |
| 2 tbs strawberry syrup | 2 tbs Kirsch or strawberry liqueur |
| 6 egg whites | |
| 3 drops of strawberry essence | TO DECORATE |
| | 75 g (3 oz) seedless strawberry or raspberry jam |
| FOR THE SABAYON | 250 g (8 oz) fresh strawberries |
| 6 egg yolks | 8 mint leaves |

$\mathcal{G}$rease 6 individual metal moulds with oil and line them with paper, without creasing, for easier removal. First prepare the cooked meringue. Boil the caster sugar, glucose and strawberry syrup to 121°C/250°F. In a bowl, beat the egg whites very stiffly and gradually pour in the syrup, at the temperature already stated. Beat for 3 minutes to cool the mixture. Add the strawberry essence.

To prepare the sabayon, in a bowl over a pan of boiling water, beat the egg yolks and sugar until the mixture begins to thicken. Gradually add the strawberry purée and the cream. Reheat the mixture in a saucepan until it is thick as a custard and whisk for 8 minutes. Remove and cool. Blend together the meringue mixture and the sabayon, smoothly and thoroughly. Fill the 6 prepared moulds to the brim with the mixture and freeze for 3 hours.

To make the sauce, flavour the cream with Kirsch or strawberry liqueur. There is no need to sweeten the cream.

On each of 6 plates, pour a pool of sauce. Put the jam in a cornet of paper and pipe a line around each plate over the cream. With a knife, make a marble effect by inserting the point of the knife in the jam and pulling it towards you; repeat this in the opposite direction. Unmould an iced pudding in the centre of each plate and decorate with halved strawberries and mint leaves.    *Serves 6*    **GERARD PERCHERON**

Note: This recipe may also be used to make raspberry soufflé. Simply substitute raspberries and raspberry products for strawberries throughout.

# Chocolate Soufflé à la Buchan

| | |
|---|---|
| 75 g (3 oz) soya margarine, softened | 1 tsp chocolate liqueur or Tia Maria |
| 50 g (2 oz) caster sugar, | 2 egg yolks |
| plus extra for dusting moulds | 1 whole egg, beaten |
| 300 ml (½ pint) milk | 6 egg whites |
| 15 g (½ oz) cocoa powder | 50 g (2 oz) icing sugar, for glazing |
| 25 g (1 oz) plain flour | 50 g (2 oz) toasted flaked almonds |
| 2 drops of almond essence | a pinch of salt |

First spread some soft soya margarine thickly inside six 200 ml (7 fl oz) capacity ramekin soufflé dishes. Dust the insides with a little caster sugar so that it sticks on the walls as well as the bottom of each mould. Turn the dishes over to remove the surplus sugar.

To prepare a panada, boil the milk and sieve together the cocoa powder, flour, and sugar. Add the almond essence and liqueur. Pour the boiling milk gradually into the flour mixture. Return it to the heat to cook in a saucepan for 2 minutes. While it is still warm, add the egg yolks and return the mixture to the boil until it bubbles. Then remove it from the heat and blend in the beaten egg to make the mixture softer.

Heat the oven to Gas Mark 6/200°C/400°F.

In a separate bowl, beat the egg whites with a pinch of salt until the mixture forms peaks. Do not beat too much. Fold in the panada lightly.

Fill the moulds to the brim. Make a circular groove close to the edges of each mould to remove some of the mixture. This will help to make the soufflés rise evenly and upwardly. Level each with a palette knife and score with the prongs of a fork in a criss-cross pattern. Place the moulds on a tray and bake for 20 minutes.

Dust each soufflé with icing sugar and toasted almonds, and return to the hot oven for 2 minutes to caramelise the sugar slightly. Serve with chocolate ice cream and almond biscuits.      *Serves 6*      **BRUCE BUCHAN**

# CHOCOLATE BAR MOUSSELINE

| |
|---|
| a little soya oil for greasing |
| 200 g (7 oz) dark chocolate, cut into small pieces |
| 5 egg yolks |
| 4 tbs strong coffee or 2 tbs coffee liqueur |
| 150 ml (¼ pint) double cream |
| 5 egg whites |
| 150 g (5 oz) milk chocolate, cut into small pieces |
| 6 Langues du Chat (page 186) |
| a little icing sugar |

Grease an oblong mould with soya oil and line it with paper. Melt the dark chocolate in a bowl over a pan of hot water. In a mixing bowl, put the egg yolks and pour in the melted chocolate and coffee or coffee liqueur. Add the cream. Beat the egg whites until they are semi-stiff and fold them into the chocolate mixture. Pour this mixture into a 1-litre (1¾-pint) capacity mould. Chill until set.

Unmould the mousseline on a board lined with silicone paper. Melt the milk chocolate and with a palette knife spread it evenly on the top and sides of the mousseline. Chill again to set the chocolate covering.

Dip a knife in hot water and cut the mousseline into slices 1 cm (½ inch) thick. Place a slice on each of 6 plates. Decorate with langues de chat dusted with icing sugar.  *Serves 6*  **WALTER RAEBER**

# APPLE, PEACH, AND LEMON SORBET

| |
|---|
| 3 tbs soya oil, plus extra for greasing |
| 5 tbs sweet cider |
| 225 g (7½ oz) apples, peeled, cored, and diced |
| 225 g (7½ oz) peaches, peeled, stoned, and diced |
| 225 g (7½ oz) caster sugar |
| 2 egg whites |
| 1 tsp ground cinnamon |
| juice of 1 lemon |
| 4 Langues du Chat (see page 186) or almond squares |

*H*eat the oil and cider. Cook the fruits and sugar to a purée. Pass through a sieve. Add the cider, egg whites, and cinnamon. Beat the mixture well. Stir in the lemon juice. Grease an oblong, metal, ice-cream mould. Line it with greased paper. Fill the mould with fruit mixture. Freeze for 4 hours.

Cut the iced fruit cake into thick slices and arrange 2 on each plate. Decorate with Langues du Chat or almond squares. Serve with soured single cream.     *Serves 4*                                    **GRAHAM MALONEY**

# *Iced Grand Marnier Soufflé*

| |
|---|
| 225 g (7½ oz) granulated sugar or sugar cubes |
| 4 tbs water |
| 4 egg whites |
| a pinch of salt |
| 1 tbs soft butter for greasing |
| 1 tbs granulated sugar to sprinkle inside the moulds |
| 50 g (2 oz) sponge fingers, diced |
| 90 ml (3 fl oz) Grand Marnier liqueur |
| 300 ml (½ pint) whipping cream |
| 2 tbs toasted flaked almonds |
| 1 tbs icing sugar, for dusting the soufflé |

*P*repare a syrup by boiling the sugar and water until they reach 118°C/244°F (measured by a thermometer). Beat the egg whites in a clean bowl with a pinch of salt until stiff. Then pour in the syrup gradually. This produces an Italian meringue.

Grease 4 ramekin soufflé dishes of 150 ml (¼ pint) capacity with soft butter and sprinkle granulated sugar on the greased part. Place 2 sponge finger cubes in each mould. Soak them with Grand Marnier. Now blend the whipped cream into the Italian meringue, folding the two lightly and thoroughly together. Wrap a band of paper round each mould, holding it in position with string. This will produce the illusion of a soufflé when the paper band is removed after the mixture has been frozen. Fill each mould with the mixture until it is about 2 cm (¾ inch) higher than the top of the paper band. Freeze for 8 hours or overnight.

When ready to serve, sprinkle the flaked almonds on the tops and dust with icing sugar. Serve as an ice-cream dessert. Alternatively, the recipe can be served inside a casing made of nougat caramel.
*Serves 4*
                                                                                              **EMANUEL PÉLERIN**

# Chestnut Mousse in a Biscuit Cup

*Pictured on page 175.*

| | |
|---|---|
| 100 g (3½ oz) chestnut purée (fresh or canned) | or mixture of both, |
| 3 drops of vanilla essence | plus extra for greasing |
| 15 g (½ oz) melted chocolate (or liqueur) | 80 g (3 oz) icing sugar, sifted |
| 100 ml (3½ fl oz) single cream | 3 drops of vanilla essence |
| 3 tbs cream, whipped (optional) | 50 g (2 oz) flour, plus extra for |
| | flouring baking tray |
| **FOR THE EGG CUSTARD** | 2 egg whites |
| 3 egg yolks | |
| 60 g (2½ oz) caster sugar | **TO DECORATE** |
| 250 ml (8 fl oz) milk | 150 ml (¼ pint) whipping cream, whipped |
| | 4 marrons glacés |
| **FOR THE TULIP BISCUITS** | crystallised violets, or other |
| 40 g (1½ oz) soya margarine or butter, | chocolate confectionery (optional) |

Prepare the custard first. In a bowl over a saucepan of boiling water, whisk the egg yolks and caster sugar together for 8 minutes until the mixture is thick. Boil the milk and gradually stir it in while whisking the egg custard. Gently reheat the mixture in a saucepan to thicken it. When it coats the back of a spoon, it is ready.

In a bowl combine the chestnut purée and the custard. Flavour it with vanilla and melted chocolate (or any liqueur of your choice). Cool. When cold blend in the single cream.

Heat the oven to Gas Mark 4/180°C/350°F. To make the tulip biscuits, whip the butter and/or margarine to a fluffy consistency with the sifted icing sugar. Add the vanilla, the flour and 2 unbeaten egg whites. The mixture should be soft.

Grease a baking tray with soft margarine. Dust it evenly with flour. Pipe the biscuit mixture in 4 rounds of about 10 cm (4 inches) in diameter. Cook for 4 minutes. Remove and place each round inside a greased individual metal dariole mould or glass (so that on cooling it will take the shape of a cup or tulips.

If you wish, to make the mousse lighter, fold 3 tbs whipped cream into the chestnut mixture when it has completely cooled.

On each of 4 plates, place 1 tulip biscuit. Fill it with piped mousse, or spoon the mousse in neatly. Decorate each with a rosette of whipped cream and place a marron glacé on top. Add other decorations according to taste. *Serves 4* **ALBERT PREVEAUX**

# Milk Tart with Sauce and Exotic Fruit

| FOR THE | 125 g (4 oz) caster sugar |
|---|---|
| PASTRY CRUST | a pinch of ground cinnamon |
| 100 g (3½ oz) soya margarine, plus extra for greasing | 50 g (2 oz) seedless raisins, soaked in 1 tbs rum |
| 40 g (1½ oz) icing sugar (sifted) | |
| 275 g (9 oz) cake (low-gluten) flour | TO DECORATE |
| 1 egg, beaten, and 2 tbs water | lemon jelly sauce: |
| a pinch of salt | 50 g (2 oz) lemon curd |
| | 150 ml (¼ pint) water |
| FOR THE | 10 g (½ oz) lemon jelly crystals |
| CUSTARD FILLING | 8 slices mango |
| 500 ml (18 fl oz) milk | 4 passion fruits, split |
| 1 vanilla stick | 4 black grapes and 4 white grapes |
| 25 g (1 oz) cornflour | 4 strawberries |
| 25 g (1 oz) plain flour | 4 large plums, stoned |
| 1 egg | 4 mint leaves |

Heat the oven to Gas Mark 6/200°C/400°F. Whip the margarine with the icing sugar until fluffy. Add the salt and flour. Mix to a dough with your fingers. Mix in the egg and water and chill. Grease a round tin with a little soya margarine. Roll the dough into a shell around 20 cm (8 inches) in diameter and 4 mm (¼ inch) thick. Line and place in tin with a circle of paper and fill it with dry beans. Bake blind for 20 minutes. Cool and remove the paper and beans.

To make the custard filling, boil the milk with the stick of vanilla. In a bowl, combine the flours with the beaten egg and the sugar. Gradually pour in the boiling milk while stirring the mixture. Reboil it until it thickens like a béchamel sauce. Cool and sprinkle with the ground cinnamon. Add the raisins soaked in rum. Fill the baked pastry case with the mixture. Finish in the oven for 20 minutes. Cool and cut into wedges.

To make the lemon jelly sauce, boil the lemon curd and water, and dissolve the lemon jelly crystals in the mixture. Pour this sauce onto 6 plates.

To serve, arrange a piece of tart on each plate. Beside each add the assorted fruits, neatly cut. Decorate each with mint leaves.    *Serves 6*

**BILL GALLAGHER**

# Compote d' Ananas Harry Chapin

*Pictured on the front cover.*

| | |
|---|---|
| 6 slices fresh pineapple, peeled, cored and | 125 g ( 4 oz ) unsalted butter |
| cut into wedges | 150 g ( 5 oz ) corn syrup |
| 250 g ( 8 oz ) caster sugar | 125 g ( 4 oz ) plain flour |
| 2 tbs Grenadine | a little icing sugar, for dusting |

| FOR THE | FOR THE PINEAPPLE AND |
|---|---|
| AVOCADO SORBET | BASIL COMPOTE |
| 1 large ripe avocado, peeled | 40 g ( 1½ oz ) butter |
| juice of 1 lime | 50 g ( 2 oz ) brown sugar |
| 250 ml ( 8 fl oz ) water | 1 tbs dark rum |
| 125 ml ( 4 fl oz ) dry white wine | 90 ml ( 3 fl oz ) light syrup |
| 125 g ( 4 oz ) granulated sugar | 1 small bunch fresh basil, shredded |

| FOR THE | TO GARNISH |
|---|---|
| LACE BISCUITS | 1 pomegranate, cut into small pieces |
| 150 g ( 5 oz ) brown sugar | sprigs of basil |

To candy the pineapple, put it into a heat-resistant bowl, cover with the caster sugar, add the Grenadine, and put into a hot cupboard. Leave for 4–5 days. Heat the oven to Gas Mark 5/190°C/375°F. Purée the avocado with the lime juice. Boil the water, wine and granulated sugar together. Allow this mix to cool and then pour onto the avocado purée. Freeze the mixture in a sorbetière. (If no sorbetière is available, place the cold mixture in a freezer, and when it is firm, liquidise it and re-freeze. Repeat twice.) To make the lace biscuits, dissolve the brown sugar, butter and corn syrup in a bain-marie or a bowl over a pan of simmering water. Remove from the heat and allow to cool slightly. Add the flour and stir for about 2 minutes. Cover a baking sheet with baking parchment and drop four heaped teaspoonfuls of the mixture onto it. Bake for approximately 5 minutes until light golden-brown. Allow the biscuits to cool before taking them off the tray. Make 12 biscuits in all.

To make the compote, melt the butter in a pan, add the sugar and cook until foaming. Add the pineapple and cook gently for 2 minutes. Flame with the rum. Add the stock syrup and the basil and cook for a further 5 minutes. Keep this mixture hot. Dust half the lace biscuits with icing sugar, and decorate with wedges of the candied pineapple and a sprig of basil. Put the remaining biscuits on 4 plates, and spoon 3 quenelles of avocado sorbet on each biscuit, and top with a plain biscuit. Spoon the hot pineapple and basil onto the sweet, allowing the sauce to run over onto the plate. Put the decorated biscuit on top, and garnish with the pieces of pomegranate.     *Serves 4*

**DAVID EVANS**

# Banana Club Sandwiches with Fruit and Cream Filling

| | |
|---|---|
| 125 g ( 4 oz ) soya margarine | 2 tbs banana liqueur or milk, warmed |
| 125 g ( 4 oz ) brown sugar | 1 ripe banana, mashed |
| 1 egg, beaten | juice of ¼ lemon |
| 1 tsp baking powder | 50 g ( 2 oz ) sifted icing sugar |
| ½ tsp bicarbonate of soda | 225 ml ( 8 fl oz ) whipping cream |
| 6 tbs lukewarm milk | 2 kiwifruit, peeled and sliced |
| ½ tsp salt | 250 g ( 8 oz ) strawberries, sliced |
| 250 g ( 8 oz ) strong bread flour | 1 ripe mango, sliced |
| ¼ tsp cinnamon | |
| 450 g ( 1 lb ) peeled ripe bananas mashed to | TO GARNISH |
| a purée and sieved | 150 g ( 5 oz ) potato crisps |
| 6 drops vanilla essence | 50 g ( 2 oz ) chocolate, melted |
| 50 g ( 2 oz ) shelled walnuts, chopped ( optional ) | 100 ml ( 3½ fl oz ) mango purée |
| | 100 ml ( 3½ fl oz ) raspberry purée |
| FOR THE FILLING | |
| 2 gelatine leaves softened in a cup of water | |

Cream the margarine and sugar until fluffy, then stir in the beaten egg. In a cup dissolve the baking powder, bicarbonate of soda and salt in the warm milk. Add this to the margarine mixture. Fold in the flour lightly without beating. Flavour with cinnamon, the banana purée and the vanilla essence. Lastly mix in the chopped nuts. Line a loaf tin with greased baking parchment. Fill the tin ⅔ of capacity to allow for expansion. Bake in preheated oven at Mark 4/180°C/360°F for 1 hour middle shelf. Cool and chill. Slice when cold into 1 cm thick and 5 cm square. You need 3 slices for each club sandwich. Toast each slice on one side only and complete with the fruit filling.

Soak the gelatine for 5 minutes in a little cold water. Remove and dissolve in the banana liqueur or milk. Blend in the mashed banana and add the lemon juice and sugar. Chill for 15 minutes. Whip the cream and fold lightly into the banana mixture, to make a spreadable mousse. Spread 8 slices of banana cake with the filling. Arrange slices of kiwifruit, strawberry and mango on top, leaving some for decoration. Toast 4 slices of the banana cake. Make 4 3-tier sandwiches, each with 2 filled slices topped with a toasted slice. Cut each club sandwich diagonally. Trim the edges. Place a half sandwich on each plate, garnished with a few slices of fruit and some potato crisps coated in melted chocolate. Place a spoonful of mango and raspberry purée side by side on each plate.

*Serves 8*                                                                                    **ANDREAS STALDER**

# $\mathcal{A}$LMOND $\mathcal{P}$ASTRY $\mathcal{C}$AKE

| | |
|---|---|
| 250 g (8 oz) plain flour, plus extra for | ALMOND CREAM |
| flouring board and tins | FILLING |
| 3 tbs caster sugar | 75 g (3 oz) soya margarine |
| 150 ml (¼ pint) milk, warmed to 27°C/80°F | 100 g (3½ oz) caster sugar |
| 5 g (¼ oz) baker's yeast (dried yeast can be used; | 100 g (3½ oz) ground almonds |
| just follow the instructions) | 1 tbs anisette liqueur |
| 1 egg, beaten | (or rum and coconut liqueur) |
| 100 g (3½ oz) soya margarine | 3 small eggs, beaten |
| 2 tbs soya oil for greasing tins | 1 tbs cornflour |
| a little water for sealing pastry | 1 pinch of salt |
| 1 egg yolk, mixed with a little water | 50 g (2 oz) single cream |
| 1 large pinch of salt | |

$\mathcal{P}$lace the flour, sugar and salt in a large mixing bowl. Make a well in the centre and pour in the warmed milk. Crumble the yeast and mix it with the beaten egg. Pour this into the well in the mixing bowl, sprinkling a little of the flour (about 1 tbs) over the liquid. Cover with a cloth and leave to let the yeast ferment for 15 minutes. Blend the ingredients together when the yeast starts to foam. Then knead the dough a little to bind, then press well together (don't knead it).

Roll the dough into an oblong shape on a well-floured pastry board. Dot small pieces of soya margarine at regular intervals all over the dough. Fold the pastry in 3, as with puff pastry. Roll it again into an oblong and rest it for 10 minutes; repeat this operation 3 times at 10-minute intervals. (This is, in fact, the technique used in making croissants.) While the pastry rests for the last time, prepare the almond cream.

To make the almond cream, cream the soya margarine and sugar, and add the ground almonds, the liqueur, and the beaten eggs. Mix to a rather soft, creamy mixture. Dust with cornflour, add the salt, and mix until smooth. It should be of dropping consistency when you lift the spoon. Stir in the cream.

Grease 2 round tins 18 cm (7 inches) in diameter. Sprinkle with a little flour. Heat the oven to Gas Mark 6/200°C/400°F. Divide the pastry dough into two rounds. Fit 1 round in each tin. Prick the bottoms with a fork. Then spread evenly with a thick layer of the almond paste, leaving an edge about 5 mm (¼ inch) all around. Wet the edge with water to seal the second round of pastry, which is placed on top. Crimp the edges to seal the two together. Make a pattern like a rosette on the top with the back of a knife.

Brush the top with egg yolk and water. Leave it to rest for 20 minutes. Then bake for 40–45 minutes. Serve hot or cold with crème anglaise or pear compote.    *Serves 6*    **CHRISTOPHER CONIL**

# CONTRIBUTING CHEFS

Michel ADDON, Executive Chef, Hyatt Regency Hotel, Brussels, Belgium.

Mrs Ungku Shirin AHMAD, Specialist Chef, Malaysian Restaurant, Holiday Inn, Marble Arch, London, U.K. She used to cook at the royal court.

Chalie AMATYAKUL, Director of the Thai Cookery School, The Oriental Mandarin Hotel Group, Bangkok, Thailand.

Ken ANDERSON, Frenchman's Cove Hotel, Port Antonio, Jamaica.

Barry ANDREWS, Food and Beverage Manager, St. Geran Sun Hotel, Mauritius. President of Mauritian Cooks Association.

Satish ARORA, Executive Chef, Taj Mahal Hotel, Bombay, India.

John ASH, American Peanut Association, California.

Javier BASELGA, Executive Chef, Hotel La Bobadila, Loja, Granada, Spain. Was highly complimented by King Carlos of Spain for the excellence of his cuisine.

Jean-Paul BATTAGLIA, Chef de Cuisine, Follet Restaurant, Place du Village, Mougins Village 06250, France.

Martin BAUMANN, Executive Chef, Suncrest Hotel, Qawra, Malta. Officer of CEM.

Joe BEAVER, Executive Chef, Malaysian Restaurant, Holiday Inn, Marble Arch, London, U.K.

Kurt BINGGELI, Executive Chef, Excelsior Hotel, Hong Kong.

Christian BODIGUEL, Executive Chef, Orient Express, Venice, Italy.

Augusto BORGHESE, Executive Chef, Hotel Danieli, Venice, Italy.

Erwin BOTTNER, Executive Chef, Hinckley Island Hotel, Leicestershire, UK.

Mesh BOYJOONAUTH, Chef de Cuisine, St Geran Sun Hotel, Mauritius.

Bruce BUCHAN, Executive Chef, Fossebridge Inn, Gloucestershire, U.K.

Howard BULKA, Executive Chef, Mandarin Oriental, San Francisco, U.S.A.

Kevin CAPE, Head Chef, Bell Inn, Aston Clinton, U.K.

Olarc CASYNS, Executive Chef, Hyatt Regency Hotel, Jerusalem, Israel.

Chan CHI-HUNG, Chef, Hotel Riverside Plaza, Shatin, New Territories, Hong Kong. Worked in Dubai and Jeddah for 4 years. Has won many medals.

Gordon CLAPPERTON, Executive Sous-Chef, Oriental Hotel, Bangkok, Thailand.

James E. COHEN, Head Chef, Lodge Hotel, Vail, Colorado, U.S.A.

Christopher CONIL, General Secretary CEM and WMCS. Havengore Residence, Leigh-on-Sea, U.K. Master Baker.

Jean CONIL, International President of CEM and WMCS.

Pierre CONIL, Retired Chef/Proprietor, Café Routier, Lille, France. Trained by father, Octave Conil, who owned several hotels in Boulogne and Paris.

Christian CONSTANT, Executive Chef, Hôtel de Grillon, Paris, France.

André DAGUIN, Chef/Proprietor, Hôtel de France, Auch, France. Runs a school of cookery of international fame. President of Chamber of Commerce and Regional Association of Hoteliers and Restaurateurs.

Mohamed DAHO, Chef Instructor, Bury Metro College, Manchester, U.K.

Serge DANSEREAU, Executive Chef, Regent Hotel, Sydney, Australia.

Peter DAVIS, Executive Chef, Hyatt Hotel, Bali, Indonesia. Graduate of the Culinary Institute of America.

Timothy DEWHIRST, St Tudno Hotel, Llandudno, Gwynedd, Wales.

Pascal DIRRINGER, Chef/Proprietor, Marmite Restaurant, Beekman Hotel, New York, U.S.A.

Bruce DUFFY, Head Chef, Maidenhead Hotel, Norwich, U.K.

Willi ELSENER, Executive Chef, Dorchester Hotel, London, U.K.

Martyn EMSEN, Executive Chef, Britannia Hotel, Manchester, U.K. Vice-President CEM and WMCS.

David EVANS, Executive Chef, International Sporting Club, Mayfair, London, U.K. Chairman WMCS and CEM.

David FELLOWES, Executive Chef, Selfridges Hotel, London, U.K.

Nigel FROST, Executive Chef, Park Lane Hotel, London, U.K.

Haruo FURUYA, Executive Chef, New Otani Hotel, Tokyo, Japan.

Bill GALLAGHER, Group Food and Beverage Director, Southern Sun Hotels, S. Africa. President of S. African Cooks' Association.

Jeremie GARLICK, Executive Chef, Ocean Cruise Liner.

André GAUZÈRE, Chef de Cuisine, Hôtel Miramar, Biarritz, France.

Wolfgang GROBAUER, Chef, Landhaus Grill, Hamburg, West Germany.

Antonio Abel GUERRERO, Deputy Director, Hotel School of Lisbon, Portugal.

Mato GUOZDEN, Chef, Croatia Hotel, Yugoslavia.

Jean Michel HARDOUIN-ATLAN, Executive Chef, Mandarin Hotel, Macao.

Edwin JOHNSON, Chef, Royal Bahamian Hotel, Nassau, Bahamas.

Hamadi KAROUI, Chef, Kuriat Palace Hotel, Tunisia.

Lewis KEAL, St Tudno Hotel, Llandudno, Gwynedd, Wales.

Jens P. KOLBECK, former royal chef, Executive Chef, Gristies Restaurant, Tonder, Denmark.

Yannis KOULOUROS, Executive Chef, Churchill Hotel, Limassol, Cyprus.

Yip KWAI-SING, Chef, South Villa Restaurant, Tsimshatsui, Kowloon, Hong Kong. Best known for his poultry dishes.

Patrick LABOULY, Chef de Cuisine, Le Moulin de Cierzac, St Fort-sur-le-Né, France.

Hugh LANG, Head Chef, Review Restaurant, Royal Festival Hall, London, U.K.

Patrick LANNES, Executive Chef, Meridien Hotel, Singapore.

Stephane LEDAY, Executive Chef, Ocean Cruise Liner.

Marc LEGROS, Chef, Royal Norfolk Court Hotel, London, U.K. Committee member CEM, Vice-Chairman WMCS.

Patrick LIN, Chef, Regent Hotel, Hong Kong. Gold medallist.

David LODGE, Executive Chef, Norfolk Hotel, Brighton, U.K. Gold medallist of Culinary Excellence Award of WMCS.

Michel LOUSTEAU, Chef de Cuisine/Proprietor, Demeure des Brousses, Montpellier, France. Trained locally. Wise not to emigrate from Languedoc, a region rich in food products.

Gordon McGUINESS, Award Chairman of CEM and WMCS, Executive Chef, International Midland Bank Catering, London, U.K.

Nel McINNES, Chef, New Zealand Tourist Board.

George McNEILL, Executive Chef, York Hotel, Toronto, Canada.

Eëro MÄKELÄ, Consultant Chef, Arctia Hotels, Finland.

Wayan MALIASTRA, Sous-Chef, Mandarin Oriental, Jakarta, Indonesia.

Graham MALONEY, Former Chef, Adelphi Hotel, Liverpool, U.K.

Lin MAN-SANG, Chef, New World Hotel, Kowloon, Hong Kong. Has worked in French restaurants as a sauce cook. Gold medallist.

Antonio MANCINI, Executive Chef, Piccadilly Hotel, Manchester, U.K. Committee member and team captain of exhibition work of CEM. Winner of many international medals for artistic culinary exhibitions.

Manuel MARTINEZ, Chef de Cuisine, La Tour D'Argent, Paris, France.

Mohamed MECHECH, Executive Chef and Manager, Hamadi Karoui, Kuriat Palace Hotel, Tunisia.

Sergio MEI, Executive Chef, Palace Hotel, Milan, Italy.

Aimé MÉTTÉTAL, Chef/Proprietor, La Dinanderie, Vendée, France.

Phillipe MILLION, Chef/Proprietor, Hotel Million, Albertville, France.

John MORRIN, Executive Chef, Imperial Hotel, Cork, Ireland. Gold medallist of many international exhibitions. General delegate of CEM and WMCS and Vice-President.

Anton MOSIMANN, Chef Patron, Mosimann's, London, U.K. Culinary author and TV presenter.
Ivica OBERAN, Belvedere Hotel, Dubrovnik, Yugoslavia.
Emanuel PÉLERIN, Chef, now Minister of Transport, Paris.
Gerard PERCHERON, Executive Chef, Hyatt Continental Hotel, Acapulco, Mexico.
Luca PISAURI, Executive Chef, Brufani Hotel, Perugia, Italy.
Patrick POMMIER, Chef/Proprietor, Le Petit Coq, Campigny, Normandy, France.
Albert PRÉVEAUX, Chef/Manager, Château Castel Novel, Varetz, France.
Hui PUI-WING, Executive Chef, Tsui Hang Village Restaurant, Hotel Miramar, Kowloon, Hong Kong.
Majalenka RACHMAN, Sous-Chef, Mandarin Oriental, Jakarta, Indonesia.
Walter RAEBER, Executive Chef, Hyatt Saujana, Malaysia.
Jean RICHARD, Executive Chef, Tyson Corner Marriott, Washington D.C., U.S.A.
Claude ROMAGNOSI, Executive Chef, Royal Festival Hall Restaurants, London, U.K. Former Chef, Hilton, Jerusalem and London.
David Thomas RYAN, Deputy Executive Chef, Park Lane Hotel, London.
George SAINT, Chef Manager, Chequers, St Albans, U.K.
Francisco Rubio SANCHEZ, Executive Chef, Palace Hotel, Madrid, Spain.
Pat SHARREN, Executive Manager, New Zealand Kiwifruit Bureau.
Makoto SHIMADA, Executive Chef, New Otani Hotel, Osaka, Japan.
Michel SIMIOLI, Executive Chef, Hotel Bernini-Bristol, Rome, Italy.
J.J. SOLLIER, Food and Beverage Manager, Hotel du Rock, Gibraltar.
Andreas STALDER, Executive Chef, Regency Hyatt Hotel, Singapore.
Keith STANLEY, Executive Chef, Ritz Hotel, London, U.K.
Richard STURGEON, Executive Chef, Marine Hotel, Troon, Scotland.
Walter SUCHENTRUNK, Executive Chef, Vienna Marriott Hotel, Austria.
René THEVENIOT, Chef de Cuisine, L'Algue Bleue, Auberge de la Calanque, Le Lavandou, France.
Angelo TORESSIN, Chef, Albergo Quatro, Fontana, Venice, Italy.
Yves THURIES, Chef Proprietor, Cordes, France. Author and producer of his own magazine. Winner of international awards.
Peter TOBLER, Executive Chef, Ocean Cruise Liner.
Simon TRAYNOR, Executive Chef, Marriott Hotel, Hamburg, W. Germany. National delegate of CEM.
Sylvano TROMPETTO, former Executive Chef and Director of Food, Savoy Hotel, London. Author and Executive Consultant.
Khunying Prasansook TUNTIVEJAKUL, Chef of the royal kitchen, Bangkok, Thailand.
William UNDERWOOD, Executive Chef, Ankara Embassy, Turkey.
Roger VERGÉ, Chef/Proprietor, Moulin, Mougins, France. Author of several cookery books and owner of several restaurants. Runs own school of cookery.
Ip WAH, Chef, Regent Hotel, Hong Kong. Has won many medal in competitions. Specialises in shellfish.
Lai Kam Lun Man WAH, Head Chef, Mandarin Oriental, Hong Kong.
Soo Peng WAH, Executive Chef. Officer of CEM and WMCS. Regional delegate for Eastern Asiatic countries.
Al WALBREKER, Executive Chef, Marriott Hotel, Amman, Jordan.
Robert WEBSTER, Executive Chef, Shoppenhanger Manor, Maidenhead, Berks, U.K. Winner of Culinary Excellence Award of WMCS.
Jean-Claude WEIBEL, Executive Chef, Hyatt Regency Hotel, Seoul, Korea.
Stephen WHITNEY, Executive Chef, Number Ten Restaurant, London, U.K. Committee member CEM and WMCS.
Ralf WIEDMANN, Executive Chef, Hyatt Kinabalu International, Sabah, Malaysia.
Anton WUERSCH, Executive Chef, Hyatt Bumi, Surabaya, Indonesia.
Ben Aydin YILMAR, Executive Chef, Ankara Embassy, Turkey.

# NDEX